An OPUS Book

Thinking About Logic

Stephen Read is Senior Lecturer in Logic and Metaphysics, University of St Andrews. He is the author of *Relevant Logic: A Philosophical Examination of Inference* (1988) and the editor of *Sophisms in Medieval Logic and Grammar: Acts of the Ninth European Symposium for Medieval Logic and Semantics* (1993).

From the reviews:

'*Thinking about Logic* is very well written. Its explanations of abstruse topics are very clear and also very well informed and accurate. This book is nicely done, and shows care and skill in writing it. I recommend it highly as excellent reading.'   *History of Philosophy of Logic*

'the author is a lucid guide to the topics . . . Read's book can be thoroughly recommended'   *Philosophical Quarterly*

Thinking About Logic

An Introduction to the Philosophy of Logic

Stephen Read

Oxford   New York

OXFORD UNIVERSITY PRESS

Oxford University Press, Great Clarendon Street, Oxford OX2 6DP

Oxford New York
Athens Auckland Bangkok Bogota Buenos Aires Calcutta
Cape Town Chennai Dar es Salaam Delhi Florence Hong Kong Istanbul
Karachi Kuala Lumpur Madrid Melbourne Mexico City Mumbai
Nairobi Paris São Paolo Singapore Taipei Tokyo Toronto Warsaw
and associated companies in
Berlin Ibadan

Oxford is a registered trade mark of Oxford University Press

First published 1995 as an Oxford University Press paperback

British Library Cataloguing in Publication Data
Data available

Library of Congress Cataloging in Publication Data
Read, Stephen, 1947- .
Thinking about logic : an introduction to the philosophy of logic
/ Stephen Read.
p. cm.
Includes bibliographical references and index.
1. Logic. I. Title.
160—dc20 BC71.R43 1995 94–5697
ISBN 0-19-289238-X

10 9 8

Printed in Great Britain by
Cox & Wyman Ltd.
Reading, Berkshire

For
Eleanor and Megan

Acknowledgements

FIRST, I must acknowledge a debt to my colleagues in the Department of Logic and Metaphysics at St Andrews for their assistance in allowing me to take research leave in Martinmas Term 1992, when most of this book was actually written. Secondly, I am pleased to express my thanks to my graduate class on Philosophy of Logic in Candlemas Term 1993, who helped me think hard about these topics, and improve my treatment of them. Especial thanks go to Christina Altseimer, Darragh Byrne, Adrian Crofton, Michele Friend, Lars Gundersen, Anja Schwager, and Allan Taggart.

Other individuals for whose individual comments on various parts of the book I am grateful are: Paul Castell, Peter Clark, Roy Dyckhoff, Andre Fuhrmann, Bob Hale, Geoff Keene, Neil Leslie, David Miller, Mark Sainsbury, Dalbir Singh, John Skorupski, and Crispin Wright.

I should also acknowledge with thanks Anne Cameron's assistance with typing the manuscript, and express my appreciation to Catherine Clarke and Simon Mason at Oxford University Press, the first for encouraging me to undertake the project, the second for seeing it through its later stages.

Contents

Introduction

THIS book is an introduction to the philosophy of logic. We often see an area of philosophy marked out as the philosophy of logic and language; and there are indeed close connections between logical themes and themes in the analysis of language. But they are also quite distinct. In the philosophy of language the focus is on meaning and reference, on what are known as the semantic connections between language and the world.

In contrast, the central topic of the philosophy of logic is inference, that is, logical consequence, or what follows correctly from what. What conclusions may legitimately be inferred from what sets of premisses? One answer to this question makes play with the notion of truth-preservation: valid arguments are those in which truth is preserved, where the truth of the premisses guarantees the truth of the conclusion. Since truth itself is arguably the third member of a closely knit trio comprising meaning, reference, and truth, the connection with philosophy of language is immediately secured.

Yet truth looks two ways. Meaning and reference are essentially linguistic notions, a function of the particular way in which language, or the language-user, chooses to express some particular idea. Asking what was meant, who or what was referred to, looks for clarification in language. Truth, in contrast, breaks free from language, and directs our attention to the world. Truth requires that what was said conform to reality, that, in the famous phrase, things be as they are said to be.

Perhaps to make this separation between how things are, the issues of truth and inference on the one hand, and how they are said to be, language, meaning, and reference on the other—is artificial. Indeed, it will be the theme of the final chapter of this book that the conception of the world as a distinct reality independent of, and perhaps forever beyond, our knowledge and understanding of it, is simply incoherent. But much work in the philosophy of logic proceeds on the realist assumption that truth marks out how things are regardless of our ability to discern it, and so we shall suppose for much of this book.

There are many books on the philosophy of language, including many excellent introductions. There are far fewer on the philosophy of logic. One reason is a widespread but regrettable attitude towards logic, one of deference and uncritical veneration. It is based on a mistaken belief that since logic deals with necessities, with how things must be, with what must follow come what may, that in consequence there can be no questioning of its basic principles, no possibility of discussion and philosophical examination of the notions of consequence, logical truth, and correct inference. Teaching in philosophy departments across the world exhibits this schizophrenia, in which the dogmatic approach to logic sits uncomfortably side by side with the ceaseless critical examination which is encouraged and demanded in philosophy.

This reverence for logic is deeply mistaken. That a principle, if true, is necessarily true, is no guarantee against error. The consequences of someone's claims are indeed consequences of them whether we in fact recognize it or not. But the principles which we work out and express, and by which we attempt to delineate those consequences, can be as mistaken as the most contingent and chancy of empirical claims. Logicians have no privileged insight into the essentials of their craft which is somehow denied to more humble practitioners of science or history or psychology.

It is with these issues of truth and correct inference that we are to engage in this book; and central to that engagement, we will find, is paradox. Paradox is the philosophers' enchantment, their fetish. It fascinates them, as a light does a moth. But at the same time, it cannot be endured. Every force available must be brought to bear to remove it. The philosopher is the shaman, whose task is to save us and rid us of the evil demon.

Paradox can arise in many places, but here we concentrate on two in particular, one set united by semantic issues, the other by a fuzziness inherent in certain concepts. In both cases the puzzle arises because natural, simple, and what seem clearly reasonable assumptions lead one very quickly to contradiction, confusion, and embarrassment. There is something awful and fascinating about their transparency, there is an enjoyment in surveying their variety, the rich diversity of examples.

But their real philosophical value lies in the purging of the unfounded and uncritical assumptions which led to them. They demand resolution, and in their resolution we learn more about the nature of truth, the nature of consequence, and the nature of reality, than any extended survey of basic principles can give. Only when those seemingly innocent principles meet the challenge of paradox and come under a gaze tutored by realization of what will follow, do we really see the troubles that lie latent within them.

We start, therefore, at the heart of philosophy of logic, with the concept of truth, examining those basic principles which seem compelling in how language measures up to the world. But I eschew a simple catalogue of positions held by the great and the good. That could be very dull, and perhaps not really instructive either. Rather, I try to weave a narrative, to show how natural conceptions arise, how they may be articulated, and how they can come unstuck. I hope that the puzzles themselves will capture the readers' imaginations, and tempt them onwards to further, more detailed reading, as indicated in the summary to each chapter. The idea is to paint a continuous picture of a network of ideas treated in their own right and in their own intimate relationships, largely divorced from historical or technical detail.

This philosophical and critical narrative leads from natural thoughts about truth and inference to puzzles about language, the world, and the relationship between them. We naturally talk about how things must be if certain assumptions are true, and so consideration of consequence leads naturally to examination of what logicians call conditionals—'if . . . then' statements. Conditionals speak of possibilities, and possible worlds seem to give substance to that sort of talk. But how things are, and how they might be, are ontological issues—issues about what there is—which feed real puzzles. Can I promise you a horse without promising any horse in particular? Can I hunt for a unicorn even if there are none—or even talk meaningfully about what does not exist?

There are many technical and formal ways of dealing with these puzzles, and the guides to further reading direct the reader to them. But what lie at the heart of these technicalities are often philosophical assumptions and insights which can be explained, and evaluated, without any great need for technicality. As the book proceeds, the reader will, I hope, come to understand the reasons behind, and even, in outline, the details of, these formal techniques. None, however, is presupposed, and the central thread is the philosophical motivation, presuppositions, and consequences of these key ideas. There are many esoteric technical details in logic. But the focus here is on those issues in logic which raise accessible and exciting issues in philosophy.

As I have said, the tendency in philosophy teaching (except where logic is omitted altogether) is to frame introductory courses in logic as dogmatic and formal. Discussions of the issues raised in this book are mostly reserved for later study. I hope I have succeeded here in making the issues comprehensible to the beginner. Thereby I wish to counteract the prevailing pedagogy. To the logic teacher I say: take the student through these questions in parallel with the formal course, so that the student can appreciate why logic has developed in the way it has, and the ways in which its development is a result of decisions which should be challenged and questioned—even if the answer is in the end, to agree with those decisions. To the student I say: here are the important philosophical issues. If you find them exciting, the next step is to proceed to the formal study of logic, to flesh out what is said here, and to provide the tools for formal analysis of logical consequence. But learn to separate what your logic teacher tells you as fact from the gloss upon it, what is logic from what is philosophical interpretation. With the help of this book, and with the aid of logicians who have preceded you, you must rethink and rework your logic, so that it has your endorsement and your stamp.

1 Truth, Pure and Simple: Language and the World

WHAT is truth? This question can be seen as one of the most typical of philosophical puzzles. We use the concept frequently and without question—we ask, 'Is that true?', we announce, 'It's true', we swear to tell the truth, the whole truth, and nothing but the truth. Sometimes truth is elusive—we find it hard to find out the real truth behind appearances, the truth can be deliberately hidden or obscured, or simply beyond our investigative abilities. Politicians can try to hide the truth, scientists aim to discover the truth behind the phenomena, historians puzzle over the remains and manuscripts to work out what was the truth about Julius Caesar or Napoleon.

In all these instances of searching for the truth, however, what is not questioned is the nature of truth itself. The truth may elude us, but we are in no doubt as to what it is we want to know. But when faced with that question, 'What is truth?' the mind goes numb—what does the question mean? We feel that we do know what the answer is, yet cannot put it into words. So it is with many philosophical puzzles: what is time? What is knowledge? What is mind? Normally we have no trouble applying concepts like time, knowledge, mind—we can look at the clock to see what time it is, we know when the next train is due to depart, we have in mind that we must remember to collect our suitcase from the left luggage. But when challenged to explain what time itself, or knowledge, or mind, or truth, is, we come to a halt. As Augustine said about time, 'I know well enough what it is, provided nobody asks me; but if I am asked and try to explain, I am baffled' (*Confessions*, bk. 11.14).

The temptation to rush to the dictionary should be resisted. There are technical terms, even in philosophy, where the dictionary is needed. Words like 'isobar', 'arcane', 'dualism' can be usefully explained to the novice. But the typical philosophical problems are not like this. We know perfectly well what truth, knowledge, time are—up to a point. But can we find how to say it?

If we can use the concept, why worry about understanding it really fully? Apart from the task in itself—there is satisfaction to be gained from overcoming such a barrier—there is another motivation. Although we may have no difficulty in most circumstances in using such concepts, there are times when puzzles arise. Take time: a science fiction writer may describe a case of time travel, where the hero travels into the distant past or future. Is this really possible, we ask? Now we need to think more deeply, about the nature of time itself. Or take knowledge: the sceptic may challenge us—Chuang Tzu dreamed he was a butterfly, and did not know, when he awoke, if he were a man who had dreamed he was a butterfly or a butterfly who now dreamed he was a man. But if all life is a dream, we can know nothing, for dreams are illusion. What happens in dreams is not real. What is real? What is truth? What is knowledge?

There are many puzzles about truth. We will look at the famous Liar paradox (would you believe me if I told you I always lie?) in a later chapter. Another, and perhaps the most challenging, is the sceptic's or relativist's claim that there is no such thing as absolute truth—all truth is relative to the one who judges. The water feels warm to me, cold to you—is there any fact of the matter as to whether it is really warm or cold? The table looks solid, but the physicist says it is mostly empty space—is there any fact of the matter? Perhaps there is no absolute truth, but only what is true for me, true for you, and so on.

Global relativism is self-refuting, as Plato observed in his dialogue, the *Theaetetus* (170e–171c). It falls to the *ad hominem* objection that, by its own lights, in rejecting it I make it right to reject it. It has to concede that it is false for me; and I—speaking as one who is not a relativist—say it is false. So either way, relativism is false. Truth is not relative, but absolute. Each of us has perceptions, makes judgements on the basis of them, views the world from his own perspective. But the world is distinct from all those different viewpoints. Truth is objective. The world is a world of facts which make our judgements objectively true or false. It is at the very least, an ideal which our judgements seek to mirror.

The Correspondence Theory of Truth

This is the crucial aspect of the concept of truth. Truth corresponds to what is real, to the facts. When we are asked to find out the truth, we must find out what is the case, the facts. Indeed, this idea can be fleshed out into one widely held theory of truth: the correspondence theory of truth. According to it, truth is a relational concept, like 'uncle', consisting in a relation of correspondence to a fact. (One becomes an uncle by having a niece or nephew.) A thought or proposition is true in those cases, and only those cases, where there is a corresponding fact of the matter. (A man is an uncle in those and only those cases where there is a matching nephew or niece.)

An answer to one question immediately gives rise to more. Here we are led on to the further questions: what is a fact? What is the relation of correspondence? Pressing as these may be, another is yet more urgent—what is it which is true or false? We said here 'a thought or proposition'—but is it thoughts, or propositions, or sentences (a string of symbols), or beliefs, or what, which should be said to correspond to the facts when it is true?

Of course, it may be several of these, and others besides. For example, if it is propositions which are true (or false) and what are believed are propositions, then derivatively beliefs are true when they are beliefs in true propositions, and false when beliefs in false propositions. The same holds for thoughts, if the object of a thought is a proposition. But what exactly is a proposition—in particular, is it the same as a sentence?

Certainly, 'proposition' is sometimes used to mean a declarative sentence, a sentence in which something is stated (as opposed to a question or command, for example). But it cannot be sentences which are true or false, or not simply so. Sentences may be uttered by different speakers, or at different times, or in different places, and be sometimes true and sometimes false. For example, anyone who said, 'Kennedy is President' before November 1963 spoke truly, but if anyone uttered the same sentence after that, they spoke falsely. When Kennedy said 'I am an American' he was without doubt speaking truly, but if Khrushchev had spoken the same sentence, it would have been false. It won't do here to say that sentences, as other objects, can change from true to false and back again from time to time—Kennedy was at one time Senator, at another President, so cannot the sentence 'Kennedy is President' be at one time true and at another false? Yet Kennedy and Khrushchev could have uttered 'I am an American' simultaneously, one truly and the other falsely. Rather than say that the sentence was true for one of them, false for the other, that truth is relative— that misses the point that it was false of Khrushchev for everyone—we should focus on what it was that each of them said that was different, in the one case true and in the other false. Kennedy said that he, Kennedy, was an American, and that was true; Khrushchev, if he had uttered those words, would have said that he, Khrushchev, was an American, and that was false. Philosophers use the term 'proposition' to pick out the different thing which each of them said. The same sentence can be used to express two different propositions, to say two different things. Conversely, different sentences can be used to say the same thing. For example, 'It is raining' and 'Es regnet', or 'Kennedy is President' uttered in 1963 and 'Kennedy was President in 1963' uttered after that date.

When a declarative sentence is uttered, in normal circumstances, a proposition is expressed—something has been said. Sometimes this doesn't happen—some sentences, though arguably grammatically well formed, fail to express any definite proposition, such as, 'Three is happy,' or the famous 'Colourless green ideas sleep furiously'; other sentences, though perfectly meaningful, may be uttered in circumstances which rob them of sense, for example, 'The President of England flew to Geneva,' which fails to say anything since there is no President of England. Philosophers introduce the idea of a proposition. What a proposition does is to make an object out of the notion of what is said or expressed by the utterance of a certain sort of sentence, namely, one in the indicative mood which makes sense and doesn't fail in its references. Accordingly, the proposition can become the object of thought and belief, the common factor between different persons and different languages.

Other philosophers object to this abstracting move, forming an abstract object, the proposition, corresponding to distinct sentences. But their objection is misplaced. Even in dealing with sentences we are abstracting from the many different but similar utterances speakers make of what we then call the same (type-)sentence. In terminology invented by the American logician C. S. Peirce in the late nineteenth century, the physical events of voicing or writing a sentence are called the separate tokens of the same type-sentence. The same distinction between types and tokens can be made in the case of words, actions, dreams, and so on. Peirce said the type 'did not exist'; it is certainly not a concrete entity, as the token is. But there are type-words, type-sentences, and there are propositions, common to all utterances (whether of the same type-sentence or not) which say the same thing. To be sure, we need to clarify the equivalence relation (same-saying) over which we abstract; but that task is also needed even for type-sentences, in articulating what is common to different utterances (by, say, a Geordie, a Cockney, and an American Southerner) of the same sentence. Its familiarity makes us overlook the theoretical difficulties; they are no greater in the case of propositions.

Propositions, taking the two truth-values as they are called, true or false, avoid the relativism of truth to place, speaker and time. Another possibility would be to take token-sentences as what are true or false, type-sentences or propositions then being derivatively so, when all tokens have the same value. But this ignores an important unifying feature which the notion of proposition brings out, namely, that the reason why all the token-sentences have the same value is because they all express the same proposition. Of course, we may not be able to tell if any particular proposition is true or false, for example 'Oswald killed Kennedy' or 'Every even number greater than two is the sum of two primes'.

Nevertheless, a clear proposition has been expressed, something suitable for assessment as true or false.

We will therefore take propositions as the bearers of truth-values. But now we must return to the other questions: what is it that gives a proposition the truth-value it has? What are facts, and what is the correspondence relation between true propositions and facts?

What I will describe is a paradigm of the correspondence theory. Once it is clear what such a theory is, variants on it can be considered, and the question raised as to how close they are to the central idea of the correspondence theory. But let us start with the correspondence theory in its cleanest, simplest, and starkest form. The correspondence theory is a realist theory in two ways—ontologically and epistemologically, that is, both in its implications for existence and in its consequences for knowledge. On this view, the world is constituted by facts, facts whose existence is independent of whether we are aware of them.

Ontology is the study of what sorts of things exist. It is not an empirical, scientific study—not some sort of natural history. It is a theoretical or conceptual study, a consideration of what implications there are for what there must be, in giving a systematic account of our experience. One philosopher might say that there are minds as well as bodies, in order to account for human action and perception—he is a dualist. Another might deny the separate existence of minds, giving an explanation of action and perception as complex operations of physical matter alone. A third may deny the existence of matter itself, suggesting that our experience can be accounted for without it, simply as the experiences of minds. These last two theories are monistic, claiming the basic existence of only one type of thing, in the first case, physicalist, in the second, idealist. The issue is an ontological one, namely, what sorts of things there are.

The correspondence theorist of truth claims there must be more than this—whether mind and/or matter. In addition to individual minds and/or bodies, there must be facts—facts about those minds and/or bodies. The minds and bodies just are—in addition, there must be facts about them. It is the existence of facts which makes true propositions true. This is a realist onto-logical claim.

Moreover, it is epistemologically realist. The facts which make true propositions true exist independently of our ability to discover them. Some we do discover—we know that Kennedy was President. Others we know not to be facts—Kennedy did not serve a second term. The one fact existed, that he was President, the other did not, that he served a second term. We know the one fact, and the absence of the other. But other facts we have not discovered—indeed, perhaps we never shall. The Warren Commission confirmed that Oswald alone killed Kennedy. Perhaps he did—but we shall never know for certain. None the less, according to the correspondence theory, there must be a fact of the matter: either it was a fact that Oswald killed Kennedy, or not. The proposition that Oswald killed Kennedy is true if there was such a fact, false if there was not. We cannot be sure that it was a fact. But either there was such a fact or there was not. Hence either the proposition is true or it is false. That is, whether a proposition is true or false, according to the correspondence theory, turns on whether there is a corresponding fact—on the existence of a certain sort of object. But either that fact exists or it does not. So either the proposition is true or it is false. The order of explanation is: it is natural to think that either an object exists or it doesn't—that's what the reference to a corresponding fact gives to the correspondence theory. So by linking the condition for truth of a proposition to a corresponding object—the fact—we are naturally led to Bivalence—either the proposition is true (for there is a fact corresponding to it) or it is false (for there is no such object). Hence every proposition is either true or false—and is so, regardless of our ability to discover it. Its truth turns simply on the question of whether there is such an object, the corresponding fact. Thus the Correspondence Theory of Truth naturally leads to epistemological realism.

The epistemological realism of the correspondence theory therefore consists in its commitment to what is known as the Law of Bivalence: every proposition is true or false. Every proposition—that is, what is expressed by a meaningful sentence uttered in appropriate circumstances—either has a corresponding fact which makes it true, or lacks such a corresponding fact, and so is false. By making truth a matter of the existence of a certain sort of object, the theory commits itself to the possibility that propositions may be true or false, but which they are we have no way of determining. Luck might have made it clear that Oswald killed Kennedy. But the circumstances clouded it. None the less, either he did or he didn't—the proposition is either true or false. (We will leave objections to this aspect of realism about truth until Chapter 8.)

So it is facts that make propositions true or false—but what is this relation? How can a fact make a proposition true? What is the correspondence between propositions and facts?

Correspondence is the Achilles' heel of the correspondence theory. Either the relation is made substantial and interesting, in which case it seems implausible that it should hold; or it is made trivial and automatic, in which case the theory evaporates into thin air. G. E. Moore, one of the main proponents of the theory, was charmingly direct about the difficulties he faced: 'the difficulty [is] to define this relation [which each true belief has to one fact and one only]. Well, I admit I can't define it, in the sense of analysing it completely . . . But . . . it doesn't follow that we may not know perfectly well *what* the relation is' (*Some Main Problems of Philosophy*, 267). The alarm signals should sound. If it is so clear that the relation must hold, yet impossible to describe it, perhaps it is a figment of the philosopher's imagination. Let us contrast two accounts of the correspondence relation, to make clear the horns of the presently impending dilemma: first, Bertrand Russell's account of propositions and facts, in which the distinction threatens to collapse; secondly, Ludwig Wittgenstein's, in which the immoderateness of the realism strains belief.

Wittgenstein came to work as a student with Russell in Cambridge in 1911. Their ideas developed in parallel, but from 1913 they did not meet, and during the Great War barely corresponded. At root, Russell's realism was always tempered by epistemology; Wittgenstein's was not—for him the correct analytic structure was what mattered, however psychologically implausible it became.

The idea in each case was to exhibit the perfect congruence between linguistic structure and the structure of the world. It was part of a metaphysical method which sought to discern the nature of reality by examining the essential nature of how that reality was described. As far as concerns us here, the structure of propositions revealed the structure of the corresponding fact. For both, the idea was that complex propositions should be analysed into, and so essentially reduced to, elementary or atomic propositions. So what are atomic propositions like? For Russell, they consisted of one or more particulars and a universal, for example, the proposition expressed by the sentence 'Kennedy is President' contains two objects: Kennedy, a particular person, and 'presidenthood', that attribute common to all things that are president (Eisenhower, Reagan, and so on). The proposition must be distinct from the sentence, because, for example, 'Kennedy is President' and 'JFK is President' express the same proposition, so that what is common to all sentences expressing the same proposition is that the same particulars are referred to. Hence, said Russell, the particulars themselves must be present in the proposition and the same universal is ascribed to them.

If the proposition consists of the particulars and universals themselves, what then is the fact? For Russell it was distinct from the proposition. For one thing, there are false propositions but no 'false facts'. Facts are how things actually are, so corresponding to each fact there are several propositions, the one it makes true, and all those it makes false. But one may reasonably be troubled at this point how exactly fact and proposition differ. There is certainly no trouble connecting them— the proposition contains the very same objects which make up the fact, so the relation of correspondence is explained. But the cost of that explanation is to erode the language/world distinction.

Wittgenstein's conception of the proposition was different— for him it was much more insubstantial. Let us start with his account of facts. Facts are facts about objects, so what is distinctive of actuality, how things actually are, is what facts there are. The objects must be common to all possibilities. Call those possibilities states of affairs, how the objects, the same in all possible worlds, are disposed. The actual world consists of those states of affairs which exist, that is, the facts. Elementary propositions get their meaning by association with—by corresponding to—particular states of affairs. The visible (or audible) part of a proposition is a sentence, a sequence of signs. These signs become symbols by an arbitrary act of correlating them with objects. Facts about those symbols then come conventionally to picture certain states of affairs about the corresponding objects. Thus at the heart of Wittgenstein's correspondence theory of truth is a picture theory of meaning. Elementary propositions are facts about names, and thereby picture (or mean) atomic states of affairs, that is, certain combinations of objects. In general, propositions (via the connection at the base level of elementary propositions and atomic facts) picture putative facts, or states of affairs.

The idea, therefore, is to use the theory of meaning to bridge the language/world gap and to correlate each proposition with a corresponding state of affairs, that correlation constituting the meaning, or sense, of the proposition. The true propositions are then simply those propositions whose pictured state of affairs actually exists, that is, is a fact. True propositions correspond to the facts.

Wittgenstein's picture theory is without doubt the best thought out and developed of all versions of the correspondence theory —or at least, to anticipate later discussion, of those versions in which true propositions straightforwardly correspond to facts. None the less, there are doubts one can raise about it. Let us focus in turn on three of these.

First, as was mentioned before, the correspondence theory is a realist theory. This is an aspect to which we will return only at the end of this book. In the final chapter, the challenge will be that realism of this sort is incoherent in that its account of truth is incompatible with plausible constraints on the theory of meaning. We noted that the realism of the correspondence theory commits one to accepting the Law of Bivalence, and consequently, to accepting that there may be propositions about which we cannot, in principle, tell whether they are true or false. In the jargon, these are verification-transcendent propositions—

their truth (or falsity) transcends our powers of verification. The question we must face later in the book is how such propositions could be understood. For propositions are what are expressed by meaningful sentences (uttered in appropriate conditions), and what is meaningful is what can be understood. The challenge will be to give an account of meaning and understanding which will embrace verification-transcendence. Realism has yet to answer that challenge.

This challenge must wait. For the remainder of this chapter I wish to develop the second and third doubts and elaborate from them alternative accounts of truth.

Reductionism

The second doubt concerns the reductionism central to Wittgenstein's account. Here was a marked contrast with Russell's theory. It was quite clear to Russell that to suppose, for example, that in addition to the facts corresponding to two true propositions, say, 'Kennedy is President' and 'Oswald killed Kennedy', there was a third fact, some sort of conjunctive fact, which made the conjunctive statement 'Kennedy was President and Oswald killed him' true, was absurdly profligate. Once one had been told the two separate facts, one was not given any further information when told their conjunction. 'I already knew that,' would be the sharp retort. There is no extra fact behind the conjunction 'A and B' of two true propositions A and B, additional to the separate facts which make A and B true. Similarly with disjunctions. If one of two propositions A and B is true, then the disjunctive proposition 'A or B' is true. But what makes 'A or B' true is not another strange disjunctive fact, but the very same fact which makes one of the disjuncts (the constituent propositions in the disjunctive proposition) true. To think otherwise would be, for Russell, to sin against Occam's Razor, a much-proclaimed methodological principle in metaphysics, dating back if not to William of Occam (or Ockham, a famous fourteenth-century thinker) alone, at least to his time. It says: do not postulate more kinds of thing in an explanation than are absolutely necessary. In the prese t case, we can explain, within the correspondence theory, why a conjunctive proposition is true without postulating a third fact additional to the two separate facts which make the conjuncts (the constituent propositions in the conjunctive proposition) true.

Moreover, there is another consideration which warns against admitting conjunctive and disjunctive facts. Suppose there were conjunctive facts, and take two true propositions, A and B. Then, in addition to the two separate facts making A and B true, there would have to be a third fact making the conjunction of A and B, 'A and B', true. But then we could ask about the relation between the first two facts and the third. How do the first two compel the third to exist? Must there be another fact which relates them? That way lies a vicious regress: to explain the relation between the first two facts and the third, we would appeal to the fourth fact relating them; to explain the relation between these four facts, we would need to appeal to a fifth, and so on. The explanation would never be completed. The central plank of atomism is that facts are autonomous: no fact should depend on any other. There should be no internal relations—logical relations like entailment—between distinct existents. The conjunctive fact would be entailed by the two facts corresponding to its components, and so cannot be a separate entity.

The best we could do would be to claim that the fourth fact was unnecessary, for the third fact was itself simply the 'conjunction' of the first two. Perhaps by 'conjunction' here (it is metaphorical, which is why the word appears in scare-quotes, because conjunctions are actually linguistic objects, and the notion has now strayed over on to the worldly side of the correspondence) we mean that the third fact has the first two as parts. But now we see that the third fact is unnecessary too. We don't need to erect a structure of facts matching that of propositions. We can simply explain the truth of the conjunction 'A and B' as resulting from, that is, reduce it to, the truth of each conjunct, and no further explanation is needed beyond the explanation of their truth, namely, that each corresponds to a fact.

The dream of the logical atomists, Russell and Wittgenstein, was that the truth of every proposition could be reduced in this way to the truth of atomic or elementary propositions. The correspondence between true propositions and facts (or between propositions and states of affairs, whether existing or not) worked in two stages: first, the truth of complex propositions was reduced to the truth of elementary propositions; secondly, the correspondence between elementary propositions and states of affairs was drawn as described earlier. It was realization that the reduction to the atomic level would not work that eventually led Wittgenstein to abandon logical atomism (and the correspondence theory and realism).

Russell was the first to accept that the reduction of all propositions to atomic propositions could not be achieved. The problem cases for him were negative propositions, such as 'Oswald did not kill Kennedy', general propositions, such as 'Someone killed Kennedy' or 'No one killed Eisenhower', and belief propositions, or propositions expressing epistemic attitudes, such as 'Ruby believed Oswald killed Kennedy' and 'Oswald knew Kennedy was in Dallas'. Take the first sort, negative propositions. An obvious reduction move would be to explain the truth of a negative proposition such as 'Ruby did not kill Kennedy' as resulting from the truth of another proposition incompatible with 'Ruby killed Kennedy'. Suppose that Oswald did actually kill Kennedy. Then that fact would make 'Oswald killed Kennedy' true, and assuming we are talking about lone gunmen, that proposition is incompatible with 'Ruby killed Kennedy'. So 'Ruby killed Kennedy' would be false, and so 'Ruby did not kill Kennedy' would be true.

Russell's objection to such an explanation was that a vicious regress threatens. The form of the explanation is (let's write 'not-A' for the negative proposition, 'Ruby did not kill Kennedy', say) that 'not-A' is true if there is a true proposition B incompatible with A. But 'B is incompatible with A' is itself a negative proposition. To explain its truth we would require a third proposition C incompatible with 'B is compatible with A'; and so on, meaning that the truth of 'not-A' would never receive a full explanation.

This is a strange objection. For the same point would apply

with equal force to conjunctions. Recall that our account of the truth of 'A and B' was that it is true if A is true and B is true. Here the truth-condition, 'A is true and B is true' (that is, the condition we have specified for the truth of 'A and B') is itself a conjunction. Similarly, the truth-condition for disjunctive propositions will itself be a disjunction. If the objection is valid that the truth-condition for negative propositions must not itself be a negative proposition, then the truth-condition for conjunctive and disjunctive propositions must not be, respectively, conjunctive and disjunctive. If there must be negative facts to explain the truth of negative propositions, then there must be conjunctive and disjunctive facts to explain the truth of conjunctive and disjunctive propositions.

In fact, we seem to be about to impale ourselves on the horns of a dilemma. To appeal to negative and conjunctive facts to explain the truth of propositions of these kinds will fail to be fully explanatory, for we will then need an account of the relation between such facts and the facts or the absence of facts corresponding to their components; while to appeal to a truth-condition reducing the truth of such propositions to the truth of their component propositions will fail to be fully explanatory until we have an account of what makes the truth-condition, a proposition of the same quality, true.

It will be helpful at this point to step back from the by now rather messy detail of the correspondence theory and try to think more generally about our aim in providing a philosophical account of the nature of truth. This is where the third doubt about the correspondence theory will set in.

Theories of Truth   *Question*.

 Our original question was: what is the difference between true propositions and false ones? We were led by the thought that to find out whether a proposition is true we should look at the facts, to propose as a general theory that true propositions correspond to the facts, while false ones do not. But perhaps a metaphor has overtaken us here and misled us. Indeed, it starts to look as if a very common philosophical mistake has been committed.

Consider the proposition, 'The whale is a mammal'. Clearly, in a sense, we are talking about whales—every whale is a mammal. But why is the sentence in the singular? Which whale are we talking about? No whale in particular. None the less, it is tempting to construe the proposition as referring to some archetype. Recall Rudyard Kipling's stories about how the camel got his hump, and the elephant his trunk. In these stories a particular elephant goes proxy for the whole species. So we find ourselves talking as if there were, in addition to each particular whale, a generic whale whose properties are those essential to all whales—as a representative of their nature. We might indeed say that this is the species whale. Literally, the species is spread across the world's oceans, and across millennia. So the species whale is not itself, literally, a whale. But talk of the horse as a quadruped, the dodo as extinct, the dormouse as nocturnal, leads us naturally by a figure of speech to understand these sentences as predicating a property of some generic individual.

Gilbert Ryle, in his review of Carnap's *Meaning and Necessity*, labelled a similar mistake in the theory of meaning, the 'Fido'-Fido Principle. Because the name 'Fido' gets its meaning by referring to a single individual, Fido, and so on for a large class of words, we are tempted to suppose that other words function the same way. Russell fell into this trap in his account of universals: we noted earlier his account of atomic propositions as consisting of a number of individuals and a universal. Consider the sentence 'Fido is a dog'. 'Fido' refers to one individual. What does 'dog' refer to? Surely, to lots of individuals—all dogs. But on the 'Fido'-Fido theory it must obtain its meaning by being correlated with a single thing—dogness, or the universal, dog. Fido is a particular; dogness is a universal, being common to many things, truly predicable of all dogs. Russell's propositions were conceived by him as constituting the meaning of sentences. Hence, he said, they must contain these generic entities, universals.

This is an unwarranted move; but a similar temptation lies in wait for us in the case of facts. If true propositions are those which fit the facts, then will there not be particular facts corresponding piece-wise to each true proposition? The word 'fact' in such a sentence as 'It's a fact that Kennedy was killed' is seen as getting its meaning by referring to a fact, some worldly correlate of the proposition, 'Kennedy was killed'. Perhaps the Correspondence Theory of Truth also commits the mistake encapsulated in the 'Fido'-Fido Principle.

Let us consider generally what we are doing when we say that a proposition is true, and what question we are asking when we ponder, what is truth? These are semantic questions, issues to do with the relation between language and the world. Semantics is generally thought to cover three aspects in particular: truth, meaning, and reference. Reference, of course, is the relation between a word or phrase, and some object in the world. For example, a paradigmatic case of reference is the use of a demonstrative phrase such as 'that cucumber', or a proper name such as 'Kennedy'. Such a phrase is used to refer to a particular cucumber, or to a particular person. More contentiously, some philosophers think that other kinds of words refer to other kinds of things. For example, we noted that Russell believed that predicate phrases, verbs, and adjectives, refer to universals, so that 'is President' refers to presidenthood, and 'runs' to whatever is common to all things that run. Other philosophers deny that reference has any application at all to such parts of speech.

Meaning is more difficult to make general remarks about. Russell and others simply identify meaning and reference, so that the meaning of 'that cucumber' is identical with what it refers to, namely, the cucumber. It followed that for Russell the meaning of a sentence is the proposition expressed by it, which itself consists of the objects referred to—the particulars and the universal. But in general, most semantic theorists distinguish meaning from reference. Some, while separating it from reference, continue to think of it as an object, correlated with the sentence, either some mental object, an idea in the mind, or some abstract object, something immaterial and non-physical, yet none the less distinct from individual mind and consciousness. It is something we can all think about, and so has some objective existence independent of the mental. Other philosophers deny that meaning is in any way a correlation of a sentence with an object. It is rather a property of the sentence—that it is meaningful.

Thirdly, there is the semantic notion of truth, again, a property of an expression, this time a sentence, in its relation with the world. Some philosophers construe this relation on the model of reference, so that (for Gottlob Frege) true sentences refer to the True, false sentences to the False. These objects, the True and the False, are truth-values. Russell, who could not accept Frege's tidy scheme, was tempted by the thought that the correspondence relation was one of reference. But if so, he believed that true propositions would refer to facts: the proposition that Kennedy was President would refer to the fact that Kennedy was President; in which case, what do false propositions refer to? Unimpressed with the suggestion that they refer to non-existing states of affairs, Russell abandoned reference as the model, and tried to give another account of the correspondence relation.

We have seen some of the problems that are involved in trying to develop a correspondence theory of truth. Our present task is to set up a framework for elaborating a semantic theory, in particular, for elaborating any theory of truth. Recall the problem we had: the truth-condition for a negative statement of the form 'not-A' is itself negative—'not-A' is true if A is not true; that for a conjunctive statement of the form 'A and B' is itself a conjunction—'A and B' is true if A is true and B is true. Is there a vicious regress, or even a circularity here? Are we already presupposing what we are trying to explain—are we presupposing an understanding of negative propositions in giving an explanation of negative propositions, and the same for conjunctions, disjunctions, and so on? Do we need to appeal to negative facts, conjunctive facts, and so on in order to account for the truth of negative and conjunctive propositions? When we say, for example, that 'not-A' is true if and only if A is not true, is that explanatorily adequate, or do we need to replace the 'truth-condition', 'A is not true', by some reference to a negative fact, such as 'it is a fact that not-A'?

It is helpful here to appeal to a distinction, introduced by Alfred Tarski, between the object language and the meta-language. Tarski's own theory is not a correspondence theory, as we shall see below. But besides a theory of truth of his own, Tarski developed a theory of theories of truth. Clearly, in developing a semantic theory, we need a language in which to express that theory, a language which may or may not be distinct from the language whose semantics we are attempting to describe. The latter, the object of our theory, Tarski called the object language; the former, the language in which the theory is stated, he called the meta-language. For example, the object language might be Polish, while the meta-language was German, or the object language might be English and the meta-language French. We might even try to develop the semantics of the object language in the language itself—so that both object and meta-language were, say, English. None the less, the same language is performing distinct tasks. This is how it has been so far in this chapter.

Tarski saw an insuperable problem in this latter course, arising from the existence of semantic paradoxes, which we will consider in Chapter 6. What he recommended was that we at least fragment the language into layers: take all those propositions not containing semantic concepts—let that be the basic object language; extend the language to contain semantic concepts applying to the basic level, that object language—but not to its own level. That is the first meta-language or meta-level. If we wish to develop a semantic theory for this level, which contains semantic concepts for the basic level, we need to move to a meta-meta-language, containing semantic concepts for the first level, but not for itself; and so on. Thus any language is seen as divided into strata, a hierarchy of language and meta-language.

We will consider in Chapter 6 whether this regimentation is necessary, or even practicable. But it provides us at this point with an answer to our present problem. In developing any theory, we need a language for that theory, and we need to presuppose that it is understood and coherent. Negations and conjunctions in the meta-language are given us—we are not attempting to give the semantics of the meta-language. We use the resources

of the meta-language to give the truth-conditions of the propositions of the object language.

It is a useful exercise to work out what resources we need in
the meta-language to do this. To begin with, we need to be able
to refer to the propositions of the object language. For example, if we are to say: ' "Kennedy is President" is true if . . .', we
need to be able to refer to the object language proposition,
'Kennedy is President'. We also wish to say: ' "not-A" is true
if . . .'; so we need a means of referring to various forms of
object language propositions, 'not-A', 'A and B', and so on. In
general, what we need is a way of referring to the expressions
of the object language, for we specify the propositions of the
object language (the abstract propositions expressed by various
particular sentences) indirectly via reference to the sentences
and expressions of the object language. The means we are
presently using, and a very common one, is to form quotation-
names. We present the expression itself, enclosed in quotation
marks, as a name of that expression. If, for example, we were
using English as a meta-language to described the semantics of
German, we would present the German expression, in quotation-
marks, as a name, in English, of that German expression: e.g.
' "Schnee ist weiss" is true if . . .'.

Other means of naming are possible, but quotation-names
are very convenient, and easily decoded. We might decide to
refer to words by their position in a certain dictionary, e.g. 'the
proposition expressed by the first word on p. 331 of vol. Si–St
of the *Oxford English Dictionary* followed by the 3rd word on
p. 499 of vol. I–K, followed by the sixteenth word on p. 70 of
vol. Wh–X'. Or we could form names by associating each letter
with an odd number, and each sentence with the product of a
string of prime numbers raised to the power of the numbers
correlated with its constituent letters. (Kurt Gödel introduced
this method of naming in a famous paper on logic in 1931, and
it is now often called the method of 'Gödel-numbering'.) On
such a scheme, the shortest sentence in the Bible receives a
Gödel number of the order of 10^{332}. These two methods are not
so easy to use, and particularly to decipher, as the method of
quotation-names. Nevertheless, the essential point is the need

for decoding: given such a name, there must be a procedure for determining what expression is named by it. (In the one case, we refer to the *OED*; in the other, we factor the number and examine the exponents of its prime factors.)

Having adopted some system for naming the propositions expressed by sentences of the object language, we now need to define a truth-predicate. There are a number of constraints on what constitutes a proper definition. The most important, perhaps, is that the power of expressibility of the meta-language be no less than that of the object language. We will not be able to specify the conditions under which each proposition is true if we cannot express in the meta-language what can be expressed in the object language. For example, to give the conditions of truth of 'Kennedy is President', we will need to be able to refer to Kennedy; to give the truth-conditions of negated propositions (in general) we will need to be able to express negation; and so on. Thus to each object language proposition will be correlated a meta-language sentence with the same meaning. We can now propose as a minimal constraint on truth-theories, one which has famously come to bear Tarski's name, a condition of adequacy: nothing deserves the title of a theory of truth if it cannot establish at the very least, all propositions of the form

S is true if and only if p,

where what replaces p is a translation into the meta-language of the object language proposition whose name replaces S.

Let us take a couple of examples. First, let the object language be Gaelic and the meta-language English. We will use quotation-names to refer to propositions of Gaelic. 'Tha an t-uisge ann' translates into English as 'It is raining'. Hence a minimal condition on a truth-theory (in English) for Gaelic is that among its consequences should be

'Tha an t-uisge ann' is true if and only if it is raining.

The theory would need to include all other such pairs, pairing a proposition of Gaelic with its translation into English, that is, a proposition of English saying the same thing, i.e. saying when that other proposition was true. For our second example, let us take English as its own meta-language (if necessary, regimented into a hierarchy of Tarski's kind in order to avoid paradox). The condition here is even more mundane. The theory must entail, at the very least, all biconditionals (i.e. 'if and only if'-statements) such as

'It is raining' is true if and only if it is raining.

Tarski called this minimal constraint the 'material adequacy condition'. Any theory which did not meet it would be giving the wrong truth-conditions for the propositions of the object language. We should see it as part of a package of conditions on the semantic theory: the formal constraints, that there be decodable ways of referring to propositions of the object language, that the definitions be formally correct, and so on; and this material condition, that the theory not correlate object language propositions with truth-conditions in the meta-language which say something different.

Minimalist Theories of Truth

Can one read more into the material adequacy condition? Can we not read the T-sentences (the set of statements of the form 'S is true if and only if p') as giving proper expression to the correspondence theory of truth? For what we have, as indicated in the last paragraph, is a correlation between propositions of the object language on the one hand, and facts—or at least, states of affairs, actual or non-actual—on the other. But this is to read too much into the T-schema, that is, the schema for the T-sentences. Certainly, a correspondence theory would meet the material adequacy condition—all the T-sentences would be entailed by it. But it is the correspondence theory, not the material adequacy condition, which interprets the right-hand side as a reference to facts, or states of affairs. There is in the schema a correlation of language and world, a reference on the left-hand side to linguistic entities and on the right—dare one say—a non-linguistic 'reference', the truth-condition. But it is a further step to read into that description a metaphysical reference to facts. The correspondence theory contains a metaphysic of facts and states of affairs correlated with propositions. That is its fundamental mistake: to construe the semantics of truth on analogy with the reference of 'Fido'. The T-schema is neutral on this question. Any semantic theory will set up a correlation of language and the world; the correspondence theory's metaphysic articulates that as a correlation of propositions with facts.

Tarski himself also presented a theory of truth, which should not be confused with his statement of adequacy conditions on any theory of truth. His own truth-theory followed the correspondence theories of Russell and Wittgenstein closely—but without the reference to facts. Setting natural languages aside, as open to semantic paradox because of their semantic closure, he showed how to give a semantics for a formal language, a language specified by first describing a class of atomic sentences, followed by a recursive account of how complex sentences are constructed out of simpler ones. (To call it 'recursive' means that given any string of symbols we can formally check if it is well formed and constitutes a legitimate sentence.) Atomic sentences consist of names and predicates, each correlated with some non-linguistic entity: names with objects, predicates with properties or relations or sets. An atomic sentence is true if the objects named have the property or are related by the relation correlated with the predicate. (For example, 'Sortes currit' is true if and only if the object denoted by 'Sortes' has the property assigned to 'currit'.) Complex sentences are dealt with as we saw earlier: 'not-A' is true if A is not true; 'A and B' is true if A is true and B is true; and so on. (In fact, Tarski gave the recursive definition on a notion of 'satisfaction'—s satisfies 'not-A' if s does not satisfy A, and so on—and defined truth in terms of satisfaction. But that is a complication we can ignore.) Two points are important: the definition of truth, though distinct from the adequacy conditions—that is, Tarski's theory of truth-theories—was shown to satisfy those conditions; and nowhere in either the definition of truth, nor in the theory of truth-theories, is there any explicit commitment to a particular metaphysics of truth.

What is more plausibly read into Tarski's account—though again, this is not entailed by it—is a metaphysically minimal account of truth. Such an account can take three forms: one calls itself 'minimalism' and asserts that the set of T-sentences exhausts what there is to say about truth; an older minimal account is the redundancy theory; and a more recent version is the so-called 'prosentential' theory. Let us consider the second and third of these.

According to the correspondence theory, the truth-predicate is a substantive predicate, attributing a relational property to propositions. In virtue of their correlation with facts, true propositions have a real property, a property which distinguishes them from false propositions. The redundancy theory denies this. Truth is redundant, it says, in that predicating truth of a proposition says no more than assertion of that proposition itself. Take an example: '"Matilda is sensitive and brilliant" is true' is not, according to the redundancy theory, and despite appearances, an assertion about a proposition, attributing the property of truth to it. It is, rather, an assertion about Matilda, saying she is sensitive and brilliant. It says no more and no less than the proposition 'Matilda is sensitive and brilliant'. No theory of truth is needed, for there is no such thing as truth. Tarski's T-sentences are true because right- and left-hand sides are essentially identical—they differ only notationally.

What does it mean to say that truth is not a real property? The familiar philosophical example of such a denial is existence, which we shall treat at greater length in Chapter 5. Descartes's version of the ontological argument for the existence of God claimed that since existence is a perfection and God has all perfections, God must exist. Kant's rejoinder was that perfections are properties (properties which make their possessor better in some way) and existence is not a property, so the argument collapses. Existence is not a property, since there is no difference between, say, a God and an existent God, or between a table and an existing table. If the table does not exist, there is no table. To have any properties at all, their possessor must exist. Hence existence cannot be a property.

Language is not always to be trusted. Consider the sentence 'It is raining': to ask 'What is raining?' is a sign of lack of understanding of English, or of philosophical obtuseness. Doubtless, an answer can be fabricated. But in fact the sentence does not serve to predicate 'raining' of something. It means that there is rain, that rain is falling. Grammatically, the sentence is of subject-predicate form. But there is no subject. Logically, there is only a predicate.

The predication of truth is similarly misleading. If we assert a proposition, we assert it as true. Hence, to say that it is true adds no more to it. That is what the T-sentences remind us of. But they are not simply a minimal condition against which to test a substantial theory of truth. Rather, they show us that there is no substance to truth.

Why then does language have a truth-predicate? If everything which can be done with a truth-predicate can be done without it, what possible use is there for it? To say that truth is not a real property, and that there is no substance to truth, is not to say that the notion has no use, nor that whatever can be done with it can be done without it. The truth-predicate allows us to make general claims which we could not make without it. Consider the remark: 'What John said is true', and suppose first that what John said was 'Oswald killed Kennedy'. Then we can rephrase our remark as '"Oswald killed Kennedy" is true', and then drop the redundant truth-predicate to obtain 'Oswald killed Kennedy'. We make the same claim as John.

But suppose we do not know what John said—we are endorsing his remark not because we know what he said and believe it too, but perhaps because we know that John never lies, or because someone else has told us to believe him. The truth-predicate enables us to endorse what he said without actually repeating it. Our remark has generality built into it. 'Whatever John said (on that occasion), . . .', that is, 'For all propositions, if John uttered that proposition (on that occasion), then that proposition—is true.' An early proponent of the redundancy theory was Frank Ramsey. He made an interesting observation. Suppose all propositions had the form $a R b$—e.g. 'Oswald killed Kennedy'. Then we could say: 'For all names and predicates, a, R, and b, if John said that $a R b$, then $a R b$.' In particular, if John said that Oswald killed Kennedy, then Oswald killed Kennedy. Here in the consequent of the conditional (the part following 'then') there is a verb (R). So we do not need to add 'is true'. But not all propositions have the form $a\ R\ b$—there is an unlimited number of different forms of propositions. To run through all possible forms would be impossible. So we say 'whatever John said, . . .', and then we need a verb in the consequent; we cannot simply conclude, '. . . that proposition'. The truth-predicate supplies such a verb: '. . . that proposition *is true*'.

So in what sense is truth redundant? It is not that everything that can be done with the truth-predicate can be done without it. In that sense, it is not redundant. It is required grammatically, as a dummy verb. But logically and metaphysically it is redundant. It adds nothing to the sentence to which it is added. There is no condition which can complete the criterion: 'True propositions are those which . . .' Following Tarski, we can take particular cases: ' "Oswald killed Kennedy' is true if and only if Oswald killed Kennedy.' Following Ramsey, we can partially generalize: 'True propositions of the form "$a\ R\ b$" are those for which $a\ R\ b$.' If we try to generalize completely, all we obtain is 'True propositions, p, are those for which . . .'—p? No, we cannot say that. It is ungrammatical: 'is true' must be added, as a dummy verb. But that, of course, is unhelpful and trivial: 'True propositions, p, are those for which p is true.'

The redundancy theory makes an important and salutary point. It restrains us from searching for an object-laden metaphysics of truth, from hunting for a real property of true propositions. But there is more to truth than repetition—the point about generality shows that. And more: for simply repeating what another has said misses out the aspect of endorsement. This is what the prosentential account adds to the redundancy theory. To say that a proposition is true is to do more than repeat it. It is to endorse it too. The redundancy theory is right to deny that truth is a real property; it is wrong to insist that the truth-predicate is really redundant. That is shown already by the point about generality. More important, however, is the anaphoric nature of truth-predication. To say, 'That's true', or 'What John said is true' is essentially to refer to another assertion—but not to predicate a real property of it.

The epithet 'prosentential' is a neologism, a word made up

by analogy with 'pronominal'. Anaphoric pronouns serve to refer to other nouns, and pick up their reference from them. For example, in 'Peter opened the door. He picked up the mail,' 'he' refers back to the use of 'Peter' in the first sentence. Similarly, in 'Peter picked up his mail', 'his' (if used anaphorically) refers back to 'Peter'. In these cases, we have what are called pronouns of laziness; their sense is essentially to stand in for a noun. Ignoring clumsiness, we could replace them by their antecedent: e.g. 'Peter picked up Peter's mail'—where we have to ignore the suggestion created by using 'Peter' twice that two different people are being referred to. Note that a pronoun's antecedent (we haven't defined this notion precisely) can come after the pronoun itself: e.g. 'When he had opened the door, Peter picked up the mail.' The antecedent of 'he' in the first (subordinate) clause, is 'Peter' in the second (the main) clause.

Not all anaphoric pronouns are pronouns of laziness. For example, in 'Someone opened the door. He picked up the mail,' we cannot—while preserving the sense—replace 'he' by 'someone'. Gareth Evans called such cases 'E-type pronouns'. To replace them with a noun-phrase, we have to construct it from the context: 'Someone opened the door. The person who opened the door picked up the mail.' Again, such pronouns serve to pick up a previous reference, and refer back to it. But they cannot be simply replaced by their antecedent. A third type of anaphoric pronoun is the quantificational use. Consider the proposition, 'All the students brought their passport photographs': 'their' is anaphoric, but we cannot replace it with its antecedent, nor is there a previous sentence or clause from which to construct a noun-phrase. It does not mean, 'All the students brought all the students' passport photos', so it is not a lazy pronoun. It refers back to the quantifier 'all' (other quantifiers are e.g. 'every', 'some', 'no', 'any', 'each', and so on), picking up its reference.

Truth has a similar anaphoric function. '"Oswald killed Kennedy", said John. "That's true," Mary responded.' We might first identify 'that' as an anaphoric pronoun. But we can go further. The whole phrase 'that's true' can be replaced by its antecedent. All Mary *says* is, 'Oswald killed Kennedy.' But in doing so, she endorses what John had said. That is what the redundancy theory overlooks. Adding the anaphoric element completes the account of truth. Other prosentential uses of truth are E-type: 'John said something. If it was true then . . .'—here we cannot replace 'it' by 'something', nor can we reduce 'What John said was true' to what he said. 'It was true' is a prosentence picking up the reference to what John said. Yet further uses are quantificational: e.g. 'Nothing John says is true'—that is, for all propositions, p, if John said that p, then p is not true. We cannot replace 'p' in 'p is not true' by any antecedent here. Yet 'p is not true' refers back to its quantificational antecedent, 'Everything John said.'

   Truth is not a property. We cannot characterize true propositions, for there is no common characteristic shared by true propositions. The T-sentences show us that predicating truth of a proposition is equivalent to asserting that proposition. What the truth-predicate adds to this fact is generality: the ability to make general claims abstracting from the particular; and endorsement: the anaphoric role of truth in responding to and commenting on other assertions.

Summary and Guide to Further Reading

Our first attempt to answer the question, 'What is truth?', led us to the metaphysical puzzle over the nature of facts, and how they related to—corresponded to—true propositions. G. E. Moore's paralysis in the face of the latter issue can be read in his *Some Main Problems of Philosophy*, ed. H. D. Lewis, chs. 14–15, lectures given in Cambridge in 1912 and the ensuing years (though not published until long after). Russell's answer, his logical atomism in which the nature of reality was read off the logical structure of language, was published in his lectures, 'The Philosophy of Logical Atomism', reprinted in his *Logic and Knowledge*, ed. R. C. Marsh. Wittgenstein's more thoroughgoing logical atomism, in which the picture theory of meaning acts as the tie between language and the world, can be found in his *Tractatus Logico-Philosophicus*, tr. D. Pears and B. McGuinness. But the style of the *Tractatus* is opaque, and a clearer overview

of correspondence theories and logical atomism can be found in
J. Urmson's *Philosophical Analysis* or in D. J. O'Connor's *The
Correspondence Theory of Truth*.

The objections to correspondence theories that I focused on
were essentially ontological: can a plausible account be given of
facts (and the correspondence relation) which shows that recognizing their existence as ontologically autonomous is essential? Gottlob Frege put forward another argument against them,
indeed against any theory of truth which claims that truth is a
substantive concept. The idea is that the equivalence between
A and 'It is true that *A*' coupled to any such claim will induce
a vicious regress (and so entail that such a theory is incoherent).
The argument is summarized, and criticized, in S. Blackburn,
Spreading the Word, ch. 7. Some see in this argument the first
mooting of minimalism in the theory of truth.

The correspondence theory has a more modern guise, inspired by a paper of J. L. Austin, 'How to Talk', reprinted in his
Philosophical Papers: it is called 'situational semantics', and is
described in *Situations and Attitudes* by J. Barwise and J. Perry.
Some directional pointers for the new theory are set out by
Barwise in ch. 11: 'Notes on Branch Points in Situation Theory'
of his *The Situation in Logic*. Keith Devlin's *Logic and Information* is a careful and gentle introduction to situation theory.

The deepest puzzles are: what is a situation, and do we really
need them? This is the original puzzle, which led us to ask:
'What is a theory of truth for?', and 'How should theories of
truth be evaluated?' Tarski's formal and material adequacy
conditions were first formulated in a long paper published
around 1930, but can be found expressed more succinctly in his
'The Semantic Conception of Truth', reprinted in *Readings in
Philosophical Analysis*, ed. H. Feigl and W. Sellars. Tarski's
own account of truth itself led to the development of model
theory in formal logic. A useful survey paper on Tarski's work,
covering the theories of both this and the next chapter, can be
found in 'Tarski on Truth and Logical Consequence' by John
Etchemendy. A reworking of the correspondence theory, inspired by Tarski's results, was presented by Donald Davidson
in 'True to the Facts', reprinted in his *Essays on Truth and*

Interpretation. A clear presentation of theories of truth including Tarski's contribution, can be found in S. Haack, *Philosophy of Logics*, ch. 7. This is also the focus of Mark Platts' discussion of truth in the first chapter of his *Ways of Meaning*.

Reflection on Tarski's material adequacy condition led us to wonder what is really achieved by the ascription of truth. Ramsey's intriguing observation which later developed into the redundancy and other minimal theories of truth was made in his 'Facts and Propositions', collected after his untimely death at the age of 27 in 1930 in *The Foundations of Mathematics and Other Essays* by R. B. Braithwaite. The redundancy theory, that the ascription of truth is essentially redundant and says no more than the sentence whose truth is averred, was developed by Arthur Prior in the 1960s and has a limpid articulation in Christopher Williams's *What is Truth?* The prosentential theory adds to redundancy the reminder of the anaphoric nature of truth: asserting truth not only reasserts what was said, it endorses it. The theory was set out by Dorothy Grover and others in 'A Prosentential Theory of Truth'. This, and others of her papers developing the theme, are collected in her book, *A Prosentential Theory of Truth*.

Recent years have, none the less, seen a strong reaction to minimalist ideas, and attempts to delineate a substantial notion of truth without the unacceptable metaphysics of the full correspondence theory. For example, Hilary Putnam, in 'A Comparison of Something with Something Else', dismisses Tarski's work as giving no philosophical insight whatever into the concept of truth. In many other places—a very readable account is given in his *Reason, Truth and History*, especially chapter 3—he has defended a form of realism he calls 'internal realism' to distinguish it from 'metaphysical realism', which he rejects. The essential idea of the internalist account, which it shares with the constructivist views we shall look at in Chapter 8, is that there is no external standpoint from which one can compare what we say and think with how things are: there is only the internal standpoint, the perspective within a scheme of description.

A general treatment (and critique) of minimalist (there called 'deflationary') treatments is given by Hartry Field in 'The

Deflationary Conception of Truth', in *Fact, Science and Morality*, ed. G. Macdonald and C. Wright. Crispin Wright has recently launched a further sustained attack on the idea that truth is not a substantial property in his *Truth and Objectivity*. It cannot account, he claims, for essential features of the concept of truth, in particular, that it is distinct from, and goes beyond, justified assertibility, in being stable (once true, always true) and absolute (so not admitting, as justification does, of degree).

2 The Power of Logic: Logical Consequence

LOGICAL consequence is the central concept in logic. The aim of logic is to clarify what follows from what, to determine which are the valid consequences of a given set of premises or assumptions. The consequence relation relates a set or collection of given propositions to those propositions or conclusions which correctly, or validly, follow from them. We can say that the premises entail the conclusion; or that the conclusion (validly) follows from the premises; or that one may correctly infer the conclusion from the premises; that the conclusion is a (valid) logical consequence of the premises; or that the argument or inference from premises to conclusion is valid. It is this essential relation, logical consequence, which is the topic of this chapter.

When broaching the topic of truth in the previous chapter, I contrasted our common lack of hesitation in determining the truth of various claims with our uncertainty when faced with the question of what truth itself is. The present situation is different. Logical consequence is not the everyday concept which truth is. To be sure, we do express a view as to whether one proposition follows from another, and whether an argument is valid or not. But logic has a task additional to that required of a theory of truth. A theory of truth requires a conceptual analysis of the concept of truth, a statement of what truth consists in. A theory of logical consequence, while requiring a conceptual analysis of consequence, also searches for a set of techniques to determine the validity of particular arguments. That is what much of logic consists in, elaborating semantic and proof-theoretic methods for establishing the validity and invalidity of arguments.

But there is another aspect to this conceptual analysis which at least must go hand in hand with, if not be prior to, the development of technical methods. This conceptual analysis is the real philosophy of logic. Particular logical theories are based on particular decisions as to the correct analysis of consequence. Classical logic, and theories based on it such as modal logic, first-order arithmetic, set theory, and so on, have at their root a particular analysis of the notion of logical consequence. Rival logical theories, such as intuitionistic logic, paraconsistent logics, relevant logics, connexive logics, and so on, are based on different philosophical analyses of this basic notion.

The contrast with theories of truth is dramatic. With a few exceptions (for example, whether to count the semantic paradoxes as true, false, or neither—see Chapter 6), there is no disagreement in truth theories about the actual truth-values which should be accorded to particular propositions. The disagreement is about what truth consists in, what the correct account of the concept of truth is. In the case of logical consequence, in addition to so differing about the proper basis of the notion, there is actual disagreement about the validity and invalidity of particular arguments.

The Classical Conception

The classical conception of consequence takes its name from its being the orthodoxy against which rivals are measured. It consists of a closely worked collection of views concerning both the extension of the concept, that is, views as to which arguments are valid and which are not, and concerning its intension, that is, as to the philosophical basis of that determination of validity.

First, on the classical view, validity is a matter of form. Individual arguments are valid only in virtue of instantiating valid logical forms; one proposition is a logical consequence of others only if there is a valid pattern which the propositions together match. For example, 'This match will light' follows from the propositions, 'All matches light when struck' and 'This match is about to be struck'. The argument exhibits the same structure as this one: 'Edmund is a mountaineer. All mountaineers are brave. So Edmund is brave.' The common pattern can be set

out, as described in many logic textbooks, as follows: '*Fa*. All
*F*s are *G*. So *Ga*.' First we let *a* mean 'this match', *F* mean 'is
(about to be) struck' and *G* mean '(will) light(s)'; secondly, we
let *a* mean 'Edmund', *F* mean 'is a mountaineer' and *G* mean
'is brave'. In each case, by replacing the schematic letters *a*, *F*,
and *G* by the English expressions according to the key, we obtain
the particular inferences in turn. And we can use alternative
keys to generate indefinitely many arguments of the same form.

The classical view makes two claims about this form and its
instances (and similar claims about other valid forms): first, that
the form is valid, and so, in virtue of instantiating a valid form,
the particular inferences are valid; secondly, that it is only in
virtue of instantiating such a form that these arguments are
valid. That is, any argument which does not conform to a valid
pattern is invalid. Its conclusion does not validly follow from its
premisses. For example, 'Edmund is brave. All mountaineers
are brave. So Edmund is a mountaineer.' Here the conclusion
is not a logical consequence of the premisses. There is no valid
form of which this is an instance.

So validity is a matter of form, and the task of logic is to
provide techniques for identifying and discerning the logical
form of various arguments, and for determining whether the
forms discovered in this way are indeed valid. But the question
remains, of course: which are the valid forms? It is fairly clear
in the above examples that the first two are valid and the third
is not. We don't need logic to tell us that. But what is the basis
of that judgement? What is the criterion by which we judge arguments, and argument-forms, to be valid? What is the correct
analysis of logical consequence?

According to the classical account, it is truth-preservation.
That is, an argument-form is valid if, however the schematic
letters are interpreted, the result does not consist of a collection
of true premisses and a false conclusion. For example, take
our third example above. We might formalize it as: '*Fa*. All *G*s
are *F*. So *Ga*', with *a* as Edmund, *F* as 'is brave' and *G* as 'is a
mountaineer'. This form is invalid. For let *a* stand for a moth,
interpret *F* as 'was once a caterpillar' and *G* as 'is a butterfly'.
Then we obtain as an instance of the form: 'This moth was once

a caterpillar. All butterflies were once caterpillars. So this moth is a butterfly', whose conclusion is clearly false, even though its premisses are true. It follows from the truth-preservation condition that the form is invalid. It has an instance (about moths and butterflies) whose premisses are true and conclusion false. Moreover, the third example can yield no other form which is valid. Hence it is not an instance of a valid form, and accordingly is invalid. Its conclusion is not a valid logical consequence of its premisses.

In contrast, the first form we looked at is a valid one: '*Fa*. All *F*s are *G*. So *Ga*.' There is no interpretation of *a*, *F*, and *G* under which the premisses come out true and the conclusion false. It follows that *Ga* is indeed a logical consequence of *Fa* and 'All *F*s are *G*', and that 'This match will light' follows logically from 'This match is struck' and 'All matches light when struck'. The classical truth-preservation criterion agrees with intuition on such simple examples as the three we looked at above, and extends it to a whole range of arguments and inferences. Logical consequence is a matter of form, namely, that however the schematic letters are interpreted, truth is preserved from premiss to conclusion: we never obtain true premisses and false conclusion.

Valid arguments need not have true premisses, nor need invalid arguments have false conclusions. Perhaps not all matches do light when struck; perhaps this match will never be struck. None the less, the claim that it will light follows from the other, possibly false, claims. Similarly, even if Edmund is a mountaineer, that he is does not follow from the fact that he is brave and all mountaineers are brave (if they are). The form is invalid, and it is so because there are instances in which the conclusion is actually false ('This moth is a butterfly') even though the premisses are true.

It is helpful here to say something about the notion of logical truth. In the early twentieth century a number of authors (perhaps under the influence of the axiomatic method) seem to have concentrated on logical truth as the primary logical notion, and logical consequence became an afterthought. This is a grave mistake, completely reversing the real situation. Consequence

cannot be defined in terms of logical truth; but logical truth is
a degenerate, or extremal, case of consequence. It can be characterized in two equivalent ways. First, a logical truth is the
conclusion of a valid inference with no premises. Clearly, an
argument can have one, two, three, or more premises. Later
we will consider the case where the number of premises in-
creases to infinity. But what if it decreases to zero? Remember
that a proposition or propositional form is a classical logical
consequence of a number of premises if, however the schematic
letters are interpreted, the result does not consist of true
premises and a false conclusion. So, if the number of premises
is zero, we obtain the following characterization: a proposition
or propositional form is a logical truth if, however the schematic
letters are interpreted, the result is not false. In other words,
logical truths are true however their constituents are interpreted.
Consider, for example, the formula (propositional form) 'A or
not-A'. Whatever sentence is substituted for A, this comes out
true: 'This match will light or it will not light', 'Edmund is brave
or not brave', and so on. Similarly, the formula 'all Fs are F' is
a logical truth. Whatever predicate is substituted for F, the result
is true: 'All mountaineers are mountaineers', 'All matches are
matches', and so on. Logical truths are the extremal case of
valid arguments with no premises or assumptions.

Another way to characterize logical truth is in terms of sup-
pression. Logical truths are those propositions in the premises
of an argument which are unnecessary, or may be suppressed.
Suppose a conclusion validly follows from a collection of
premises, and suppose one of those premises is true under
any interpretation. Then the conclusion logically follows from
the other premises alone. For if the argument is valid, then
any interpretation which makes the conclusion false must make
one of the premises false too. But that cannot be the logical
truth, the particular premiss under consideration. So validity
will not be affected by omitting it—it will still be true that any
interpretation making the conclusion false will make one of the
premises in the new argument (omitting the logical truth) false.
So the logical truth is redundant, and can be suppressed.

Our description of the classical account is not yet complete, however. For there are a number of ways in which the notion of truth-preservation is articulated which are distinctive of the account. First, note that as presently outlined, truth-preservation is essentially a substitutional criterion. We take an argument, M. We replace a certain amount of terminology in M by schematic letters, to obtain an argument-form, M'. We then interpret the schematic letters in M' in various ways, looking to see whether any instance of M' has true premises and false conclusion. Suppose it does, that is, that there is an instance N of M' with true premises and a false conclusion. Then N results from M by substituting one or more terms for others—by replacing certain expressions in M by different ones. For example, we obtained our counterexample to the validity of the third example above by replacing 'Edmund' by 'this moth', 'is brave' by 'was once a caterpillar' and 'is a mountaineer' by 'is a butterfly'. By such a substitution we would obtain an argument which led from truth to falsity. Hence the original example could not be guaranteed to lead us from truth only to truth (since another of the same form does not). So it must be invalid. That is, in general an argument is invalid if there is some substitution for the terms in it which yields true premises and a false conclusion; and an argument is valid if there is no such substitution.

This raises an immediate problem, of course: which substitutions are permissible—that is, which terms may be replaced? For the classical account does not permit every term in an argument to be open to substitution. This restriction is contained within the notion of form, of which we have perhaps said too little. Note that in all the forms above, one word was not replaced by a schematic letter, namely, the word 'all'. This is, on the classical conception (and indeed all others) a reserved term, part of the logical vocabulary. In exhibiting the logical form of an argument, we replace all expressions other than those in the logical vocabulary by schematic letters. Logical words include 'all', 'some', 'if', 'and', 'or', 'not', and a number of others. Indeed, some words are treated sometimes as logical, sometimes not, yielding different logics. For example, if 'necessarily' is treated as a logical word, we obtain modal logic, an extension of classical logic; if not, non-modal, that is, standard logic. If the 'is' of identity (as in 'The morning star is the evening star') is taken as a logical term, we obtain classical logic with identity, if not, not. Many extensions of classical logic (so themselves essentially classical) are obtained by extending the logical vocabulary.

The classical account is not, however, purely substitutional. The substitutional criterion dates back to Bolzano in the early nineteenth century. But it cannot stand as it is—it gives absurd answers, for it declares valid certain inferences which are clearly invalid. A simple example takes an apparent logical truth, but the point can be generalized straightforwardly to inferences with one or more premisses. Consider the proposition, 'There are at least two things'. It's not a matter of logic that there are at least two things. None the less, the Bolzano or purely substitutional criterion characterizes this as a logical truth, given the usual acceptance of the quantifier 'some' or 'there are', negation, and identity as logical expressions. For the proposition is equivalent to 'There are two things which are not identical', and in this proposition there are no non-logical expressions. In other words, there are no schematic letters in its form for which to make differing substitutions, and so the question of its logical truth reduces to that of its truth. Since there are in the world at least 10^{80} atoms, the proposition is true—and similarly, arguments such as 'There are two things, so there are 76 things', 'It is raining, so there are 10^{26} things' and so on, turn out valid. This is clearly absurd.

Tarski's solution was to add to the substitutional account a varying domain of interpretation (and to lift the requirement that every element of the domain have a name). An interpretation is now to consist of a domain (which may not be empty—the non-emptiness of the domain is characteristic of classical logic, in which 'There is at least one thing' continues to be taken as a logical truth—see Chapter 5) and an interpretation of the schematic letters over that domain. The proposition 'There are at least two things' may now be falsified, as may the conclusions of the inferences in the last paragraph, while their premisses are kept true, by suitable choice of domain and interpretation. For example, 'There are at least two things' is false when interpreted over a domain containing only one thing.

There are two further aspects of the classical notion of logical consequence which need to be brought out before we turn to consider alternatives. Both elaborate further what is classically understood by 'truth-preservation'. Consider the notion of logical truth as characterized above. It is an immediate consequence of its explanation that a logical truth is not only a consequence of the empty set of premisses, but that it is also a consequence of any set of premisses whatever. For if it cannot be made false by any substitution or interpretation, then whatever the premisses, it cannot be made false jointly with the truth of those premisses. Hence every argument whose conclusion is a logical truth is valid. For example, the proposition 'All matches are matches' logically follows from any set of propositions whatever. Similarly, any proposition of the form 'A or not-A' is a logical consequence of any other proposition or set of propositions.

Conversely, take any proposition or formula which cannot be made true by any substitution or interpretation, such as one of the form 'no Fs are Fs' or 'A and not-A'. Then there will be no interpretation making it true jointly with the falsehood of another proposition. It follows that any proposition whatever is a classical logical consequence of such a contradictory proposition. A contradiction entails any proposition whatever. This principle is often known as *Ex Falso Quodlibet*, which in Latin means, 'from the false, anything whatever', that is, anything follows from what is (logically) false. It is also sometimes called the 'spread law', that an inconsistency spreads to every proposition. Define the *logical closure* of a set of propositions as the set of all propositions which logically follow from those propositions, and call any logically closed set of propositions a *theory*. Thus a theory encompasses all its logical consequences. We say that a theory is consistent if it contains no proposition and its negation, and that it is trivial if it contains every proposition. It follows from the classical account of logical consequence that any inconsistent theory is trivial.

Compactness

In its purely substitutional version, that of Bolzano, the classical view is found to overgenerate: it counts as valid inferences which are clearly invalid; for example, as we have seen, any inference with the conclusion, 'There are at least two things'. So the prevailing view, the classical account as deriving from the work of Tarski, has been amended to avoid such overgeneration. Later, I will argue that in accounting any inconsistent theory trivial and any logical truth a consequence of any set of propositions the classical account also overgenerates—but this feature is essential to and characteristic of the account here called 'classical'. The third and final aspect of the classical view which remains to be brought out is an aspect in which it undergenerates, that is, in which it fails to count as valid, arguments which plausibly should be recognized as valid logical consequences. I will use the phrase 'classical view' to cover that view which rejects such inferences as not being logically valid. But there are proponents of what is really at heart the classical account who are willing to extend it to cover these inferences.

The aspect in question is known as compactness: classical logical consequence is compact. To understand this notion, we need to generalize the idea of an argument's having a number of premisses, so that this collection of premisses can be infinite. We have implicitly done this already in introducing the notion of a theory. For any single proposition has infinitely many consequences—on the classical account, every logical truth (of which there are infinitely many) is a consequence of any proposition, and even setting that fact aside, any proposition entails itself, its double negation, the conjunction of itself with its double negation, the disjunction of itself with any proposition, and so on. But a theory was defined as a set of propositions which contains all its logical consequences. So we have recognized that the relation of logical consequence can hold (and fail to hold) between a theory, that is, an infinite set of premisses, and a proposition. We say that a consequence relation is *compact* if any consequence of an infinite set of propositions is a consequence of some finite subset of them. The compactness of classical consequence does not mean that it denies that an inference can have infinitely many premisses. It can; but classically, it is valid if and only if the conclusion follows from a finite subset of them.

Compactness can be seen as a virtue—it makes the consequence relation more manageable. But it is also a limitation—it limits the expressive power of a logic. So far we have concentrated on the semantic aspect of classical logical consequence, namely, truth-preservation. Consequence can, however, also be thought of in purely syntactic terms. As such, one thinks of one proposition as a consequence of a set of others if one can derive it from them in a series of steps, where these steps accord with certain rules. This is proof-theory, where the correctness of an application of a rule of inference is entirely a matter of its form, abstracting from the meaning of the symbols involved. Of course, ultimately the rules one accepts will be answerable to the semantic notion, so that one wants assurance that falsehood cannot be derived from truth. But in itself a proof has no meaning; its correctness is defined in terms of its shape and structure.

The idea of a proof, therefore, is that one can check whether a given formula is a consequence of certain others by recursively checking that the proof is well formed. Soundness—that if the proof is correctly formed the conclusion really is a logical consequence of the premisses—is paramount; its converse, completeness, that a derivation should exist matching every case of consequence, though highly desirable, cannot be given the same importance. Given that our proof-methods are sound, a proof can establish with certainty that one proposition is a consequence of others.

Kurt Gödel's first significant result, his Completeness Theorem, proved in 1930, established that there was a complete proof-method for classical consequence. His second important result, his Incompleteness Theorem of 1931, showed that result up for the empty victory it was. Compact consequence has a matching proof-method; but compact consequence undergenerates—there are intuitively valid consequences which it marks as invalid. The clearest and most famous example is the ω-rule. Suppose some formula A is true of every natural number, 0,1,2,..., that is, $A(0)$ holds, $A(1)$ holds, and $A(n)$ holds for every natural number n. Then it obviously follows that the formula 'for every n, $A(n)$' is true. 'For every n, $A(n)$' is a logical consequence of the infinite set of formulae, $A(0)$, $A(1)$, $A(2)$, and so on. But it is not a classical logical consequence of them, for it does not follow from any finite subset of that collection. The ω-rule would permit one to infer 'for every n, $A(n)$' from the premisses $A(0)$, $A(1)$, and so on. It is not a rule, however, that one could ever use—it would require that a proof be an infinite object, containing proofs of each of $A(0)$, $A(1)$, and so on. The ω-rule is not accepted as a rule of orthodox classical proof-theory, and its validity is not accepted in orthodox classical consequence.

How is this possible? For a rule is valid according to the classical account unless by some interpretation over some domain the premiss may be made true and the conclusion false. How can the premisses $A(0)$, $A(1)$, and so on be true but 'for every n, $A(n)$' be false? How can $A(n)$ be true for every n while 'for every n, $A(n)$' is false? The explanation is the limitation on expressibility which follows from choosing a compact logic. The aim of logicians at the turn of the twentieth century was to axiomatize mathematics—to find a finite set of axioms, or at least a finitely specifiable such set, from which the whole of mathematics could be derived, and only that. It was a foundational endeavour to establish the consistency and coherence of mathematics and to complete a task which had occupied mathematicians throughout the nineteenth century: to remove the unclarities and uncertainties in mathematics which they had inherited from their predecessors, and exhibit by proof-theoretical methods a clear, certain, and consistent theory. Gödel's 1931 result showed that even for arithmetic this could not be done. The standard model of arithmetic, usually called ω, consists of the natural numbers 0,1,2, and so on, with operations of successor, addition, multiplication, and exponentiation on them. The aim was to find a set of formulae which characterize this model exactly—in the jargon, 'categorically', meaning that up to isomorphism, that is, purely structurally and ignoring renaming of elements, the axioms should have only one model, the standard model, ω. Gödel showed that no compact logic can do that—in fact, he showed that no proof-methods in any logic can do it. In a non-compact logic there can be a categorical set of formulae for arithmetic, but as we noted, proof-methods (as usually understood) require compactness.

There is another way to see the difference between compact and non-compact logic. Orthodox classical logic is first-order; a categorical set of axioms for arithmetic must be second-order. What does this mean? We need to think a little more carefully about the notion of form, and in particular about schematic letters (used to replace non-logical predicates) and quantifiers. Quantifiers are the words such as 'all', 'some', 'no', 'any', 'every', 'there are', which qualify a predicate, as in 'every F is G', or a dummy-predicate, as in 'There are two things which are not identical'. In general, in classical logic the use of quantifiers is regimented so that they 'bind' or are tied to variables; the two examples become 'For every x, if x is F (or Fx) then Gx' and 'There are x and y such that $x \neq y$', using = for 'identical to' and $\neq$ for 'is not identical to'. Here the quantified variables range over or refer to things, objects, separate from the properties referred to by the predicates which stand in for the schematic letters (F, G, etc.). This is first-order logic; in second-order logic we allow quantifiers to range over and refer to properties as well. For example, to formalize 'Napoleon had all the qualities of a great general', we would quantify over properties (or qualities). What it says is that Napoleon had all those qualities which only great generals have, that is all those qualities, anyone who possessed which was a great general. That is, 'For every quality f, if for every person x, if x was a great general then x had f, then Napoleon had f', that is, 'For every f, if for every person x, if Gx then fx, then f (Napoleon)'. Here 'f' is a first-order variable, distinct from the individual variable, x, and from the schematic letter G, representing 'was a great general'. In first-order logic, only individual variables, ranging over things (and people) are allowed in addition to schematic letters; in second-order logic, first-order variables, ranging over properties of those things, are also permitted.

Actually, it is more subtle than this. For syntactically, one cannot tell whether a formula such as 'For every f, if for every x, if Gx then fx, then fn' is first-order or second-order. It could be a formula of a many-sorted first-order theory, where f ranges over one sort of object, x over another. What distinguishes first-order from second-order logic is its semantics, and the crucial question is, what constitutes the range of a variable such as f here. We've commented on the fact that in setting up an interpretation, one must specify a domain, and that that domain may be arbitrary (provided it is non-empty). So if f is an individual variable, its range of interpretation can be arbitrary. Only if it is first-order must it range over all properties; the defining factor of second-order logic is that, while the domain of its individual variables may be arbitrary, the range of the first-order variables consists of all properties of the objects in its domain (or if we are thinking extensionally, of all sets of objects in the domain). That is why second-order arithmetic is categorical—indeed, there is a single formula of second-order logic whose only model is the standard model, ω, consisting of just the natural numbers. Every arithmetic truth is a (second-order) consequence of this formula. None the less, second-order arithmetic is incomplete, in the sense (which Gödel was interested in) that there is no set of inference-rules by which all those truths may be derived from that formula, or from any finitely specifiable set of axioms.

If we return to first-order logic, the classical orthodoxy, we can now understand why the ω-rule fails to be valid. The standard model of arithmetic, ω, is an initial segment of every model of the first-order truths of arithmetic. That is, ω forms the first part of every model—and in the case of the standard model, all of it. But the other models contain additional, non-standard numbers, all larger than the standard natural numbers (for it is a truth of arithmetic, which we can state in a formula, that every non-zero natural number is larger than zero, and if a non-standard number were less than some standard number, n, say, it would have to be identical with one of the n standard numbers less than n). That is why the ω-rule fails: whatever proposition instantiates $A(n)$, it can hold of all the standard numbers, 0,1,2, and so on, and still fail to be true of every number in the model—so that although all the premisses of the ω-rule, $A(0)$, $A(1)$, and so on are true in this model, the conclusion, 'for every n, $A(n)$' is false.

One might be led by this explanation actually to object that the ω-rule really is (logically) invalid. In citing the ω-rule as an objection to the compactness of classical logic, it was crucial that we accept both that the ω-rule is classically invalid, and that it is really valid. But its validity depends on the sequence 0,1,2,... exhausting the natural numbers. So we might suppose that the ω-rule as it stands is invalid; it needs an extra premiss: 'and these are all the numbers'. This additional clause is arithmetically true; but the non-standard models show that as a matter of logic it must be stated explicitly (in first-order, i.e. logical, terms).

There are two ways of seeing that this response is inadequate as a defence of classical logic and its compactness. First, the extra clause, 'and these are all the numbers', cannot be expressed in first-order terms. This is clear, since we have seen that no set of formulae of first-order logic has ω as its only model. So again, first-order logic is inadequate to capture the validity of the ω-rule—seen this way, it cannot even be expressed in first-order terms.

The other response (which is not essentially a different one) is to relate the issue to a problem in logic of some antiquity. Wittgenstein in his logical atomism proposed a reduction of 'every F is G' to 'this F is G and that F is G and ...', an indefinite conjunction ranging over every F. Russell objected that the two propositions are not equivalent, for the second (the long conjunction) needs a final clause, 'and these are all the Fs'. I believe he was wrong. If the conjunction was exhaustive (that is, contained reference to every F), the two propositions were equivalent; if not, the extra clause is ineffective, since it is false. So too with the ω-rule. Since 0,1,2,... is a complete list of the natural numbers, it is unnecessary to add that claim as an extra premiss. It does no extra work. If $A(n)$ is true for every n, then 'for every n, $A(n)$' is true. The non-standard models of first-order logic are just that, non-standard. They contain objects which are not numbers.

Second-order arithmetic is able to rule out these non-standard models, and the non-standard numbers they contain, because we can express in it the fact that the standard model is an initial segment of all the other models, and that it is this initial segment, ω, in which we are interested. We express it in the induction axiom, which says that any property possessed by zero

and by the successor of any number with the property belongs
to every number. It is crucial to the success of this axiom that
we mean 'any property'. In the first-order induction axiom, only
a schematic letter is used, and that might only range over a
subset of properties, a subset which does not exclude the funny
non-standard numbers. The semantics of second-order logic
ensures that 'any property' means 'any property', and so gives
the needed categoricity.

First-order logic is complete in the Pickwickian sense that
there is a set of inference rules by which a proof can be constructed deriving from given premises every first-order consequence of these premises. It is incomplete in that not every
intuitively valid consequence of these premises is indeed a
first-order consequence of them. Second-order logic is complete
in the sense that its consequence relation matches the intuitive
one. It is incomplete in that there is no set of proof-methods
and inference rules adequate to derive all those formulae from
the premises whose consequences they are.

Matter and Form

We now have a clear conception of the account of logical
consequence supplied by classical logic. Logical consequence is
a matter of form: one proposition is a logical consequence of
others if all propositions of the same form are consequences
of others of the same form; and one formula is a consequence
of others if there is no domain and interpretation of the schematic letters rendering the one true and the other false.

Even setting aside the incompleteness we looked at in the
last section, one might well query this account. For it appears
cavalierly to dismiss a whole range of valid consequences,
namely, those which though valid are not valid in virtue of their
form. Take the case of logical truths, in particular. Is it really
the case that all logical truths are so purely in virtue of their
form? Consider, for example, 'Nothing is both round and square
(at the same time)'. Neither 'round' nor 'square' is a logical
expression, so the proposition's form is 'nothing is both F and
G', which can clearly be made false by suitable interpretation

of *F* and *G*. But that must have overlooked something, for 'Nothing is both round and square' cannot be false. It is a necessary truth.

The classical criterion of logical consequence makes no mention of necessity. Indeed, that is seen by its champions as a virtue. It avoids talk of necessity by speaking instead of permissible interpretations or substitutions. An argument is valid if it instantiates a valid form; and a form is valid if there is no (permissible) interpretation of the schematic letters (over some domain) under which the premisses are true and the conclusion false. It might be thought that this captures the same notion as to say: an argument is valid if it is impossible for the premisses to be true and the conclusion false. For is it not the same to say '*A* might be false' and 'There is an interpretation of *A* under which it is false'? Suppose *A* is 'Edmund is a mountaineer': what we did earlier was represent its form as *Ga*, then interpret *a* as 'this moth' and *G* as 'is a butterfly'. So interpreted, *Ga* is false. Effectively, what we have done is substitute 'this moth' for 'Edmund' and 'is a butterfly' for 'is a mountaineer', and see whether any such substitution renders the proposition false. It seems that *A* might be false if and only if there is a substitution for the non-logical expressions in *A* which makes it false.

In fact, we have already seen that it cannot be as simple as that. For varying the interpretation of constituent expressions cannot represent a variation in the number of things there are, yet such a variation can show the failure of an entailment. So the interpretational criterion, if we may call it that, needs to be modified by the addition of a varying domain of interpretation. Nevertheless, we now find that the interpretational account still fails to represent the possibilities which are relevant. It is just not true that 'Nothing is both round and square' could be false because one can replace 'round' and 'square' by suitable expressions and obtain a proposition which is false.

The interpretational account, as represented by the classical criterion, is an attempt to avoid a certain modal metaphysics. We will discuss it further in Chapter 4. The problem is thought to be this: one account of modal propositions, propositions that say what might or what must be the case, is that they refer to possible situations in which those things really are the case. For example, to say that Edmund might be a mountaineer is to say that there is a possible situation, or as it is often called, a possible world, in which Edmund really is a mountaineer. A possible world is a complete determination of the truth-values of all propositions over a certain domain. Classically it is required to be consistent and complete—that is, no proposition and its contradictory take the same truth-value, so one or other of them must be true and not both.

Modal Platonism is the philosophical claim that such possible worlds are more than simply a specification of the truth-values of propositions: they are real worlds, as full in their elaborate complexity as the one in which we live. Our world is special only in that it is actual—ours is the actual world. But these other worlds exist and are real since, it is claimed, their existence is needed for modal propositions to have the value they do. The 'metaphor' of possible worlds must be taken literally. 'Edmund might be a mountaineer' is true if and only if there really is a possible world in which Edmund really is a mountaineer. That world may not be actual—that is, Edmund may not actually be a mountaineer—but the truth of the modal proposition (and surely it is true) requires that there be such a world.

Modal Platonism is ontologically profligate and epistemologically problematic. Occam's Razor recommends that we include no more in an explanation than is strictly needed. Of course, the modal Platonist believes that possible worlds, in their full reality, are indeed needed. The classical criterion of validity tries to show they are not. Moreover, modal Platonism raises its own problems, epistemological ones as to whether, if modal Platonism was true, we could ever know the truth of a modal proposition. For how would we ever discover the truth-values of propositions in other worlds? We are inhabitants of this world, the actual world, so our sensory processes represent to us information about how things actually are. Edmund is, let us suppose, not a mountaineer. According to modal Platonism, to find out if he might be, requires us to know whether there is a world in which he is one. Indeed, we seem to have the cart before the horse. Surely, to find out if there is such a world, we think about Edmund (the actual Edmund) and mountains (actual mountains) and whether he could climb them. But that not only tells us whether there is a possible world in which Edmund climbs mountains, it also and directly tells us whether Edmund might climb them. In other words, the reality of possible worlds is irrelevant to discovering the truth of modal propositions.

That does not show that modal Platonism is false. The modal Platonist (like the mathematical Platonist) will deny that knowledge always depends on a causal relation. The reality of possible worlds is an ontological requirement, to secure the truth-values of modal propositions. None the less, if it were the only plausible account of modality (and we will explore another in Chapter 4) one would obviously be led rapidly to consider ways of avoiding modality altogether. The classical account is one such: to replace talk of necessity and possibility, and of possible worlds and possible situations, with talk of permissible interpretations and substitution. For this brings everything within our epistemological compass. It is we who interpret expressions and give them their meaning; it is we who take other expressions and substitute them to produce new propositions from old ones; it is we who look to see whether the resulting propositions are actually true. The interpretational account promises to reduce metaphysically problematic language to clear and hygienic forms of expression.

The reduction fails, however. For 'Nothing is round and square' is necessarily true, but its non-logical components can be interpreted in such a way as to make it false. One might appeal to the earlier point about varying domains to urge that some minor revision would overcome the problem. For that seemed to be a good strategy with the converse problem, that 'There are at least two things' is not necessarily, and so not logically, true. But in fact we can now see that admitting varying domains was a disaster for the classical account. When varying the interpretation, or making a substitution, one looked to see if the proposition was actually true or false; when varying the domain, one has to look to see if the proposition would be true or false—modality has returned. We can change the actual interpretation of the terms; we can effect a substitution of one expression for another. But we cannot actually vary the domain. One might reply that one can: one interprets the variables as ranging over a subset of the actual universe—for example, in showing that 'There are at least two things' might be false. Yet to suppose this is always possible requires fudging the question of how big the actual universe is. However big it is, one can find inferences whose invalidity is shown only by considering a bigger universal domain. We can only speculate or calculate or divine what the truth of a proposition would be in such a situation. And if we can do that, then we can also speculate or calculate or divine what would be the case if Edmund, and all mountaineers, were brave. In particular, we can see that Edmund would not necessarily be a mountaineer.

Logical consequence is really a matter of what would be the case if the premisses were true. One proposition is a logical consequence of others if it would be true if those others were true, that is, if it is impossible for the one lot to be true and the other false. Logical consequence provides a guarantee that their conclusions are true if their premisses are true, that is, that their conclusions cannot be false when their premisses are true. Classical logic tries to replace this talk of necessity and impossibility by interpretations and substitutions, but it is inadequate. In particular, by insisting that all logical consequence is a matter of form, it fails to include as valid consequences those inferences whose correctness depends on the connections between non-logical terms. Given that an object is round, it follows that it is not square; but this inference is not valid in virtue of form, but in virtue of content, of what it means to be round. We can say that the inference is materially valid, that is, valid in virtue of matter, not of form.

Such connections between terms are often called analytic connections. In keeping with the insistence on the formal nature of consequence, the nature of analytic connections has come under attack from classical logicians during this century. One way to defend classical logic, and the claim that all valid consequence is validity in virtue of form, is to dismiss analytic connections, and analytic truths, as lacking the firmness and immutability of logic.

Another way of defending the formal nature of validity is to dismiss examples such as 'Nothing is both round and square' as not logical truths, but truths about meaning. Compare it with 'Every plane map can be coloured with at most four colours' (the Four Colour Theorem); though true, and necessarily true, that is not a logical truth, but a truth of mathematics. Its proof requires substantial mathematical assumptions, which we believe to hold of necessity. So not all necessary truths are truths of logic. In the same way, 'This is not square' might be said not to follow logically from 'This is round', but only with the addition of an extra premiss, this time a fact about meaning, namely, 'Nothing is both round and square'. Actually, the case of mathematics is a difficult one: in particular, one explanation of our ability to grasp the truth of mathematical propositions is that they can be reduced to logic. Much of mathematics can be developed in second-order logic, which I argued earlier was logic—and conversely, those who believe mathematics goes beyond logic use that fact to argue that classical logic is right to exclude second-order logic. The ω-rule is then seen not as a logically valid inference, but one which is substantially mathematical.

What we should recognize is that first-order classical logic is inadequate to describe all valid consequences, that is, all cases in which it is impossible for the premisses to be true and the conclusion false. Whether the theories which complete it should be called logic, or whether they are substantial theories—of mathematics, or of meaning—is arguable.

Relevance

Finally, let us turn from these cases in which classical logic appears to undergenerate, that is, not to recognize as valid, consequences which are intuitively valid, to others in which it appears to overgenerate, that is, cases which are intuitively invalid but come out as valid on the classical criterion. The most notorious of these is *Ex Falso Quodlibet* (*EFQ*, for short), which I mentioned earlier. It permits the inference of any proposition whatever from a contradiction. The form is '*A* and not-*A*, therefore *B*'. Whatever propositions are substituted for

A and *B* here, there is no resulting instance in which the premiss comes out true and the conclusion false, for the simple reason that no proposition of the form '*A* and not-*A*' is true. (Some logicians, *in extremis*, have denied this last point—see Chapter 6. But for the moment, let it pass.) Hence the inference is valid, according to the classical criterion. That means we should accept the following inferences as valid, for example,

> Ernest is brave and Ernest is not brave. So Ernest is a mountaineer,

or even worse

> Ernest is brave and Ernest is not brave. So this match will not light.

Yet what has Ernest's bravery, or his cowardice, to do with whether the match will light? The contradictory claims about Ernest's bravery provide no support for the conclusion—one might say, they are not even relevant to the conclusion. The objection, therefore, is that the truth-preservation criterion in the classical account endorses inferences in which the premisses are not relevant to the conclusion. Logical consequence should recognize not only that valid inferences are truth-preserving, but that they require relevance between premiss and conclusion.

A similar case of irrelevance arises when the conclusion is a logical truth. For logical truths cannot be false—however the schematic letters are interpreted, they come out true; or whatever substitution is made on the non-logical terms, the result is true. So whatever the premisses are in an inference, if the conclusion is a logical truth, no interpretation will make the premisses true and the conclusion false. Hence a logical truth is a logical consequence of any set of propositions whatever. That means that the following inferences are valid:

> This match will light. So either Ernest is brave or he is not,

and

> All mountaineers are brave. Ernest is a mountaineer. So a moth is a moth.

Once again, the premisses do not seem even to be relevant to the conclusion, and therefore, not such as to entail it.

This problem does not only affect the interpretational version of the classical account of logical consequence. It also arises—indeed, even more so—for the account that makes reference to impossibility. For if one proposition is to be a logical consequence of others if it is impossible for it to be false when the others are true, then any proposition is a consequence of a set of propositions which cannot all be true, and any proposition which cannot be false is a consequence of any other propositions whatever. It follows that logical consequence also embraces the following inferences:

> All squares are round. So Ernest is brave,

and

> Some athletes are mountaineers. Some mountaineers are brave. So every effect has a cause.

How can relevance be incorporated into the criterion of logical consequence? One method might be to give an account of relevance in terms of subject-matter which can then be conjoined with the truth-preservation criterion to give a stricter account in which relevance is a necessary component. This is unlikely to be successful, however. Consider

> All squares are round. So all round things are square.

As far as subject-matter goes, premiss and conclusion seem here to be as closely related as any propositions can be. Yet the only thing that makes the inference valid—if it is—is the logical impossibility of the premiss. That is, the inference could satisfy the relevance and truth-preservation principles separately; yet it seems as objectionable an instance of valid inference as any of the others.

A better route to a solution of the difficulty is to diagnose the real problem with the truth-preservation account, and then to revise it in the light of the diagnosis. The account has the form 'it is impossible that both A and not-B'—or 'under no interpretation is it that both A and not-B'—where A is 'the premisses are true' and B is 'the conclusion is true'. This seems to capture our intuitions until we realize that, if it is impossible that *A* (or necessary that *B*), then it is impossible that both *A* and not-*B*. At first we thought the impossibility would consist somehow in a relation between *A* and not-*B*—that *B* is a logical consequence of *A*. That thought is then subverted by the isolated impossibility of *A* or necessity of *B*.

As we said before, what a valid argument must do is provide a guarantee that the conclusion is true whenever the premises are, that is, that it be necessary that if the premises are true the conclusion is too. We might think that the condition 'if the premises are true so is the conclusion' (if *A* then *B*) is the same as 'it's not the case that the premises are true and the conclusion false' (not both *A* and not-*B*). Since 'it is necessary that not . . .' is the same as 'it is impossible that . . .', we think we can safely express the truth-preservation criterion as 'it is impossible that both *A* and not-*B*', that is, 'it is impossible that the premises are true and the conclusion false'. It turns out that that was a mistake. For whereas if it is impossible that *A*, it is impossible that both *A* and not-*B* (and similarly if it is necessary that *B*), that it is necessary that if *A* then *B* does not so obviously follow from the claim that *A* is impossible (or that *B* is necessary). We will look at these inferences in more detail in Chapter 3, when we come to discuss conditionals directly. Such inferences are as implausible as *EFQ* itself, for example,

> It is impossible that all squares are round. So if all squares are round, all round things are square.

(Note that this is not a case of *EFQ*: 'It is impossible that all squares are round' is not itself impossible—indeed, it is necessarily true.) It follows that the truth-preservation criterion is actually correct—what was wrong was the way it was expressed, and the belief that it validated such inference-patterns as *EFQ*. We do not need to add relevance as an extra necessary condition on logical consequence alongside the truth-preservation condition. If we express the latter correctly, it already excludes those implausible and irrelevant inferences. One proposition is a logical consequence of others if it is necessary that if the latter are true, so is the former.

This is not how classical logic understands the criterion, however, and it can fight back. One way to understand the classical response is that perhaps we have been overhasty in our judgements of what is relevant to what. After all, if one proposition really is a logical consequence of others, then the latter must be at least logically relevant to it—what better mark of relevance could a logician ask for? A putative valid inference cannot, therefore, be challenged on grounds of relevance, for if there are grounds for endorsing the inference, those grounds themselves equally show that a relevant connection exists. The result is a stand-off between the classical logician and his opponent, the one using the truth-preservation criterion (interpreted in his own way—'it is impossible that *A* and not-*B*') to bear out his endorsement of *EFQ*, the other appealing to intuition to reject it.

We will consider further arguments against the classical position in the next chapter, when we turn to the proper analysis of conditionals. We can close this chapter by examining an argument in favour of accepting *EFQ* as valid, and an attempt to parry it from the other side. So far in this chapter the notion of proof has received very little attention. At one time, defenders of classical logic, in their antipathy to the notion of necessity, went so far as to define a valid inference as one that accorded with the rules of logic. The problem then arises, of course, of justifying the rules of logic. Ultimately, for classical logic, as I am presenting it here, the basis of logical consequence has to be semantic. The notion of proof will come into its own when later in the book (Chapter 8) we consider the objections to the realist notion of truth and the support there is for epistemic constraints on such concepts.

Nevertheless, it's open to the classical logician to produce a proof of the conclusion of *EFQ* from its premises, that is, to produce a succession of steps in accordance with certain inference rules, and to challenge his opponent to fault one of those rules. For if all the steps in the proof are valid, it would seem plausible to infer that the proof as a whole is valid, that is, its conclusion follows from its premises. The argument is as follows, and takes an arbitrary contradiction, of the form '*A* and not-*A*', and moves step by step to a conclusion *B*, that is, a conclusion not apparently relevantly connected with the premiss:

Suppose we have	*A* and not-*A*
Then by Simplification, we have	*A*
and so by Addition,	*A* or *B*
But by Simplification again, we have	not-*A*
and so by Disjunctive Syllogism,	*B*

Three rules of inference are referred to here by their traditional names. Simplification is a name for the inference of *P* from '*P* and *Q*', and equally of *Q* from '*P* and *Q*'. Addition names the inference of '*P* or *Q*' from *P*, or equally from *Q*. Finally, Disjunctive Syllogism says that one may infer *Q* from '*P* or *Q*' and 'not-*P*'. Each of these rules seems intuitively valid, and is certainly truth-preserving. If '*P* and *Q*' is true, then *P* must be true and *Q* must be true. If *P* is true, then either *P* is true or *Q* is true, and so '*P* or *Q*' must be true. If 'not-*P*' is true, then *P* cannot be true, and so if '*P* or *Q*' is also true, it must be *Q* which is true. Thus we have a succession of steps in each of which, if the premiss is true the conclusion must be true. One might reject the assumption that a succession of valid steps builds into a single valid step from beginning to end—the so-called 'transitivity of proof'. If not, then unless one can fault one of these very plausible steps, *B* does indeed follow from '*A* and not-*A*', for arbitrary *B*, that is, *EFQ* is valid.

Of course, there must be more to this argument than that the steps are truth-preserving. We know that *EFQ* meets the truth-preservation conclusion—indeed, that is the problem. The question is whether truth-preservation is enough. It is beside the point for the classical logician to challenge the objector to produce a counterexample. It is agreed on all sides that there is no case where the premiss is true and the conclusion false. What is in contention is whether producing such a counterexample is a necessary condition for invalidity—that is, whether inability to produce one is sufficient for validity. In fact, each of these steps has been queried at some time by some logician. I wish to concentrate on one step above, the final one.

Disjunctive Syllogism says that from '*P* or *Q*' and 'not-*P*' one may validly infer *Q*. Let us pause for a moment and think generally about this move. Suppose one wishes to infer *Q* from 'not-*P*'; what more must one know in order to do so? The answer has to be: 'if not-*P* then *Q*'. The very minimum one must know in order to move from 'not-*P*' to *Q*, is that if not-*P* then *Q*. Hence, if Disjunctive Syllogism is to be valid, the major premiss, '*P* or *Q*', must be equivalent to (or entail) 'if not-*P* then *Q*'. And that seems to be the case: 'Either Edmund is cowardly or Edmund is a mountaineer' does seem to say 'If Edmund is not cowardly, he is a mountaineer'. Either Edmund is cowardly or he is not, in which case, he is a mountaineer.

But there is a problem here. For '*P* or *Q*' was inferred from *P*—we agreed that either Edmund was cowardly or a mountaineer on the ground that he was cowardly. While it seems fine to argue that 'Edmund is cowardly or a mountaineer' follows from 'Edmund is cowardly', it is not so plausible to say that 'If Edmund is not cowardly then he is a mountaineer' follows from the premiss that he is cowardly. Given that he is cowardly, it follows that either he is cowardly or—whatever you like. But simply from the fact that he is cowardly, it does not follow that if he is not cowardly—whatever you like. The issue here is again one which directly affects conditionals, and we will need to examine it in the next chapter. But the conclusion has to be that the argument given above equivocates on the formula '*A* or *B*'. In one sense, '*A* or *B*' follows from *A* alone—but is then not equivalent to 'if not-*A* then *B*'. In the other it is equivalent to the conditional, and with the minor premiss, 'not-*A*', entails *B*. But these senses cannot be the same—or at least, that they are is as contentious as the claim that *EFQ* is a valid consequence.

We leave the issue of relevance—for the time being—like this: there is a cogent challenge to the classical interpretation of the notion of truth-preservation, that it has been interpreted too loosely, and that inferences which classical logic admits as valid are in fact not so. The premisses are not, for the purposes of logical consequence, relevant to the conclusion.

Summary and Guide to Further Reading

In this chapter I have claimed that the central logical concept is that of logical consequence. For much of this century this has not been the prevailing view. Rather, the notion of logical truth has held centre stage. In very many books on logic, the phrase 'logical consequence' (and equivalent phrases) will not be found in the index. In them, 'validity' will be identified with logical truth. Logic was seen as a set of truths, to be derived from self-evident axioms by two or three rules of inference—*modus ponens*, Universal Generalization, and (usually) Uniform Substitution. A paradigmatic example is Quine's *Methods of Logic*.

This was not always so, as my reference to Bolzano (see his *Theory of Science*) indicates. Indeed, Aristotle's syllogistic, and the medieval theory of *consequentiae* both gave the theory of inference its rightful supremacy. Nor was logical consequence entirely ignored even during the early years of this century. None the less, the ground-breaking work of Gentzen and Tarski in the 1930s has only much more recently been properly recognized. Tarski's papers on logical consequence, especially the one 'On the Concept of Logical Consequence' (all in the collection of his papers translated into English and entitled *Logic, Semantics, Metamathematics*), make rewarding reading.

The classical paradigm that was developed in the works of Frege, Russell, Tarski, and others has three features which I tried to bring out: logic is formal, truth-preserving, and compact. It is also symbolic, but that should not be confused with its being formal. Logic is formal when it uses schematic letters to identify the formal structure of arguments, leaving only the logical expressions ('logical constants' as they are often called) in place; it is symbolic when those logical constants are represented by symbols (and technical methods for manipulating those symbols soon follow). But most modern textbooks use the titles 'Formal Logic' or 'Symbolic Logic' interchangeably. There is a vast selection of texts. Mark Sainsbury's *Logical Forms* has an unusual and enlightening slant, and brings out the importance of form to the classical paradigm. G. B. Keene gives a spirited defence of the restriction of logic to the study of form alone in his *Foundations of Rational Argument*, ch. 2 sect. 2.

I attributed the prominence given to logical truth to the pre-eminence of the axiomatic method in the early development of modern logic. That probably also accounts for the late development of semantic methods. The cloudy history of the concept of truth-preservation can be read in John Etchemendy's survey article on Tarski referred to in Chapter 1: 'Tarski on Truth and Logical Consequence'. This is also a useful introduction to his sustained attack on the Tarskian conception in his *The Concept of Logical Consequence*.

The expressive limitations of first-order logic (the classical paradigm) are not emphasized by its exponents. An important (and technical) paper in 1969 by Per Lindström gave a useful double characterization of those limitations: on the one hand we have compactness, and the consequent inability to express such notions as 'finiteness' or to give a set of first-order formulae characterizing the standard model of arithmetic, that is, the set of natural numbers, categorically. Compactness is so called by analogy with the corresponding topological property: every cover of a compact space has a finite subcover; equivalently, if the intersection of a family of closed sets is empty, so is the intersection of a finite subset (the finite intersection property, f.i.p., or finite meet property, f.m.p.). The history of the slow recognition of the importance of the notion of compactness is intriguingly recounted by John Dawson in 'The Compactness of First-Order Logic: From Gödel to Lindström'. The other limitative aspect of first-order logic is what is referred to as the Löwenheim–Skolem–Tarski property, and the consequent Skolem paradox, showing the inadequacy of any first-order theory of sets. An interesting discussion can be found in a pair of papers by P. Benacerraf and C. Wright, both entitled 'Skolem and the Skeptic'. Hilary Putnam makes great play with it in his 'Models and Reality'. It is a major plank in his argument against metaphysical realism referred to in Chapter 1 above. One of the first intimations of first-order undergeneration came in K. Gödel's famous paper of 1931: among many elementary expositions, that in D. Hofstadter's *Gödel, Escher, Bach: An Eternal*

Golden Braid can be particularly recommended. One can read about Gödel's, and other famous limitative results, in another OPUS book, *What is Mathematical Logic?*, by J. Crossley *et al.* However, the reader should also consult the review by J. Corcoran and S. Shapiro in *Philosophia*, where some inaccuracies in Crossley's account are noted. None the less, Crossley's book does uniquely succeed in conveying hard (and very important) technical results in a very clear and approachable way. An exemplary discussion of the whole issue of expressibility is found in Leslie Tharp's 'Which Logic is the Right Logic?'

Complaints about the overgeneration associated with the classical view have a much older ancestry, but alternative accounts have only been systematically worked out in this century. The most fully worked-out development of the theme of relevance dates from a paper by Wilhelm Ackermann in 1956, and led to the programme of 'relevance (or relevant) logic'. An encyclopaedic survey can be found in a two-volume work by the two main proponents, A. Anderson and N. Belnap, *Entailment: The Logic of Relevance and Necessity*. A more recent, and briefer, exposition was given by the present author in *Relevant Logic*.

Other notable attempts to avoid the overgeneration found in classical logic are the development of the logic of analytic implication (see W. T. Parry, 'Analytic Implication: Its History, Justification and Varieties'), which rejects Addition; and the so-called 'intuitionistic relevance logic' of Neil Tennant, presented in his *Anti-Realism and Logic*, in which the transitivity of valid inference is restricted.

3 To Think But of an If: Theories of Conditionals

CONDITIONALS are propositions of the form 'if A then B', such as

> If the pound is not devalued, the recession will continue
> If Oswald had not killed Kennedy, someone else would have

and

> If Aristotle wrote any dialogues, they have not survived.

Sometimes the form is not so clear, and reordering is needed to produce the 'if A then B' form:

> We will catch the 9.20 bus if it comes on time
> Charles, if he was to clear his name, had to make an honest confession
> Provided that the unemployment figures are satisfactory, the Government will survive the vote of confidence
> A sufficient condition for obtaining a grant was taking a First Class degree.

All these can be put in the form 'if A then B'. A marks the antecedent of the conditional, and B the consequent. All but the second are in the indicative mood—the second is in the subjunctive. Conditionals can also take questions, commands, and other modes of speech in their consequents:

> If the buzzer sounds, turn off the oven
> If there was no alternative, why does the President claim credit for making hard decisions?

and

> If the bus does not arrive by 10.30, let's walk.

In this chapter, we will not consider conditionals of this last type—commands, questions, and optatives will need separate consideration, whether conditional or not. Moreover, at first, we will concentrate on indicative conditionals, but later in the chapter we will need to say something about subjunctive conditionals.

When we make assertions of conditionals with indicative antecedent and consequent which themselves can be uttered and evaluated as true or false, we seem to be uttering a proposition which is itself true or false. We treat

> If you take a First, you will get a grant
> If Aristotle wrote any dialogues, they have not survived
> If it was on time, they will have caught the 9.20

as making assertions which are true or false. We can agree or disagree with them, and we can adduce evidence for or against them—they constitute propositions themselves composed of propositions. They are complex, or molecular propositions.

Disjunctions and conjunctions are also complex propositions; and in those cases, whether the complex proposition is itself true or false depends straightforwardly on whether its constituents are true or false. If either part of a disjunctive proposition is true, the whole disjunction is true; if both parts of a conjunctive proposition are true, the whole conjunction is true; and in all other cases, these complex propositions are false. The standard, or classical account of conditionals gives a similar account of conditional propositions, at least for the case of indicative conditionals. The whole conditional is true if either the antecedent is false or the consequent is true.

Consider the three conditionals immediately above. The first says

> Either you won't take a First, or you will get a grant

which would seem to be true either if you don't get a First or if you obtain a grant, that is, if you both obtain a First and a grant. In the same way, the second says

> Either Aristotle wrote no dialogues or they have not survived

and again, this is surely true if either he wrote no dialogues or he did but they have not survived. Lastly, the third conditional is true either if the bus was not on time, or it was and they caught it. That is, each conditional is true if either the antecedent is false or the consequent is true. This is because, as we noted in the previous chapter, a conditional, 'if A then B', seems to be in general equivalent to a disjunctive statement, 'either not-A or B', that is 'either not-A or A, in which case B', or 'either not-A, or A and B'.

Conjunctions and disjunctions are said to be truth-functional, because their truth depends immediately and straightforwardly on the truth of their constituents. A disjunction is true if either disjunct is true, otherwise false; a conjunction is true if both conjuncts are true, otherwise false. ('Disjunct' and 'conjunct' here are technical terms for the parts of propositions of these forms). There is a 'function' from the truth-values of the constituents to the truth-value of the whole complex proposition. These functions, that is, the dependencies of the truth-value of the whole on that of its parts, are often displayed in the form of truth-tables. For disjunction, the function yields the value 'true' if either part is true, and the value 'false' only if both parts are false:

'A or B':

A \ B	T	F
T	T	T
F	T	F

that is, 'or' maps the pairs of truth-values, <T,T>, <T,F>, and <F,T> to T, and the pair <F,F> to F, letting 'T' stand for 'true' and 'F' for 'false'.

Similarly, the function modelling conjunction yields 'true' only when both parts are true:

'A and B':

A \ B	T	F
T	T	F
F	F	F

that is, 'and' maps the pair <T,T> to T, and the pairs <T,F>, <F,T>, and <F,F> all to F.

The standard view of conditionals is that they too are truth-functional, that is, that their truth-values are determined by the truth-values of their constituents. This is immediate from their equivalence to disjunctions, and the truth-functional nature of disjunction. The truth-table for conditionals is accordingly like this:

'If A then B':

A \ B	T	F
T	T	F
F	T	T

that is, 'if ... then' maps the pairs of truth-values <T,T>, <F,T>, and <F,F> to T, and the pair <T,F> to F.

The Conversationalist Defence

Nevertheless, treating conditionals as truth-functional leads to a number of puzzles. Suppose the pound will be devalued, but the recession will none the less continue. Does that suffice to bear out the claim that if the pound is not devalued, the recession will continue? According to the truth-functional account, it should. Translated into disjunctive terms, this conditional says that either the pound will be devalued or the recession will continue. If the pound is devalued, that disjunction is true; equally, if the recession continues (regardless of what happens to the pound), the disjunction is true. But the conditional suggests a closer connection between antecedent and consequent. The truth-functional account implies that a conditional is true simply in virtue of the truth-values of its constituents. When we think of it generally, we assume that they will take those values as a result of such a connection. But now we see that there may be no connection, even though the values may coincidentally turn out such as to entail the truth of the conditional, on the truth-functional account. Consequently, a doubt sets in as to whether the truth-functional account has captured the full story.

The argument given for truth-functionality was a quick one; it depended on the equivalence of the conditional 'if A then B' to the disjunction 'either not-A or B', and on the truth-functionality of disjunction. We might now wonder whether these links hold. The doubt arose in the previous chapter. 'If Edmund is not cowardly then he is a mountaineer' seems to mean that either Edmund is cowardly or he is a mountaineer—either he is cowardly or he is not and so is a mountaineer. But the disjunction is torn apart by, on the one hand, the requirement that it be equivalent to the corresponding conditional, and on the other, that it be truth-functional. The premisses of the quick argument (equivalence and truth-functionality) cannot be simultaneously satisfied by a univocal disjunction.

There is, however, a more extended argument for the truth-functionality of conditionals. It takes as its premiss the standard account of logical consequence, which we examined earlier, and adds the observation that conditionals are used to express the dependency of the conclusion of an argument on its premisses. That is, a conditional is true, on certain assumptions, just when its consequent is true conditionally on its antecedent in addition to those assumptions:

'If A then B' follows from some propositions
        if and only if
B follows from those other propositions in conjunction with A.

For example,

'If Edmund is brave then he is a mountaineer' follows from 'Everyone brave is a mountaineer'
        if and only if
'Edmund is a mountaineer' follows from 'Everyone brave is a mountaineer' and 'Edmund is brave'.

Conditionals not only match valid arguments, they are often used to say that those arguments are valid. We can say that a valid argument is one in which, if the premisses are true, so is the conclusion—where the connection is reinforced by a reference either to necessity or to generality: the classical account of validity in the previous chapter said that, however the schematic letters are interpreted, if the premisses come out true so does the conclusion. Let us call this relationship between conditionals and consequence (or validity), the 'Conditionality' principle.

Between them, the standard account of consequence and the Conditionality principle entail that conditionals are truth-functional. First, suppose A is true and B false. Then if 'if A then B' were true, B would be true (by *modus ponens*). So, since

B is false, 'if *A* then *B*' must be false too, given that *A* is true. Indeed, that is agreed on all hands: if *A* is true and *B* false, 'if *A* then *B*' cannot be true.

What if *A* is false or *B* true? We treat the cases separately. Suppose *A* is false. By *ex falso quodlibet*, *B* follows from *A* and 'not-*A*'. So by Conditionality, 'if *A* then *B*' follows from 'not-*A*'. But, since *A* is false, 'not-*A*' is true, and so 'if *A* then *B*' must be true. On the other hand, suppose *B* is true. Again, by the standard account, *B* follows from *A* and *B*, so by Conditionality, 'if *A* then *B*' follows from *B*. Hence, since we are assuming that *B* is true, it follows that 'if *A* then *B*' is true. Hence either way, whether *A* is false or *B* is true, the standard account of consequence coupled to the Conditionality principle, entails that 'if *A* then *B*' is true.

All cases have been covered: if *A* is false, the conditional is true; if *B* is true the conditional is true; and if *A* is true and *B* false, the conditional is false. Thus the truth-value of the conditional is completely determined by the truth-values of its constituents.

This reinforces the classical account of conditionals; but it does not explain the counterexamples. It does not explain the puzzle that, for example, Edmund's possible cowardice does not seem sufficient for the claim that if he is brave, he is a mountaineer. The conversationalist defence is an attempt to explain this phenomenon consistently with the truth-functionality thesis. The idea is simple: conditionals, it is maintained, are truth-functional; what the counterexamples show is not that a conditional with false antecedent or true consequent is not in fact true—rather, they show that such a conditional may not be assertible in such circumstances. A distinction is drawn between truth and assertibility. What is true may not, in certain circumstances, be assertible—and vice versa: what is assertible may not be true.

The conversationalist doctrine has a much wider sphere of application than simply to conditionals. Some of its primary examples are very familiar. If in reply to the question whether you know the young woman who was recently appointed

Professor of Classics you reply, 'She's quite good at Latin' or 'She's fond of a game of croquet,' you might well be understood to be implying that her academic achievements were not as high as they should be. Of course, in an appropriate context, this might not be the interpretation. If it was clear that her research stature was excellent, this might simply be interesting additional information. Moreover, even if your audience did infer a slight on her achievements, you could cancel it—'Of course, I did not mean to imply that her many books are not first class.' None the less there are inferences and implications (or in the jargon—since 'implication' is often used in place of 'entailment'—the technical term 'implicature' is used) in any conversational situation. One needs to be aware of them, and their existence will affect what is asserted. Two maxims in particular were identified by H. P. Grice as guiding conversation, the maxim of quality, that one should assert only what one believes to be true and is justified, and that of quantity, that one should not assert less than one can. The reason is, in the first case, that in making an assertion one implies that one believes what one said, and has good grounds for saying it. These implicatures can be cancelled; one can go on to point out that one does not believe this oneself, but others maintain it; or that one believes it, but so far has no evidence for it. But in the absence of such disclaimers, the implicature is there. So, too, in the second case: in making the assertion, one implies that no more helpful and relevant information can be given. For example, in saying that either Bush or Clinton won the election, one implies that one does not know which of them it was; or in the remark about the Professor of Classics, there is an implicature that one has no opinion about her academic standing; or even that one is hiding one's beliefs about it (though the latter example perhaps offends against Grice's maxim of relevance).

Grice's idea, therefore, is that although what makes a disjunction true is the truth of one of its disjuncts, knowledge of one disjunct is not sufficient for its assertion. In asserting a disjunction, there is an implicature that one believes it and has a ground for believing it (by the maxim of quality) but that that ground does not consist simply in knowledge of one of its components (by the maxim of quantity). There must be a reason why one has chosen to assert the disjunction rather than one disjunct, and the obvious explanation is that one does not have comparable grounds for asserting either disjunct. In other words, when asserting 'A or B' there is an implicature that one knows neither A nor B, yet does know that one or other of them is true, that is, that if A is not true, B must be true; that is, one knows that 'if not-A then B' is true (equivalently, that 'if not-B then A' is true).

The link between conditionals and disjunction serves to extend the conversationalist account from disjunctions to conditionals. 'If A then B' corresponds to—indeed, is equivalent to—'not-A or B', and each is true if A is false or B is true. But neither is assertible simply on the grounds of the falsity of A or the truth of B. If Edmund is a coward, it follows that both 'Edmund is a coward or a mountaineer' and 'If Edmund is brave he is a mountaineer' are true. But it will not follow that either is assertible, for to assert them will imply that the ground of the assertion is some connection between his cowardice and mountaineering. We therefore have an explanation of why the succession of inferences looks problematic, but an explanation consistent with its correctness. If A is true, then 'A or B' is true, and so 'if not-A then B' is true; if 'not-A' and 'if not-A then B' are true, B must be true. So if both A and 'not-A' are true, B must be true, whatever B is. That is not a problem, for no proposition and its negation are both true, so for no proposition A is it the case that both A and 'not-A' are true.

Let us think more, however, about the idea of distinguishing the assertibility of a proposition from its truth. The idea is to accept the arguments for the truth-functionality of 'if . . . then', and so to accept that any conditional with false antecedent or true consequent is true, but to explain the unacceptability of the counterexamples as due not to their being false but to their being unassertible. The reason for their being unassertible will be that they are uttered in circumstances where the antecedent is known to be false, or the consequent is known to be true, in contradiction of the conversational implicature which will result from asserting the conditional, namely that no stronger assertion was possible (namely, denial of the antecedent or assertion of the consequent).

There is a variation on the approach. Grice attributed the unassertibility of the examples to a conversational implicature. Frank Jackson attributes it to a conventional implicature. The difference is that whereas Grice sees the implicatures as a consequence of general conversational maxims (in particular, the maxim of quantity), Jackson identifies it as a specific aspect of conditionals. He defines a notion of 'robustness': a proposition is robust with respect to a piece of information if high assertibility of the proposition is unaffected by acquiring the information. Some disjunctions are robust with respect to the denial of both disjuncts; some are not. For example, if I say, 'Churchill ordered the bombing of Dresden' and you deny it, one of us must be right, that is, 'Either I am right or you are right' has high assertibility, and it will remain high when the evidence reveals which of us was right. The disjunction is robust with respect to the denial of each disjunct. On the other hand, if I know that Mascagni wrote *Cavalleria rusticana*, but choose to assert the weaker, 'Either Mascagni or Leoncavallo wrote *Cavalleria rusticana*', that disjunction, with high assertibility, is not robust with respect to the denial of its first disjunct. On learning (if I were to) that Mascagni did not write it, I would retract the disjunction, not move to infer Leoncavallo's authorship.

For Jackson, this is where Disjunctive Syllogism and *modus ponens* come in. The point of conditionals, he says, is to show that one will accept *modus ponens*. 'If Mascagni did not write *Cavalleria rusticana*, Leoncavallo did' is not for me assertible, for it is not robust with respect to its antecedent. A conditional 'if *A* then *B*' is robust with respect to its antecedent if it is highly assertible and will remain so on discovering that its antecedent is true. Only in such a case could *modus ponens* operate. But in the present case, I would not continue to believe the conditional on learning that its antecedent was true. My only reason for believing it (given the thesis that it is equivalent to the corresponding disjunction) is my belief that its antecedent is false. So I would be reluctant to detach the consequent on learning that the antecedent was true. In contrast, 'If I am wrong you are right' in the Churchill example is robust with respect to its antecedent, for I did not assert it simply because I disbelieved the antecedent. But conditionals are not, says Jackson, robust with respect to the falsity of their consequents. This is a consequence of his belief that the assertibility of conditionals is given by the conditional probability of their consequents conditional on their antecedents, a notion we will discuss in the next section. If the low assertibility of true conditionals were a consequence of conversational implicature, they would be robust with respect to both the truth of their antecedents and the falsity of their consequents, for the fact of their having been asserted would, by the maxim of quality, imply that not only was their antecedent not known to be false, neither was their consequent known to be true. If Jackson is right, therefore, about their assertibility being measured by the conditional probability, that maxim can be the ground of their low assertibility only in the case of known false antecedent, not true consequent. (We will look at the calculation which yields this at a later point.) Jackson's proposal is that there is a specific convention about conditionals, namely, that they are robust with respect to their antecedents, and so not assertible in circumstances where their antecedents are known to be false. That they support *modus ponens*, that is, that on learning the truth of the antecedent one is invited to detach and infer the consequent, is a matter of convention.

Neither Grice's nor Jackson's theory is tenable, however. The reason is that the problematic conditionals—conditionals which appear false despite having false antecedent or true consequent—occur in embedded contexts. For example, recall the example about Churchill, and consider the disjunction:

> Either if I was right so were you, or if you were right, so was I.

Since you were pictured as flatly denying what I said, neither conditional here is plausibly true. However, on the truth-functional analysis, if you were right, the first disjunct is true (true consequent), while if you were wrong, the second is true (false antecedent). The Gricean explanation is to say that though one or other is true, neither is assertible. But neither of them was asserted—what was asserted was their disjunction. Assertion and assertibility are notions which apply to complete propositions, not to parts of them. The reason why the above disjunction seems to be false is not that, though true, it is not for some reason assertible, but that it is false; and the reason it is false is that, despite the argument for the truth-functionality of conditionals, conditionals are not truth-functional. For all that the apologists may protest and try to explain the examples away, it seems clear that there are false conditionals with false antecedent or true consequent.

Conditional Probability

To defend this position, we need both to give an alternative account of conditionals, and to say where the argument for their truth-functionality went wrong. One such account develops an idea which can be traced back to Frank Ramsey. His thought was this: to decide whether to believe a conditional, provisionally or hypothetically add the antecedent to your stock of beliefs, and consider whether to believe the consequent. This reduces the question of whether to believe conditionals to the question of whether to believe non-conditional, that is, categorical or apodeictic, propositions. (Antecedent and consequent are sometimes referred to as 'protasis' and 'apodosis'.) A conditional should be believed if a belief in its antecedent would commit one to believing its consequent.

Those who have made use of Ramsey's idea, or Ramsey's Test, as it is often dubbed, have been of two kinds. Some, like Jackson or David Lewis, believe indicative conditionals are truth-functional; but they admit that subjunctive conditionals cannot be. One major type of subjunctive conditional is the counterfactual conditional, whose antecedent is known or conceded to be false. For example, if one says

> If Oswald had not killed Kennedy, someone else would have

one is conceding, or presupposing, that Oswald killed Kennedy. If all such conditionals were truth-functional, they would all be true in virtue of the falsity of their antecedents (or at least, would be considered true by all those who shared the presupposition). That would make nonsense of them. One who asserted the above would wish to deny

If Oswald had not killed Kennedy, no one would have

If counterfactual conditionals were truth-functional, that conditional would be true too.

The other group who have adopted Ramsey's Test are among those who have been persuaded that indicative conditionals are not truth-functional, and so look to Ramsey's Test to provide an account of both indicative and subjunctive conditionals. Indeed, Robert Stalnaker, the primary advocate of this view, plays down the distinction between indicative and subjunctive conditionals, seeing it as an essentially pragmatic aspect, reflecting not a deep difference in the truth-conditions of the two, but rather, simply a reflection of the fact that the falsity of the antecedent has been conceded, and perhaps a wider range of possibilities is open. (We will return to this in the next section.) Let us follow Stalnaker and develop Ramsey's Test for indicative conditionals, since we are interested in alternatives to truth-functionality.

In presenting Ramsey's Test there has been a switch from truth and truth-conditions, to belief and whether to believe—to credence and credibility. We can model belief, and relate it to truth, by interpreting it as a probability-function. The probability of a proposition is the probability that it is true. It is a measure of how likely it is that the proposition is true. A probability-function is a function which assigns to each proposition a number between 0 and 1, where totally improbable propositions, for example, logical contradictions are assigned 0, and logically certain propositions, that is, tautologies, are assigned the maximum value, 1. The probability of a disjunction of two propositions which cannot both be true, is equal to the sum of their probabilities. Thus, for example, the probability of 'not-A', for which we write 'p (not-A)', is equal to $1 - p(A)$, since 'A or not-A' is a tautology (and so has probability 1), and A and 'not-A' cannot both be true.

Given a probability measure p_1 and a proposition E we can form another measure p_2 by conditionalizing on E. The idea here is that the distribution of probability assignments measured by p_1 will have been made on the basis of certain evidence, and will measure the beliefs arrived at on the basis of that evidence. Subsequently, further evidence, E, is obtained; and on the basis of E, we wish to revise our probability assignments, and to arrive at a revised distribution of probability judgements, p_2. For each proposition A, we set $p_2(A)$ to be the ratio of the prior probability, p_1 (A and E), that both A and E are true, divided by the prior probability of the evidence, $p_1(E)$. (Clearly, for conditionalizing on E, $p_1(E)$ must not be zero. It must not have been impossible that this evidence was obtained.) This ratio,

$$\frac{p_1(A \text{ and } E)}{p_1(E)}$$

is called the conditional probability of A on E, and is written $p_1(A/E)$. Thus

$$p_2(A) = p_1(A/E) = \frac{p_1(A \text{ and } E)}{p_1(E)}, \text{ provided } p_1(E) \neq 0$$

Let us look at an example, the probabilities of drawing a card from a standard pack of 52 cards—four suits of 13 cards each, no joker. Probability theory has two interpretations, what one might call the objective probabilities arising from the frequencies or ratios of particular outcomes, and the subjective probabilities which correspond to someone's beliefs as they form themselves in the light of evidence. The former is what is illustrated by the pack of cards (and similarly by tosses of a coin or throws of a dice); the latter is what is referred to in Ramsey's Test. It is far from obvious that they match, or that actual beliefs correspond to objective frequency distributions. None the less, the objective frequencies usefully illustrate the use of probability-functions, and can be seen, if you like, as measuring the beliefs of an ideal and objective observer.

On drawing a single card at random from a well-shuffled pack, the probability of drawing a heart, $p(\text{heart}) = \frac{1}{4}$; $p(\text{ace}) = \frac{1}{13}$; $p(\text{ace of hearts}) = \frac{1}{52}$. For there are 13 ways of drawing a heart, out of 52 ways of drawing a card altogether; 4 ways of drawing an ace; and only 1 way of drawing the ace of hearts. The probability of not drawing a heart, p(not-heart) $= \frac{3}{4}$, for there are 39 such outcomes, which is $1 - p$(heart). Also, p(not-heart) $= p$(club or diamond or spade), and since club, diamond, and spade are mutually exclusive, we can sum these probabilities separately, that is, p(club or diamond or spade) $= p$(club) $+ p$(diamond) $+ p$(spade) $= \frac{1}{4} + \frac{1}{4} + \frac{1}{4} = \frac{3}{4}$, as it should be. Another illustration of the summing of probabilities—which can only be done when the outcomes are exclusive—is the probability of drawing a court card, p(court card) $= p$(king or queen or jack) $= p$(king) $+ p$(queen) $+ p$(jack) $= \frac{1}{13} + \frac{1}{13} + \frac{1}{13} = \frac{3}{13}$. However, note that p(heart or ace) $= \frac{4}{13} \neq p$(heart) $+ p$(ace) $= \frac{17}{52}$, for the outcomes of drawing a heart and drawing an ace not exclusive—I might draw the ace of hearts.

To illustrate conditional probabilities, consider the probability of drawing a king given that one has drawn a court card:

$$p(\text{king/court card}) = \frac{p(\text{king and court card})}{p(\text{court card})} = \frac{(1/13)}{(3/13)} = \frac{1}{3},$$

for p(king and court card) $= p$(king); and this is clearly right—there is a 1 in 3 chance that a given court card is a king. On the other hand

$$p(\text{ace/court card}) = \frac{p(\text{ace and court card})}{p(\text{court card})} = \frac{0}{(3/13)} = 0$$

for no court card is an ace, while

$$p(\text{ace/not-court card}) = \frac{p(\text{ace and not-court card})}{p(\text{not-court card})}$$

$$= \frac{p(\text{ace})}{(1 - p(\text{court card}))} = \frac{(1/13)}{(10/13)} = \frac{1}{10}$$

and again, the calculation obtained by the theory agrees with a direct measurement of frequencies, for there are four ways of drawing an ace among the 40 non-court cards.

Ramsey's Test equates the credence we give to a conditional

with the credence we give to its consequent on assuming its antecedent. Stalnaker's proposal was to use probability-functions
to articulate this idea, so that what has become known as
'Stalnaker's hypothesis' is this: $p(\text{if } A \text{ then } B) = p(B/A)$. A
weaker proposal, sometimes called 'Adams's hypothesis' after
the work of Ernest Adams, is that $p(B/A)$, while it does not
measure the probability of the conditional, measures its
assertibility. Note that Adams's hypothesis is consistent with
maintaining that the conditional is truth-functional—indeed, this
is Jackson's position as we saw it in the last section. On the
other hand, Stalnaker's hypothesis is not consistent with hold-
ing that the conditional featuring in it is truth-functional, for
$p(B/A) \neq p(\text{not-}A \text{ or } B)$ (for example, $p(\text{king}/\text{ace}) = 0$, but
$p(\text{not-ace or king}) = p(\text{not-ace}) = \frac{12}{13}$).

Whether one is following Stalnaker or Adams, the attractive-
ness of $p(B/A)$ as a measure is that it avoids many of the
unintuitive consequences of a slavish attachment to a truth-
functional account of conditionals, in particular, that any conditional with false antecedent or true consequent is true. For
$p(B/A)$ can be low even though $p(\text{not-}A)$ or $p(B)$ are high, that
is, high probability of falsity of antecedent or truth of consequent of the corresponding conditional does not entail a high
value for the conditional probability. For example, $p(\text{ace}/\text{court}$
card$) = 0$ but $p(\text{not-court card}) = \frac{10}{13}$ is high; similarly, $p(\text{not-court}$
card$/\text{king}) = 0$, while $p(\text{not-court card})$ is high. What breaks
down is the equivalence—in probability-value—between the
conditional (or conditional probability) and the corresponding
disjunction. Whatever one thinks of the arguments of the last
section for the truth-functionality of the conditional, they do
not work when probabilities are involved. Take the conditionality principle (relating the truth of conditionals to the validity of the corresponding argument): whenever $p(A \text{ and } B)$ is
high, $p(B)$ must be high too; but it does not follow that if $p(B)$
is high, so too is $p(B/A)$, as the above example, $p(\text{not-court card}/$
king$)$, shows.

The probabilistic analysis gives, therefore, an alternative
account of conditionals, and in addition can provide a diagnosis
of the error in the arguments for truth-functionality. In the first

argument, it was the equivalence between conditional and corresponding disjunction which was at fault; in the second, the use of the conditionality principle.

We noted in the previous section that Jackson claims that the robustness of conditionals with respect to their antecedent is a matter of conventional, not of conversational implicature. We are now in a position to understand his reason. It hinges on the difference between $p(\text{not-}A \text{ or } B)$ and $p(B/A)$ (reading the disjunction truth-functionally). The robustness, as Jackson defines it, of a proposition H some evidence E is a measure of the difference E makes to the probability of H, that is, of the difference between $p(H)$ and $p(H/E)$; $p(H/E)$ must not be significantly lower than $p(E)$. A simple calculation shows that

$$p(B/A) = p(\text{not-}A \text{ or } B) - (p(\text{not-}A \text{ or } B) - p(B/A))$$

But also

$$p((\text{not-}A \text{ or } B)/A) = \frac{p(A \text{ and } (\text{not-}A \text{ or } B))}{p(A)}$$

$$= \frac{p(A \text{ and } B)}{p(A)}$$

$$= p(B/A)$$

Hence

$$p(B/A) = p(\text{not-}A \text{ or } B) - (p(\text{not-}A \text{ or } B) - p((\text{not-}A \text{ or } B)/A)).$$

This factor, diminishing the probability of what for Jackson is the truth-condition of 'if A then B'—namely, 'not-A or B'—is exactly the measure of the robustness of the conditional (taken truth-functionally) with respect to its antecedent, $p(\text{conditional})$ – $p(\text{conditional/antecedent})$. Thus, if $p(B/A)$ does correctly measure the assertibility conditions of conditionals, as Jackson believes, then only the robustness with respect to the antecedent, and not that with respect to falsity of consequent, should be taken into account. That can only happen if the implicature is conventional, not conversational. If it were conversational (governed by the maxims of conversation), it would be affected both by the falsity of the antecedent and by the truth of the consequent. But then there would be an additional factor, $p(\text{conditional}) - p(\text{conditional}/\text{not-consequent})$, and the result would not be $p(B/A)$. If Jackson is right to adopt Adams's hypothesis, then the implicature which explains it must be conventional.

However, we saw that Jackson's account, retaining truth-functionality in the truth-conditions of conditionals, stumbles over the question of embedded conditionals. In place of that account, Stalnaker's hypothesis identifies the truth-condition differently, by equating the probability of conditionals with the conditional probability. Over the past twenty years, David Lewis has mounted a sustained attack on this equation. Lewis aims to show that there is no proposition whose probability is measured by the conditional probability, that is, given any propositions A and B, there is no proposition, C, for which $p(C) = p(B/A)$. So in particular, the conditional probability does not measure the probability of conditionals. Hence Stalnaker's hypothesis is untenable; one must either adopt Adams's version—as Lewis and Jackson do—or abandon the probabilistic account altogether.

Lewis's argument is somewhat technical; and it has undergone a succession of refinements over the years. What we can do here is look at the simplest version of it. First, note that there are propositions A and B such that none of $p(B)$, $p(\text{not-}B)$, $p(A \text{ and } B)$, and $p(A \text{ and not-}B)$ is zero. For example, let A be 'I draw a court card' and B be 'I draw a king'. Then $p(B) = \frac{1}{13}$, $p(\text{not-}B) = \frac{12}{13}$, $p(A \text{ and } B) = \frac{1}{13}$ and $p(A \text{ and not-}B) = \frac{2}{13}$. The crucial point to note is that $p(B/A) = \frac{1}{3} \neq p(B)$. What Lewis will show is that if there were a proposition C such that, for every probability-function p in some reasonable class (e.g. those modelling a range of speakers' beliefs), $p(C) = p(B/A)$, then $p(B/A) = p(B)$. Since the latter is clearly false, there can be no such proposition C, in particular, $p(\text{if } A \text{ then } B) \neq p(B/A)$.

Suppose the Stalnaker hypothesis holds for all probability-functions in some class. Let q be the probability-function defined by $q(D) = p(D/B)$ for every proposition D. q plausibly belongs to the class of probability-functions in question (in the example, it is the revised belief-state on learning that one has drawn a king). So

$$p(C/B) = q(C) = q(B/A) = \frac{q(A \text{ and } B)}{q(A)} = \frac{p((A \text{ and } B)/B)}{p(A/B)}$$

$$= \frac{p(B \text{ and } A \text{ and } B)}{p(B \text{ and } A)} = p(B/(A \text{ and } B)).$$

Similarly (supposing r defined by $r(D) = p(D/\text{not-}B)$ for all D, belongs to the class—when I have learned I have not drawn a king), $p(C/\text{not-}B) = p(B/(A \text{ and not-}B))$.

To complete the proof, we need two further facts of probability theory, which can be easily derived from the postulates we gave. First, since

$$p(D/E) = \frac{p(D \text{ and } E)}{p(E)},$$

it follows that $p(D \text{ and } E) = p(D/E).p(E)$ for any D and E. Secondly, since 'D and E' and 'D and not-E' cannot both be true, yet D is equivalent to 'either D and E or D and not-E', it follows that $p(D) = p(\text{either } D \text{ and } E \text{ or } D \text{ and not-}E) = p(D \text{ and } E) + p(D \text{ and not-}E)$. We now apply this last point to C and B (where C is the proposition whose probability we assume to be measured by $p(B/A)$):

$$p(C) = p(C \text{ and } B) + p(C \text{ and not-}B)$$
$$= p(C/B).p(B) + p(C \text{ not-}B).p(\text{not-}B)$$
$$= p(B/(A \text{ and } B)).p(B) + p(B/(A \text{ and not-}B)).p(\text{not-}B)$$
$$= \frac{p(B \text{ and } A \text{ and } B).p(B)}{p(A \text{ and } B)}$$
$$+ \frac{p(B \text{ and } A \text{ and not-}B).p(\text{not-}B)}{p(A \text{ and not-}B)}$$
$$= p(B)$$

since $p(B \text{ and } A \text{ and } B) = p(A \text{ and } B)$ and $p(B \text{ and } A \text{ and not-}B) = 0$. (Note that our assumptions of non-zero probabilities for B, 'not-B', and so on ensure that none of these denominators is zero.) We have thus arrived at Lewis's so called 'triviality' result, that C is apparently probabilistically independent of A, a result which is clearly false in cases such as that of the court card and the king. The culprit is Stalnaker's hypothesis. The probability of the conditional cannot be measured by the conditional probability.

The Similarity Account

One might be tempted to go further, and conclude that Ramsey's idea has been refuted. But that would be too hasty. Stalnaker's hypothesis is only one way of trying to give precise expression to it. Both Stalnaker, for conditionals generally, and Lewis, for subjunctive conditionals, have developed what at first appears to be a very different articulation of the Ramsey Test. It draws on ideas from the semantics of modal logic whose philosophical implications we will consider in the next chapter.

The Ramsey Test proposes that we evaluate a conditional by assuming the antecedent and evaluating the consequent under that supposition. We can take that as suggesting that a conditional is true not in virtue of how things actually are, but of how they would be in an appropriate revision: if the antecedent is true, things will be somewhat different—indeed, the conditional claims that the consequent will then be true. How different must they be?—just enough, Stalnaker proposes, to make the antecedent true. Thus he put forward this truth-condition: a conditional is true if its consequent is true in the minimal revision in which the antecedent is true, that is, in the most similar possible world in which the antecedent is true. A possible world is a maximal state of affairs—a complete specification of how things might be. (Quite what a possible world is, will be considered in Chapter 4.) What is needed is a function, a 'similarity'-function, which given any proposition and a possible world, has as value the most similar world in which the proposition is true. He called it a selection-function: $f(A,w)$ takes as input a proposition A and a world w, and yields as value the world most similar to w in which A is true. A conditional 'if A then B' is true in a world w if B is true in $f(A,w)$, the closest A-world to w.

For example, 'If you take a First, you will get a grant' is true if the most similar world to this one in which you do take a First is one in which you obtain a grant. 'If Oswald did not kill Kennedy, someone else did' is true if in the minimal revision of how things are in which we suppose Oswald did not kill Kennedy, Kennedy was none the less still shot. 'If the pound is not devalued, the recession will continue' is true if in a world as close as possible to this one but in which there is no devaluation, the recession continues.

If A is actually true in w, then $f(A,w) = w$; that is, the world most similar in respect of some proposition to a world where that proposition is already true, is that world itself. Hence, on the present analysis, conditionals with true antecedent are true if and only if their consequent is true; in particular, conditionals with true antecedent and consequent are true. In this respect, the possible worlds analysis agrees with the truth-functional one, and with the probabilistic analysis too, for $p(B/A) = p(B)$ if $p(A) = 1$. (Conditionalization—forming $p_2(B) = p_1(B/A)$ for all B by conditionalizing on A—only changes prior probabilities if the new evidence really is new.) It is when the antecedent is false that the possible worlds analysis diverges from the truth-functional one. On the standard, truth-functional, account all conditionals with false antecedent are true. That is not the result obtained by the above truth-condition in terms of similarity of worlds. Consider, for example, the earlier example: 'If Edmund is brave he is a mountaineer'. That Edmund is a coward does not automatically (as the truth-functional account determines) mean that the conditional is true. What we need to do is to consider that possible world most similar to ours in which Edmund is brave, and find out if in such a situation he is a mountaineer. That situation will be found by working out the minimal revision that is needed to turn Edmund from a coward to a brave hero. It may well be that, given Edmund's particular interests and personality, an immediate manifestation of his bravery will be his taking up mountaineering—all that was stopping him was his cowardice.

A number of logical principles which are classically valid, fail on the similarity analysis. One example is Contraposition, that 'if B then not-A' follows from 'if A then not-B'. Take this instance: 'If it rains, it won't rain heavily. So if it rains heavily, it won't rain'. The premiss could be true, but the conclusion is absurd. The closest world in which it rains can easily be one in which the rain is light; but the closest world in which it rains heavily cannot be one in which it does not rain at all. Another principle which fails is that of Strengthening the Antecedent. It has the form: 'If A then B. So if A and C then B'. Classically, it is valid, for if the premiss is true, either A is false or B is true, in which case, either 'A and C' is false or B is true, and so the conclusion is true. A counterexample is: 'If I put sugar in my tea it will taste fine. So if I put sugar and diesel oil in my tea it will taste fine.' In the closest world in which I put sugar in my tea, the tea tastes fine; but in the closest world in which I put diesel oil, as well as sugar in it, it tastes awful.

It follows that Transitivity must fail, that is 'If A then B, and if B then C. So if A then C' will be invalid. For clearly 'if A and C then A' must be true; Transitivity would give: 'If A and C then A. If A then B. So if A and C then B'; Strengthening the Antecedent would follow. Transitivity fails on the similarity account because the closest A-world need not be the closest B-world, and so need not be a C-world.

These principles also fail on the probabilistic analysis. Indeed, the logical principles which are valid on the two accounts are the same, even though the terms in which the truth-conditions of conditionals are framed on the two theories are so different. The failure of Strengthening the Antecedent and Transitivity also show that the Conditionality principle breaks down. 'If A then B. A and C. So B' is a valid principle on both the similarity and probability accounts. The counterexample about diesel oil worked because the world in which I put both sugar and diesel in my tea was non-actual. But if the antecedent of the conclusion is brought into the premisses, the counterexample will not work. If 'A and C' is true, then this world is an A-world, so 'if A then B' is true only if B is true. Therefore, if the premisses are true, so is the conclusion. The same point applies to Transitivity: when the antecedent of the conclusion is brought into the premisses, the resulting inference is valid. We thus have as valid inferences:

If A then B. A and C. So B

and

If A then B. If B then C. A. So C

but the results of applying the conditionality principle are invalid:

If A then B. So if A and C then B

and

If A then B. If B then C. So if A then C

The reason Conditionality fails on the similarity analysis is because the conditional has become a modal connective; the principle commits a modal fallacy. If 'if A then B' is treated as a modal connective of some sort (that is, its truth-value depends not only on the actual values of A and B, but on their possible values), then to infer 'if A then B' from some other propositions we need to know not only that B follows from those other propositions in conjunction with A (as the conditionality principle requires) but that those other propositions are strong enough in some appropriate modal sense. For example, even given that 'if A then B' is true; if 'A and C' is not actually true, the closest world where 'A and C' is true may not be the closest world where A is true, and so B may not be true there. To ensure that the closest 'A and C'-world is the closest A-world, we would need to know, for example, that C is true everywhere.

We should now have a feel for how the 'similarity' theory works. However, among its supporters there is disagreement over a couple of principles. One of these is Conditional Excluded Middle. We have met Excluded Middle itself before: it says that one or other of a proposition and its contradictory must be true, that is, that every proposition of the form 'A or not-A' is true. Conditional Excluded Middle is a stronger principle, that one or other of a pair of conditionals differing only in that the consequent of one is the contradictory of the consequent of the other, must be true, that is, that every proposition of the form 'if A then B or if A then not-B' is true. Conditional

Excluded Middle is central to Stalnaker's way of developing the Ramsey Test, and corresponds to the assumption that there always is a unique closest world, that is, that $f(A,w)$ is always uniquely defined for any A and w. For if so, then if B is true in $f(A,w)$, 'if A then B' is true (in w), while if 'not-B' is true in $f(A,w)$, 'if A then not-B' is true in w. Since (by Excluded Middle) either B or 'not-B' is true in $f(A,w)$, it follows (from the uniqueness of $f(A,w)$) that Conditional Excluded Middle always holds.

There are pairs of conditionals for which this result looks implausible, however. David Lewis's much-repeated example is:

> If Bizet and Verdi were compatriots, Bizet would be Italian

and

> If Bizet and Verdi were compatriots, Bizet would not be Italian

(because Verdi would also be French). On Stalnaker's account, one or other of those must be true (though he admits that he does not know which). Lewis claims they are both false. (Recall that Lewis thinks only subjunctive conditionals are not truth-functional—the indicative counterparts would for him both be true, having a false antecedent. I follow Stalnaker here in taking the indicative/subjunctive distinction simply to reflect one's knowledge of Bizet's and Verdi's nationalities. The indicative counterparts would be quite acceptable in the mouth of those unaware of their nationalities—or repeat the example with Menotti and Ligeti, say.)

In fact, one might be inclined to think the second of the pair, with the negative consequent, was the true one. That may be, however, because one understands it not as a proposition of the form 'if A then not-B'—as Conditional Excluded Middle requires—but as 'not-if A then B', that is,

> It is not the case that if Bizet and Verdi were compatriots, Bizet would be Italian

in which case it is Excluded Middle itself, and not its Conditional version, which requires that it be true (given that the instance with affirmative consequent is false). Another way of expressing one's thoughts here is to say

>If Bizet and Verdi were compatriots, Bizet might be Italian

and

>If Bizet and Verdi were compatriots, Bizet might not be Italian

If these can be true together, and Lewis is correct to identify 'if *A* it might be not-*B*' with 'Not-if *A* it would be *B*', then Conditional Excluded Middle must be abandoned, and the uniqueness assumption about a most similar world with it.

Stalnaker's semantics builds in another assumption, that there always is at least one closest world. But as well as ties for closeness, as in the Bizet/Verdi example, it is conceivable that there will not always be any world at all which is closest. Consider an adaptation of another of Lewis's examples:

>If Lewis is over 2 m. tall, he can join the basketball team.

(Those who have met him, can put 'was' and 'could' here.) What is in play here is the limit (or existence) assumption, that among more and more similar worlds there be a limit, one than which there is none more similar. But worlds in which Lewis is 2 m. 2 cm., 2 m. 1 cm., 2 m. 0.5 cm. and so on, are progressively more similar to the actual world, yet there is no limit to this sequence (other than one in which he is 2 m. tall, and that is not compatible with the antecedent). To accommodate the two revisions—abandoning uniqueness and the limit assumption—Lewis replaces the selection function *f* with a similarity relation, and proposes that 'if *A* then *B*' is true in *w* if either there is no '*A* and *B*'-world or some '*A* and *B*'-world is closer to *w* than every '*A* and not-*B*'-world; that is, there is a world more similar to *w* where *A* and *B* are true than is every world where *A* and 'not-*B*' are true. Taking the above example, the conditional is true if there is a world more similar to ours in which Lewis is over 2 m. tall and can join the team than is every world in which he is over 2 m. tall and cannot join it. In the Bizet/Verdi case, where there is no unique closest world, the 'would'-conditionals are false because for each of those matched most similar worlds in which Bizet and Verdi are compatriots, there is no more similar world in which Bizet's nationality is different. Consequently the 'might'-conditionals are both true: 'if A it might be B' is true in world w if there is an 'A and B'-world than which no 'A and not-B'-world is more similar to w.

This revision relinquishes Conditional Excluded Middle, but does not otherwise alter the basic theory. For example, taking our original examples, 'If you take a First, you will get a grant' will be true if for every world in which you take a First and fail to obtain a grant there is a more similar one in which you get both. If there is a most similar one, then whether or not you obtain a grant there determines the issue; if not, the new theory supplies an answer which the earlier one did not. Similarly, 'If Oswald did not kill Kennedy, someone else did' is true because every world in which neither Oswald nor anyone else killed Kennedy is less similar to ours than one in which Kennedy was still shot, but by a different assassin—whether this world or a revision of it. Once again, the revised theory agrees with the old theory except in the cases—no unique most similar world—which the earlier theory could not accommodate.

So much for the 'similarity'-theory. Is it acceptable? Does it give an adequate account of the truth-conditions of conditionals? There are two reasons to suppose not. The first has come out already, namely, that it makes all conditionals with true antecedent and consequent, true. But in this regard, it is mistaken. Many such conditionals are false. For example,

If the Sun is larger than the Earth then the Earth orbits the Sun

and (supposing John is in Alaska)

If John is not in Turkey then he is not in Paris.

These conditionals come out true on the 'similarity' account because it asks only if the consequent is true at the closest world where the antecedent is true (or whether they are both true at a closer world than any where the one is true and the other false), which, since the antecedent is true, amounts simply to asking if the consequent is true. But intuitively, in thinking about the examples, we actually ignore the fact that the antecedent is true, and consider whether the (possible) truth of the antecedent would imply the truth of the consequent—as the Ramsey Test asks us to. The Ramsey Test does not lay down that only the actual world be considered. It enjoins us to suppose the antecedent true, and consider the consequent. Restriction to the most similar world, and to the actual world if the antecedent is true, are aspects that have been added—added for what seemed good reasons, but none the less additional to the basic idea. The counterexamples with true antecedent and consequent suggest we should reconsider the test and how it should be applied.

In fact, if we now think again about the Ramsey Test, the Conditionality principle and Conditionalization, it should seem surprising that Conditionality fails on both the similarity and probability accounts. For the three principles appear to be but different ways of spelling out the same point. In each case, we are considering our commitment to a conditional, 'if A then B'. Conditionalization proposes raising the probability of A to 1 and seeing what difference that makes to the probability of B; the Ramsey Test proposes that we consider B in the context of adding A to our beliefs; and Conditionality proposes adding A to the propositions whose putative entailment of 'if A then B' is in question, and asking whether the augmented set entails B. The reason the similarity and probability accounts divorce Conditionality from the trio is the special treatment they give to the case of true antecedent. The core idea of the trio is, however, this: let a set of propositions together with all its consequences be a theory (perhaps a possible world), and let $\circ$ be a means, so far unspecified, of combining two theories, u and v, to form a new theory $u \circ v$. Then 'if A then B' belongs to a theory u if whenever A belongs to a theory v, B belongs to the composite theory $u \circ v$. The theories u, v, and $u \circ v$ here can be probability distributions, states of belief, or possible worlds. Given a theory of such theories, the Ramsey Test and its cognate principles tell us how to express the truth-condition for conditionals in that theory. (I am using 'theory' in both its nontechnical sense, to characterize a philosophical account of some sort, and in a technical sense, for a logically closed set of propositions. Which sense is appropriate to any single use of the word should be clear from the context.)

Such a theory has yet to be worked out. Let us close this chapter by turning to the second reason for believing that the 'similarity'-theory needs revision, which will provide some detail of how the new theory of conditionals should be phrased, and will at the same time link back to ideas at the close of Chapter 2. The question is, what about conditionals with contradictory antecedent, antecedents which cannot be true? For example,

> If the square root of 2 is rational, it can be expressed as a fraction in lowest terms.

The square root of 2 is not rational, and cannot be. None the less, this conditional is true. If $\sqrt{2}$ were rational, it would, as is definitive of rationals, be expressible as a fraction. However, because $\sqrt{2}$ cannot be rational, there is no possible world in which it is rational, and so in particular no closest such world. Stalnaker, therefore, adapts his theory by including among the worlds in his model an 'impossible' world, which he dubs λ, where every proposition is true. Conditionals with contradictory antecedents are evaluated there, and since every proposition is true at λ, all such conditionals turn out true. Lewis's theory has the same consequence, that all conditionals with contradictory antecedents are true, by making them vacuously true.

This should remind us of *ex falso quodlibet* and the objections to it on grounds of relevance in Chapter 2. Some conditionals with contradictory antecedents are indeed true; but not all are, for example:

> If all squares are round then all round things are square

and

> If Edmund is both brave and not brave then we will have to take the bus

The theory needs to be adapted so that it can distinguish true from false conditionals with contradictory antecedents. That adaptation is not difficult, but it does raise philosophical problems. It means we have to include in our theory a suitable range of 'impossible' worlds. Stalnaker's theory already includes one such world, but when a range is included they need not (all) be so extreme as to make every proposition true—providing one's theory of consequence does not include *ex falso quodlibet*. Worlds (or theories) are closed under logical consequence— they contain all logical consequences of propositions they contain (or make true)—so there is only one impossible theory (or world) on a classical account of logical consequence. But if we reject *EFQ*, and in keeping with that rejection wish to set up a theory in which conditionals with contradictory antecedents can be false, we need to include in that theory a range of worlds or theories, both possible and impossible. This also makes good sense if the theories are thought of as models for states of belief, for most people have contradictory beliefs without being aware of these inconsistencies, but not everyone's belief-state is the same, as would be the classical consequence of that admission.

The philosophical problem in entertaining such a theory of worlds is whether such impossible worlds can in any way be real. This takes us on to the topic of the next chapter, modal logic and its semantics, and the correct philosophical understanding of the notion of possible worlds.

Summary and Guide to Further Reading

The classical orthodoxy is that conditionals are truth-functional, true if the antecedent is false or the consequent true, and false only if the antecedent is true and the consequent false. We looked at two arguments for this claim, a quick argument via the equivalence between a conditional and a corresponding disjunction and the truth-functionality of disjunction; and a longer argument using the Conditionality principle and the classical account of validity, going through the three cases of true antecedent and false consequent, false antecedent, and, finally, true consequent. Both these arguments seek to show that the truth-conditions of conditionals are given by the material conditional or material implication, often symbolized by ⊃. '$A \supset B$' is by definition true if either A is false or B is true, otherwise false.

Despite these arguments there are reasons to suppose that conditionals are not truth-functional. Propositions of the form 'if A then B or if B then A' do not seem to be universally true, as they would be if the conditional were truth-functional. Again, if conditionals were truth-functional, the argument-form

If A then B. So either if A then C or if D then B

would be valid (suppose the premiss is true: then either A is false, in which case the first disjunct of the conclusion is true, or B is true, in which case the second disjunct of the conclusion is true). But there are intuitively invalid instances, such as

If John is in Paris he is in France. So either if John is in Paris he is in Turkey or if John is in Istanbul he is in France,

where both disjuncts of the conclusion seem clearly false, despite the obvious truth of the premiss. A whole catalogue of such counterexamples can be found in W. Cooper, 'The Propositional Logic of Ordinary Discourse'.

There have been many attempts to defend the truth-functionality thesis and to explain away the counterexamples. One with increasing popularity is the conversationalist defence, due originally to H. Paul Grice. He expounded and developed his theory of conversational implicatures over many years; perhaps the best account is found not in his own writings but in R. C. S. Walker's 'Conversational Implicatures'. See also Mark Platts's *Ways of Meaning*, ch. 3 sect. 2. Jackson's adaptation of Grice's ideas, tracing the unassertibility of true conditionals (on the truth-functional account) to a conventional implicature of their failure of robustness with respect to their antecedents, can be found in his monography, *Conditionals*. (My definition of 'robust' is the revised version (robust$_2$) offered by Lewis (with Jackson's assent) in the 1986 Postscript to his 'Probabilities of Conditionals and Conditional Probabilities' I.)

The real problem with such defences of truth-functionality lies in their adaptation for embedded conditionals. It is a version of the difficulty for expressivist theories pointed out by Peter Geach in his paper, 'Ascriptivism', reprinted in his *Logic Matters*. What in his 'Assertion' (ibid.) he calls 'the Frege point' is that not every case of predication is one of assertion; embeddings of propositions in conditionals and so on, require us to explain the function of 'good', 'intentional', 'if', and other words in cases where no assertion is made.

Jackson's monograph with the title, *Conditionals*, should not be confused with his edited collection of papers with the same name, which contains a paper of his own presenting his account of robustness, 'On Assertion and Indicative Conditionals'. It also contains one of Grice's papers, 'Logic and Conversation'. This is a very useful collection, as is the older collection edited by W. Harper *et al.*, *Ifs*. Both concentrate, the earlier one exclusively, on the probabilistic and similarity theories, which accept that conditionals are not truth-functional and set out to develop a non-truth-functional account, and to explain the fallacy in the two arguments for truth-functionality. Both originate in the work of Robert Stalnaker, as developments of Ramsey's Test, found in brief remarks by Frank Ramsey in his paper, 'General Propositions and Causality'. The probabilistic account was presented in Stalnaker's 'Probability and Conditionals', reprinted in Harper's collection, where Stalnaker proposed that the probability of a conditional, $p(\text{if } A \text{ then } B) = p(B/A)$, the corresponding conditional probability. Stalnaker's hypothesis was repeatedly criticized by David Lewis in two papers with the title, 'Probabilities of Conditionals and Conditional Probabilities' (I and II), reprinted in Jackson's collection, on the basis of his triviality proofs, that there can be no proposition whose probability is measured by the conditional probability, on pain of trivializing the whole assignment of probabilities.

Two reactions to Lewis's results are possible: to look for an alternative account of the truth-conditions of conditionals; or to revert to an idea of Ernest Adams's, that conditionals do not have truth-conditions and that $p(B/A)$ measures not the probability of truth of 'if A then B' but simply its credibility or assertibility. He presented this account in *The Logic of Conditionals*. What it is for a conditional to have a probability without its being a probability that it is true is unclear, but the idea is developed further by Dorothy Edgington in 'Do Conditionals have Truth-Conditions?', reprinted in Jackson's collection, where she claims they do not. If they did, they would be truth-functional, she argues, on the basis of Adams's hypothesis, that a person's confidence (as she puts it) in the conditional 'if A then B' is measured by $p(B/A)$. Since conditionals are not truth-functional, they must lack truth-conditions altogether.

Stalnaker's other elaboration of the Ramsey Test was into the similarity theory, proposing that 'if A then B' is true (in a possible world w) if B is true in the world most similar to w in which A is true. He presented this idea in 'A Theory of Conditionals', reprinted both in Jackson and in Harper. David Lewis criticized it for assuming the existence and uniqueness of a most similar world, and proposed an alternative account in 'Counterfactuals and Comparative Possibility', reprinted in Harper and developed more fully in his *Counterfactuals*. Stalnaker responded in defence of Conditional Excluded Middle, the focus of the disagreement, and the dispute can be followed in Harper's collection.

I have taken the view in this chapter, following Stalnaker, that the difference between indicative and subjunctive conditionals is essentially epistemic and pragmatic, reflecting a different epistemic view of the antecedent, and not imparting a difference in truth-conditions (though there may be a difference in truth-value). Lewis and Jackson disagree. So too, in a different way, does Vic Dudman, whose iconoclastic ideas the reader should be aware of. He believes that philosophers have systematically misclassified conditionals, and their theories are consequently in grave error. An interesting paper, 'Interpretations of "If"-sentences', is included in Jackson's collection.

My view, however, was that the Ramsey Test did give an interesting insight into the semantics of conditionals, and that the possible-worlds account was moving in the right direction. However, it needs to be revised in two ways, to accommodate the fact that not all conditionals with true antecedent and consequent are true, nor are all those with contradictory antecedent (as happens on Stalnaker's and Lewis's theories). This revision can be achieved by looking not only at the closest world where the antecedent is true (or at sufficiently close worlds, on

Lewis's theory), but more generally at worlds where the antecedent is true, and combining the 'theories' or worlds where antecedent and conditional are putatively true into a world where the consequent should be true. The development of such theory-revision or composition will need to be informed by the work of Alchourron, Gärdenfors, and Makinson; see, for example, Gärdenfors's *Knowledge in Flux*. The Ramsey Test can then be rephrased into essentially the form of the Conditionality principle, to articulate the acceptance-condition for conditionals in such a theory. A paradox threatens, generalizing Lewis's triviality results, given some plausible assumptions about theory-revision (see Gärdenfors, ch. 7). If they can be overcome, one may hope in this way to obtain a theory of conditionals which can fit with the account of logical consequence at the end of Chapter 2 in requiring a connection of relevance, between premisses and conclusion in the one case and between antecedent and consequent in the other.

4 The Incredulous Stare: Possible Worlds

W E H A V E mentioned possible worlds more than once in earlier chapters. In Chapter 1, I introduced the idea of maximal states of affairs, ways in which objects are placed so as to make every proposition either true or false. They are complete realities, ways the world might have been if the class of propositions had a certain assignment of truth-values. On one version of the correspondence theory of truth, they constitute the union of all the states of affairs which would have to exist, or obtain, if propositions were to have that set of truth-values. In Chapter 3, the same conception of a complete state of affairs, covering every eventuality, was needed for the 'similarity'-theory of conditionals, so that the consequences of supposing the antecedent true could be correctly explored. A theory, a deductively closed set of propositions, corresponded to its concrete realization, a possible world in which every situation was determinately specified. The alternative conception of conditionals at the end of the chapter replaced talk of a relation of similarity by an operation on worlds, forming a new world or theory $u \circ v$ from worlds u and v, but its basis, a class of alternative scenarios, was at least the same, despite its also encompassing 'impossible' worlds, ways in which the consequences of contradictory assumptions could be studied. Throughout all these ideas, and throughout the play with the notion of 'possible world', lies the conception of alternatives to the actual world, different ways the world might have been.

So much for the logic of possible worlds. What is the metaphysics which underlies it? Is there here a coherent philosophical picture of reality? At its most extreme, the use of possible worlds in logic presents us with a staggering immensity of alternative versions of reality. It is the very stuff of science fiction. Several science fiction writers have elaborated this conception, and woven it into their stories. One particularly striking example is *The Gods Themselves* by Isaac Asimov. Samples of a 'physically impossible' element are discovered—one which is unstable and immediately decays to form a stable element, giving off useful energy in the process. What is the origin of these samples? They come, it turns out, from a parallel universe, one in which the laws of nature are subtly different, so that the 'physically impossible' element is not, in that world, impossible. In that world, the strong nuclear binding force is two orders of magnitude stronger than in ours, one consequence of which— besides the differences in which elements (which combinations of protons, neutrons, and electrons) are stable—is that the nuclear fusion powering their stars has proceeded very much more rapidly. Only seven stars are now visible in the night sky; all the stars are going out, and the end of their universe is at hand. One of their scientists has discovered how to transfer matter from that universe to its neighbours—our world. In this transaction, both parties benefit—at least, at first glance. For each element exchanged, while stable in its own world, is unstable in the world of different nuclear binding force, and so gives off energy in its decay into a stable element. The scientists on earth have discovered, co-operating in this exchange, a free source of energy; the 'para-scientists' can stave off the death of their civilization by becoming independent of their sun for energy, and by effectively importing energy can survive the heat-death of their universe.

Asimov is also able, as a novelist, to incorporate delightful parallels between these alternative worlds, different ways in which, in the context of different laws of nature, the evolution of stars, worlds, and people has led to close but contrasting similarities in their histories. Thus the earth (and moon) scientists, Hallam, Denison, and Selene have their parallel in Tritt, Odeen, and Dua in the para-universe. There is a catch, however, in the exchange of matter. The importation of these alien elements into each world brings other changes, changes which threaten our world, threaten to bring forward—drastically forward—the explosion of the Sun. The solution hinges, as Denison puts it, on the fact that 'the number two is ridiculous and can't exist'. If our world is not the only world there is, then there is not only one alternative universe, there are infinitely many.

The picture Asimov paints for us is, therefore, one of a plethora of distinct but parallel universes, each comprising a total history of stellar evolution, each incorporating a difference in how things might have been if a variable in a physical law had been different, if stars had been differently composed, if life had evolved differently, if different decisions had been made and actions performed. Each world is a complete universe, unrelated to the others except by their place in the 'space' of alternative possibilities.

Modal Platonism

Such is the metaphysics of what is known as modal realism, or as I prefer to call it, extreme realism or modal Platonism—for I wish to defend a different realist metaphysics, later in this chapter. What is distinctive of Platonism—which takes its name from the Greek philosopher, Plato, of the fourth century BC whose theory of Forms had this character—is that it seeks to ground objectivity in self-subsistent objects. The idea is that conditionals, for example, have objectively obtaining truth-values, values independent of our ability to determine those values—that much is realism—and that the explanation for that objectivity resides in the fact that—on say, the 'similarity'-theory—antecedent and consequent have the values they do in worlds appropriately (and objectively) similar to ours. Similarly, propositions have meaning objectively—on the picture theory of Wittgenstein's mentioned in Chapter 1—in virtue of their correspondence to real and mind-independent states of affairs, segments of complete world-histories only one of which is actual but all of which are real.

Hallam, Denison, and Selene have counterparts in the para-universe, counterparts who at the same time are a single counterpart, Estwald. The different worlds are real concrete universes, containing physical matter extended in space and time. It is natural to picture them in this way in the Platonistic conception. Alternative conceptions of worlds, that see worlds as 'ways the world might have been', often suggest that objects in one world do not have mere counterparts in other worlds, but are identical with them. If we wonder what would have happened if Edmund had been brave, we are wondering what would have happened if our Edmund, the real Edmund, had been brave, not some mere counterpart of him. But taking Platonism seriously strongly suggests that this is incoherent. It is certainly a natural concomitant of Platonism, and supported by argument, to reject the idea that Edmund might inhabit different worlds. If each world has concrete reality, then Edmund cannot be in two worlds at once. When we wonder what Edmund would be like if he were brave, we are thinking about someone very like Edmund—or as much like him as anyone could be— who was brave. Dua fled not from our Sun, but from a counter-part of the Sun—like it, but much smaller and cooler.

How do we identify a counterpart? Some might say that Dua is not Selene's counterpart, rather, she is the counterpart of Peter Lamont. They are the pair who in their respective worlds try to stop the exchange process. Selene, on the Moon, has no counterpart in the para-universe, for in that world the Earth has no moon. On the other hand, Dua has the female charac-teristics of the trio, and is an 'Emotional' in the way Selene is an 'Intuitionist'. Identifying a person's, or a thing's, counterparts in another world seems to rely on the matching of features. In thinking what would have happened if Edmund had been brave, we cast around to find the person, in the other situation, most like Edmund except in possessing the quality of bravery, and our question is answered by discovering what other qualities that person has. A person or thing might have no counterpart in some other situation—if the nuclear binding force were one hundred times stronger, says Asimov, the Earth (the counter-part of the Earth) would have no moon. There would be no Moon. Conversely, when Dua and Odeen think about our world, they find the number of its stars, and the numbers of its people, unimaginable. From their perspective, there are many possible but non-existent things and persons—possible objects which have no actual counterpart.

What this thought brings out is a disturbing symmetry in the modal Platonist conception. What is actual, what really exists, is relative to each world. Denison and Selene believe our world is the actual world; the para-universe is only how things might have been if the laws of physics had been different. Similarly, Odeen and Dua believe they are real; our world for them is merely a remote possibility. But once the positron Pump is working, exchanging matter between the two universes, the others become real, and an object for concern. What will happen to the people—us—in the other world if their—our—Sun explodes? In the Platonist conception each and every world is real. 'Actual' connotes only 'the world I belong to'; 'real' is ambiguous between 'actual' and 'all'. All the worlds are real; all the worlds really exist; 'possible' is no longer contrasted with reality. Every possibility is realized.

The Platonist conception is at first glance compelling. We explain 'possible' by saying, 'it is possible that A' means that there is a possible world where A is true; 'it is necessary that A' means that in every possible world A is true. We here quantify over every possible world—'there is ...', 'in every ...'. Must there not be this infinity of possible worlds in order to explain the notions of possibility and necessity? Yet if we take the metaphor seriously, and develop a metaphysical theory really containing all these possible worlds, as really existing concrete realities, we ultimately find that we lose our grip on the very distinction we set out to illuminate. We wondered what would be possible if Edmund had been brave; we find that it would not be Edmund, but some *doppelgänger*, who would take up mountaineering. Edmund is here among us; he cannot also inhabit another world. Worse, we now have difficulty identifying his counterpart. Edmund cannot be too different—his counterpart cannot differ too much from him, or we shall not be able to find him and track him down. How different can Edmund be, and still be (a counterpart of) Edmund? Moreover, this is Edmund, the real Edmund, how Edmund actually is. His counterpart should only be a shadow, how Edmund might have been, a possibility. The possibility is now real—the counterpart thinks he is the real Edmund, how Edmund actually is. We are but a remote possibility to him. Our Edmund is how Edmund might have been had he not been brave. But this is not the conception of possibility which we sought at all.

In identifying Edmund, or whatever is the object of our modal reflections, the Platonist about possible worlds will resort to one or other of two strategies. The haecceitist (pronounced 'hex-ee-it-ist') believes that each thing has an individual essence, a set of properties which are essential to it. For example, Edmund is essentially a human being, and no counterpart of Edmund can be other than human; but Edmund is not essentially a coward—his counterpart can be brave. But more: Edmund has a defining essence, something more distinctive of him than his being a human being, for that is a trait he shares with other people. Edmund must also have the essential property of 'being Edmund', and that is shared by no one other than his counterparts in other worlds. It is this necessity (from the Latin *haecceitas*, a neologism coined by Duns Scotus in the late thirteenth century, literally 'thisness') which enables us to pick Edmund (that is, Edmund's counterparts) out in other worlds. Their properties are what determine Edmund's modal properties.

The anti-haecceitists object to this ultra-essentialist talk. They may or may not admit that some properties are essential. For example, few would claim that Edmund might have been a sports car, or a disease, or a line of longitude. That may be because being a human being is, in some deep way, essential to him; or it may simply be that Edmund's counterparts are identified by their similarity to him, by their being more similar to him than other things in their world. Whether essentialist or not, the anti-haecceitists deny that there are any individual essences. If there were, they say, it would make sense to suppose that Edmund and his brother Edgar should change places in another world—that in that world, Edmund's counterpart could behave there as Edgar does here and vice versa. Indeed, it would seem that two worlds might be identical except in so far as there was a permutation of identities, that is, of counterparts. That, the anti-haecceitist retorts, is a distinction without a difference. Between two worlds, there must be a real difference in so far as some object lacks a property in one and gains it in the other. Identity, or the counterpart relation, is not such a difference. What objects are counterparts of which is dependent on the properties they have, not on some hidden essence underneath those properties.

Many years ago, Willard van Quine rejected modal logic in its entirety on the grounds that it committed its proponents to a belief in essences. He was willing to admit that some propositions are necessarily true (at least, he could make sense of the idea, even if he did not rest content with that description of it). For example, the proposition 'Nine is greater than seven' is necessarily true, for it is a truth of arithmetic. This is modality *de dicto*, modality attaching to a proposition (*dicto* comes from the Latin *dictum*, for 'proposition'). The *de dicto* interpretation of 'Necessarily, 9 > 7' is that the proposition '9 > 7' cannot conceivably be false. But nine is the number of planets. Are we warranted in inferring that necessarily, the number of planets is greater than 7? The proposition 'The number of planets is greater than 7' does not seem to be necessarily true, for it is conceivable that there have been fewer than 7 planets. None the less, the principle we have followed in the inference is, in general, safe and useful. Colloquially, it is Shakespeare's reassurance through Juliet to Romeo that 'that which we call a rose | By any other name would smell as sweet'. 'What's in a name?', Juliet asks. Just as, since nine is greater than seven it follows that the number of planets is greater than seven, so too, it would seem, from the fact that necessarily, nine is greater than seven, it follows that necessarily, the number of planets is greater than seven. The technical designation for this principle is the Indiscernibility of Identicals, sometimes called Leibniz's Law. (The converse, the Identity of Indiscernibles, that no two different things can share all their properties, is much more contentious.) If *a* and *b* are identical, then their properties are the same. If two names mean one and the same thing, then its properties are just those properties regardless of how it is named.

None the less, the principle appears to take us from the true claim that necessarily nine is greater than seven, to the false claim that necessarily, the number of planets is greater than seven. But surely, there might have been only six planets? There is an explanation, one of which Quine is aware, but which does not allay his fears. The response is to distinguish two different kinds of name, genuine names and non-genuine names (or we could say the latter are not names at all). Only genuine names permit the substitution found in the Indiscernibility of Identicals. That principle says that, given a proposition of the form Fa, that is, the attribution to an object a of a property F, and given the minor premiss '$a = b$' (that is, that the names a and b name the same thing), we may infer Fb. The move from 'Cicero denounced Catiline' (ascribing the property of having denounced Catiline to Cicero) and 'Cicero was Tully' (reminding us that 'Cicero' and 'Tully' were different names of one man, Marcus Tullius Cicero) to 'Tully denounced Catiline' has this form, and takes us from true premisses to a true conclusion. 'Cicero' and 'Tully' are both genuine names. But 'the greatest Roman orator' and 'the number of planets' are not genuine names, it is said. (We will look more closely at the reasons for this claim in the next chapter.) They are descriptions. The proposition 'The greatest Roman orator denounced Catiline' does not have the form Fa, conjoining a predicate with a name, but makes a much more complex statement, namely, 'There was among Roman orators a greatest and he denounced Catiline'. Similarly, 'The number of planets is greater than 7' has the complex form 'for some x, x is uniquely G and x is F', that is, 'Some number uniquely numbers the planets and it is greater than 7'. When analysed in this way (and Russell's analysis of descriptions which this is, paved the way for analytical philosophy to develop in the early years of this century), the propositions 'The number of planets is 9' and 'Necessarily, the number of planets is greater than 7' are found not to contain names—genuine names (apart from '9' and '7')—and so cannot be minor premiss and conclusion of the principle of the indiscernibility of identicals.

The initial problem has been evaded. 'Necessarily, $9 > 7$' is true and 'Necessarily, the number of planets is greater than 7' is false. The latter does not follow from the former by the Indiscernibility of Identicals, since 'The number of planets is 9' is not the identity proposition it appears to be and which the principle requires. But, says Quine, we are here simply out of the frying pan into the fire. For let us apply the analysis of descriptions to the proposition, 'Necessarily, the number of planets is greater than 7'. We can do it in two different ways. In the analysis, we implicitly give to the non-genuine name a scope, for the analysis consists in replacing an apparent form $A(d)$, where a description d occurs in a proposition A, by a proposition B containing no constituent corresponding to d. We say that the proposition A is the description's scope. In our example, the description 'the number of planets' occurs both in the proposition 'Necessarily, ... is greater than 7' and in the contained clause, '... is greater than 7'. Replacing the description in the wider proposition 'Necessarily, ... is greater than 7' we obtain,

> Some number uniquely numbers the planets and necessarily, it is greater than 7;

while replacing it in the narrower contained clause, we obtain,

> Necessarily, some number uniquely numbers the planets and it is greater than 7.

(In the first, 'necessarily' has narrow scope, thus giving wide scope to the quantifier which has replaced the description; in the second, 'necessarily' has wide scope, and so the quantifier replacing the description has narrow scope.)

The latter proposition is certainly false. It is not necessary that there be a number greater than 7 which numbers the planets. Had there been only six planets (as, for example, Newton believed) there would have been no such number. That proposition causes no trouble, and dissolves the initial puzzle. But what of the former proposition? Recall the premisses of the puzzle argument: 'Necessarily, $9 > 7$' and 'Some number uniquely numbers the planets and it is 9'. The expression '9' is a genuine name (so it was conceded, in contrast with 'the number of planets'). The principle of indiscernibility therefore yields, 'Some number uniquely numbers the planets and necessarily, it is greater than 7', the very proposition above. So it is true—entailed by true premisses. But what does it say? It says that some number is necessarily greater than 7. What number, asks Quine? 'Nine,' he replies, '—that is, the number of planets.'

That last quip is pure rhetoric. We have seen that we cannot straightforwardly replace '9' by its description. But there is a serious question behind the oratory. The acceptance of genuine names commits one to *de re* modality, the ascription to objects of modal properties. Quine is willing (pending further analysis) to accept *de dicto* modality, the ascription to propositions of modal properties. But true *de re* ascriptions (*re* from *res*, Latin for 'thing') are altogether different. It means that objects themselves, independently of how described, have properties necessarily, and that is essentialism, which Quine believes is a vestige of Aristotelian science, rightly rejected by the scientific revolution of the seventeenth century and its emphasis on experiment and empirical method.

Actualism

Quine's solution is to restrict the range of application of the Indiscernibility principle, and his justification lies in effectively renouncing modal logic and the metaphysics of possible worlds which goes with it. Logic is restricted to the classical paradigm of Chapter 2, and the theory of modalities becomes a questionable theory, ultimately to be dismissed by his arguments against analyticity and meaning. Before that happens, Quine construes all modality as *de dicto*, and takes that literally as quotational. That is, modal propositions of the form 'necessarily, A' are taken to be of the form Fa, where a names the proposition A and F is the predicate 'is necessarily true'. So 'Necessarily, $9 > 7$' becomes '"$9 > 7$" is necessarily true'. The names '9' and '7' are now hidden within quotation, protected from the Indiscernibility principle. There is no dispute that quotation is 'opaque' to substitution, as Quine puts it. That Tully was Cicero does not warrant us in inferring from the fact that 'Tully' has five letters that 'Cicero' does too.

We have considered two extremes: extreme realism on the one hand, and at the other, the outright rejection of modal discourse. Neither is satisfactory, however: Platonism treats possibilities as concrete realities, eroding the distinction between what is actual and what is only possible; and it either restricts the range of possibilities in order to permit the identification of counterparts by their similarities, promoting one kind of unjustified essentialism; or it postulates haecceities, inner hidden essences shared only by counterparts, a kind of magical essentialism. No wonder Quine shies away from it. Need the rejection of Platonism be so violent, however? Is there no sensible middle ground?

There is, and it constitutes some form of actualism, sharply distinguishing the actual world from the range of possible worlds. There are two main forms of actualism: reductionism, itself having many variants, which seeks to construct possible worlds out of some more mundane and familiar materials; and moderate realism, in which the actual concrete world is contrasted with abstract, but none the less real, possible worlds. The faults with reductionism can be typified by considering two varieties of it. In one, possible worlds are identified with set-theoretic combinations of the basic elements of the actual world—for example, space-time points, or atoms, or whatever. The problem here is the limitation this imposes. It means that the basic constituents of all worlds are the same, and that conflicts with our intuition, namely, that the world might at the very least have had somewhat different constituents, if not in fact totally different ones. (None the less, recall from Chapter 1 that Wittgenstein denied this: for him, the objects were common to all worlds.) Such forms of reductionism, therefore, fail to provide sufficient variety in the range of possible worlds constructed. The other major fault with reductionism about possible worlds parallels a similar problem in reductionism about numbers. The so-called von Neumann numbers have a structural isomorphism to the set of natural numbers—we construe each number as the set consisting of all its predecessors. Thus 0 (zero) is taken to be the empty set; 1 is the set whose only member is 0; 2 is the set consisting of 0 and 1; and so on. This is very elegant, and indeed, treating the numbers as such von Neumann numbers has technical advantages, enabling certain proofs to proceed more smoothly. But philosophically, it is unacceptable. Whatever the number 2 is, it is not a set with two members, nor is it a member of the number 3. So too with possible worlds. One can construct possible worlds out of propositions (e.g. identify a possible world with the set of propositions true at it), infinite decimals (a description of a world can be coded up as such an infinite expression), and in countless other ways. But 'being true at' is not the same as belonging to, and with all of them, the pretence that this is a theory of possible worlds is thin. They are mathematical games.

When we reflect that Edmund might have been brave, or that 9 must be greater than 7, we quantify over possible worlds: there is a way things might have been in which Edmund was brave; however things are, 9 will be greater than 7. It is our ability to quantify over properties (recall 'Napoleon had all the qualities of a great general' from Chapter 2) which shows that we must take talk of properties seriously. Not too seriously: properties inhere in their subjects, and cannot exist without them. Particular objects are the primary substance of the world, yet properties are real existents too, albeit only in abstraction from the objects they qualify. Similarly, ways things might be are real, but only when abstracted from the actual way things are. They are brought out and distinguished by mind, by abstraction, but are not dependent on mind for their existence. It is an objective fact that Edmund might have been brave, and that consists in the real possibility that he be brave. But he isn't brave, and there is no concrete, independent world in which he is. In considering the possibility, we are thinking about a real but abstract possibility. Worlds other than our own are abstract entities, as real as numbers or qualities, which we can think about by abstracting away from the actual way our own world is. But they are not concrete, physically inaccessible entities, whose 'actual' inhabitants can think about us in a symmetrical way. Their reality is only moderate—as ways our world might have been.

Only moderate realism can do proper justice to the intuition that when we suppose Edmund might have been brave, it is Edmund himself whom we suppose to be brave. We saw that Platonism populates alternative worlds with counterparts; so too does reductionism—if it provides worlds with domains at all. There are many abstract possibilities concerning Edmund: that he be brave or cowardly, a mountaineer or a squash-player or a yachtsman or whatever. One set of these possibilities is exemplified in concrete reality. Through them all it is Edmund who is the recurrent subject. *De re* modalities are intelligible— Edmund has the property that he might have been brave, for there is a world, a way things might have been, in which he, Edmund, is brave. The number 9 has the property that it must be greater than 7. Moreover, identifying objects in other worlds is not a problem. Since it is Edmund himself who is brave in some non-actual state of affairs, we identify him in that state of affairs by identifying him in the actual world. Having identified him as things are, our linguistic hold on him cannot go wrong in describing him in another world. Kripke calls this a stipulation, which in a way it is. The world we are interested in is 'stipulated' to be one where Edmund is brave. One should not misunderstand this to suggest a magical way of identifying Edmund by stipulation. Rather, we identify Edmund in the ordinary way and the identity of Edmund ensures that it is he who is supposed brave.

This puts a different complexion on the earlier example, 'Necessarily, the number of planets is greater than 7'. When the description is given narrow scope, we take it to designate different objects in different worlds, namely, whatever number there is of planets in that world, six, nine, ten, or whatever. Taking the description to have wide scope means taking it to designate the same object in all worlds regardless of how many planets there are in that world, namely, the actual number of planets, nine. (Recent reports suggest there are actually ten planets in the solar system, but until this is solidly confirmed, let us take it there are actually nine.) Genuine names have wide scope always—they pick out an object, and the modal properties are ascribed to it, in a sense directly. We don't wonder, 'Which object is 9 in another world?', whereas we do need to ask, 'Which object is the number of planets?' Kripke calls genuine names 'rigid designators', their rigidity consisting in the fact that they pick out the same object in every world, at least, in every world in which they pick out anything. (For example, 'Edmund' always picks out Edmund, except in situations where he is supposed not to exist.)

A note of clarification may be in order here. When we say that a designator may pick out different objects in different worlds, we are not thinking of different uses of language in different worlds. In that sense, any expression, 'Edmund', say, might have been used to designate different objects from that which it does actually designate. We are not referring to other possible language-users' use of expressions, but our own use. Our use is such that genuine names pick out an item in the actual world and maintain that reference in any modal context. In general, descriptions do not. They can be so taken, by taking them to have wide scope; and some descriptions designate rigidly regardless of how construed, for example, 'the square of 3'. The concept of a rigid designator covers these three ideas: constant reference *de jure*, in the case of genuine names; constant reference *de facto*, in the case of taking descriptions to have wide scope; and constant reference *de facto* again, in what might be called the case of essences, where, say, a description used to pick out an object connotes an essential property of it, one which it possesses in every world—as 'the square of 3' refers to 9 in virtue of its relation to 3, a relation which holds of necessity.

We have seen that genuine names—and in fact it holds of rigid designators generally—can create *de re* modal truths. A notorious example is identity. Take two rigid designators of the same object, for example, 'Cicero' and 'Tully'. 'Cicero is Cicero' is necessarily true. But 'necessarily, Cicero is Tully' is true too, for 'Cicero' and 'Tully' designate the same object, and by hypothesis, they are rigid designators, and so each designates the same object in all possible worlds (in which they designate anything). Hence they designate the same object as one another in all worlds. The simple truth, 'Cicero is Tully' becomes the *de re* modal truth, 'necessarily, Cicero is Tully'.

The Necessary and the A Priori

This may seem surprising, for not everyone knows that Cicero was Tully. It is not an obvious truth, but one which needs to be discovered. Does that not mean that it is contingent? It does not. It only shows that it is empirical, or a posteriori (these words are equivalent). 'Necessary' means 'true in all worlds'; 'contingent' means 'true in some but not all worlds' (so 'contingent' means 'possible but not necessary'). 'A priori' means 'capable of being known to be true without empirical investigation'; 'empirical' (or 'a posteriori') means 'can be discovered only by experience'. A priori truths are not always self-evident. The four-colour theorem is a good example. Consider the cartographer's problem of drawing a map on a sheet of paper. Each area (representing a country, say, or a state, or county, or parish) needs to be coloured differently from its neighbours. Any single region can border indefinitely many others. Cartographers had discovered, however, from experience, that with sufficient ingenuity, they never needed more than four colours. Four colours were enough to colour any map they could conceive of, in such a way that no two adjacent regions received the same colour. But thus far, it was only an empirical, a posteriori, discovery, based on an inductive leap from particular maps (very, very many particular maps, with no exceptions) to a hypothesis about every map. If they knew that no map needed more than four colours—and I am willing to concede that they did know this —their knowledge was empirical. None the less, one can prove them right. The proof was obtained only in the early 1980s. The proof was a priori; it did not depend on empirical investigation, but analysed the various possible configurations of maps into (a very large number of) different types, and showed how each type required at most four colours. The proof showed that all along, knowledge of the four-colour theorem was a priori—that it was capable of being known independently of empirical investigation, as well as showing that the judgement based on experience which cartographers had formed was indeed knowledge. Their knowledge was empirical, but the theorem, the truth itself, and knowledge of it, was a priori.

Two other closely related technical terms are 'analytic' and 'synthetic'. An analytic truth is one true solely in virtue of its meaning; a synthetic one is not analytic. Thus 'necessary' and 'contingent', 'a priori' and 'empirical' and 'analytic' and 'synthetic' make pairs of opposites, exclusive and exhaustive. Primarily they are epithets applied to truths, but can also distinguish between falsehoods, the necessarily false and the contingently false (false but possibly true), the a priori false and the empirically false, the analytically false (implicitly contradictory, false in virtue of meaning) and the synthetically false. Characterizations of the terms 'analytic' and 'synthetic' have varied more perhaps than those of the other pairs; what is important to be aware of is first, that the terms 'necessary', 'a priori' and 'analytic' have quite distinct characterizations, while, secondly, many philosophers have believed them to be coextensive. This belief has, indeed, led to somewhat cavalier and imprecise use of the terms. But if they are coextensive (in which case there is nothing actually wrong in interchanging them, other than the engendering of confusion of which no philosopher should be content to be accused), that claim needs argument—it is a strong metaphysical thesis.

There were reasons for adopting this thesis, of the coextensiveness of necessity, apriority and analyticity—empiricist and reductionist reasons, in the main. So far in our thoughts about possible worlds we have tended to ignore epistemological considerations. They are particularly problematic in the case of modal Platonism. 'Necessary' has been identified with 'true in all possible worlds'. How, then, are we to establish that something is necessarily true? The model suggests an inspection of each world. But that is impossible, for two reasons: first, there are too many, infinitely many; secondly, they are inaccessible. According to Platonism, each world is a concrete reality, spatiotemporally disjoint from every other. Science fiction writers like Asimov may postulate communication between them, but this is fantasy. They are logically connected, but actual connections are necessarily within a world. Talk of possible worlds, far from assisting in establishing necessities and possibilities, threatens to make them undiscoverable. If necessity is not to be rejected as obscurantist, it seems we can only salvage it by identifying it with the a priori.

The a priori, in its turn, came under attack. Rationalist philosophers, such as Kant, had claimed that certain truths, though a priori true, were none the less synthetic. Their truth was not a trivial matter of meaning, but a substantial fact of metaphysics. The empiricist could not accept this: agreeing that analytic truth is essentially trivial, his tenet is that all substantial truth is empirical. He denies the possibility of a substantial metaphysics (real truth is scientific truth) and identifies the a priori with the analytic. Clearly, if something is a matter of meaning, we can work it out independently of experience; the empiricist urges the converse, that what can be discovered independently of experience must result from the meanings of the words in its expression.

The necessary truth of empirically discovered identities blocks the first step of this reduction of the necessary to the analytic. That Cicero was Tully was an empirical discovery; their identity is none the less necessary. Two rigid designators of the same object, must, in virtue of their rigidity, designate the same object in all worlds, so their identity is a matter of necessity. This is an immediate consequence of what is meant by rigidity. The substantial part of Kripke's thesis is the proof of a particular term that it is rigid. This is Kripke's main theme, that the proper names of natural language do not have sense and cannot be replaced by descriptive phrases, for descriptive phrases behave differently in modal contexts. Proper names are, he said, rigid designators.

Part of the difficulty with this claim is the lack of clarity in the two opposing views of names, one associated historically with John Stuart Mill—that names are purely denotative, lacking connotation—the other with Gottlob Frege—that names have sense. Kripke, while urging that names do not have a sense given by a description, none the less accepts that the reference of a name may be 'fixed' by a description; those defending Frege deny that the sense which all names have may always be given by a description, and may even concede that names in their connotative function (whether descriptive or recognitional) are by convention always given wide scope. At this point the theories have become equivalent. The nineteenth-century metaphysician F. H. Bradley pointed out that unless a name had associated with it a means of reidentifying its referent, we could not use it. But if we concede (as the 'wide scope' convention concedes) that this method of reidentification applies only to the actual world and not to possibilities, the 'sense' theory has mutated into a denotative one. For Kripke's evidence that names do not have sense was that simple (i.e. non-modal) propositions containing them might have had different truth-values. Kripke denies that this is the same as considering their behaviour in modal contexts. But how do we decide whether 'Cicero denounced Catiline' might have been false? The question seems to reduce to asking whether Cicero might not have denounced Catiline, and that is to ask after the behaviour of 'Cicero' in the modal context 'might not have'. Kripke's argument that names do not have sense observes that whatever sense, F, a name a might be supposed to have, 'a might not have been F' is true; for example, Cicero might not have denounced Catiline, or have written *De Lege Manilia*, or whatever there is about him which as a matter of fact we use to fix our reference to him. So senses serve only to pick something out as it actually is, and do not provide an expression with the same meaning—except under the convention of wide scope. Proper names have their reference fixed by description (or other recognitional means) in the world as things are, but maintain that reference rigidly in modal contexts.

If any true identity statement like 'Cicero was Tully' has to be necessarily true, what can we make of 'Cicero might not have been Tully'? It has to be necessarily false, as much as 'Cicero might not have been Cicero'. Our inclination to suppose it true reflects an epistemic possibility, not a metaphysical one. Since the truth of 'Cicero was Tully' is a posteriori, we do not immediately recognize its truth. But our doubt, 'Was Cicero Tully?' reflects ignorance, not a contingent possibility. If Cicero was Tully, he was so of necessity; if not, then necessarily not. Anastasia claimed to be the last of the Romanovs. If it really were possible that she was the surviving youngest daughter, then there was a possible world in which she was and so she was of necessity that daughter and consequently in actuality too. Hence, if she was not actually the survivor, it was not even possible that she was. The 'possibility' we entertain is an epistemic possibility—we just do not know whether she was or not.

Other essential properties also yield a posteriori necessities. For example, Kripke and others believe in the doctrine of necessity of origin—Margaret Thatcher could not have been

Stalin's daughter, for she was actually the daughter of Mr Roberts, the Grantham grocer. Of course, we might discover a conspiracy, which revealed that the British Prime Minister was a KGB mole, part of a long-term plan to destroy the British economy. But that, Kripke urges, is an epistemic possibility; there is no metaphysical possibility that the actual person who was born in Grantham might have been the daughter of Stalin. If a is a rigid designator, and F is an essential property which the object actually denoted by a actually has, then a and F keep pace with one another through all worlds. Being rigid, a denotes the same object in all worlds; and F, being essential, belongs in every world to any object which possesses it in any world. So there is no world in which a is not F, and so a could not have failed to be F.

Kripke does not only deny that all necessary truths are a priori; he also denies that all a priori truths are necessary. His primary example concerns the standard metre rod in Paris. At least at one time, a metre was defined by reference to this rod, which was kept at a standard temperature and pressure. Hence we could know a priori that the rod was one metre long. None the less, it could have been longer or shorter than it was, so there are worlds in which it has a length other than one metre. That its length in those worlds would consequently have defined one metre to be different from its actual length is irrelevant, as was the thought that the word 'Edmund' might have been used to denote someone else. What is relevant is our use of the word 'metre' and that is determined by the actual length of the rod. What length it might have had is reflected in its length in other worlds. So contingency and apriority come apart. 'The standard metre rod is one metre long' is only contingently true, but knowable a priori.

The radical divorce between the necessary and the a priori which has now sprung up has surprising consequences. One is that every proposition is a priori equivalent to a contingent proposition. Take any proposition, A: if A is contingent, the result is immediate, for A is a priori equivalent to itself; if A is necessarily true or necessarily false, consider the proposition 'A has the same truth-value as "The standard metre rod is one metre long"'. If *A* is necessarily true, this proposition is true but contingently so, and *A* is a priori equivalent to it (for all it really says is '"*A*" is true'); if *A* is necessarily false, that proposition is false, yet still contingently so, and again *A* is a priori equivalent to it. So any proposition is indeed a priori equivalent to a contingent proposition.

A little ingenuity can extend this result to establish that every proposition is a priori equivalent to a proposition which is necessarily true or necessarily false (depending on whether the original proposition is true or false). Let us call such a proposition, one which is either necessarily true or necessarily false, a necessitive. The ingenuity needed is in the construction of an appropriate rigid designator. What we need is, for every proposition, an expression which rigidly designates the truth-value of that proposition. The phrase 'the truth-value of *A*' will not do, for this will designate, for each world, the truth-value of *A* in that world, so is not a rigid designator. But 'the actual truth-value of *A*' will do the trick; whatever world we are considering, it designates the truth-value of *A* in the actual world. So 'the actual truth-value of *A*' is a rigid designator. (It is a case of rigidity by essence, the third of the three types we noted, like 'the square of 3'.) *A* is either true or false, so 'the actual truth-value of *A*' designates either truth or falsity. Consider the proposition 'The actual truth-value of *A* is truth'. Call this proposition act(*A*). If *A* is true, then act(*A*) (a true identity between rigid designators) is necessarily true; if false, it is necessarily false. So act(*A*) is a necessitive. Moreover, we can tell a priori that *A* is equivalent to act(*A*), which says essentially that *A* is actually true. So *A* is a priori equivalent to a necessitive.

Similarly, we can show that *A* is necessarily equivalent to an a posteriori proposition, and that it is necessarily equivalent to an a priori proposition. In the first case, pick *A* if *A* is a posteriori and pick '*A* is equivalent to act(*A*)' if *A* is a priori; in the second, pick '*A* is equivalent to act(*A*)' if *A* is true and '*A* is not equivalent to act(*A*)' if *A* is false.

What do these games show? They serve to emphasize how different the necessary and the a priori are. It also takes us back to Chapter 1. The idea there was that the equivalence between

A and '*A* is true' showed that truth is not a substantial property of propositions (consisting, for example, in their relation to facts) but a device to enable us to refer to, and refer back to, other claims and endorse them. The equivalence between *A* and '*A* is true' is both necessary and a priori. Take an example: suppose *A* is 'Someone killed Kennedy'. We noted earlier that whether 'Someone killed Kennedy' is true in a particular world depends on whether someone did kill Kennedy under those circumstances, not on what we might have meant by 'killed' and 'Kennedy' in those circumstances. One might think the case was different with ' "Someone killed Kennedy" is true', for we appear here to be referring to the sentence 'Someone killed Kennedy'. We need to distinguish between use and mention. In 'Fred has seven letters' we are using the name 'Fred' and referring to the person Fred—perhaps he is playing Scrabble; in ' "Fred" has four letters' we are mentioning the name 'Fred' and referring to it. The inverted commas round 'Fred' serve to remind us that we are mentioning the name rather than using it. If we were mentioning the sentence 'Someone killed Kennedy' when we said ' "Someone killed Kennedy" is true', then the truth of that proposition would depend on the meaning of 'killed', 'Kennedy', and so on, and so could vary independently of the truth of 'Someone killed Kennedy'. But we argued in Chapter 1 that we should not take sentences to be truth-bearers. If we did, '*A* is true' would differ from 'It is true that *A*'; ' "Someone killed Kennedy" is true' would ascribe truth to a sentence, whereas 'It is true that someone killed Kennedy' would not. We decided to construe '*A* is true' as predicating truth of the proposition expressed by *A*, and that means, the proposition actually expressed by *A*. So *A* and '*A* is true' keep in step as we move from world to world, evaluating them in each, but preserving their actual meaning. In contrast, *A* and '*A* is actually true' do not stay in step. 'Someone killed Kennedy' takes different values, depending on whether, in other circumstances, Kennedy was killed, whereas ' "Someone killed Kennedy" is actually true' does not. If Kennedy had died peacefully in his bed, 'Someone killed Kennedy' would be false; but even if Kennedy had died peacefully in his bed, 'Actually someone killed Kennedy' would still be true—that is, 'Someone killed Kennedy' would still actually be true, for Kennedy was killed. Remember, it is our utterance and what it expresses which is to count.

The standard metre rod might not have been a metre in length; but we can tell, a priori, that it must be a metre long. The necessary and the a priori are not coextensive.

Summary and Guide to Further Reading

Modal Platonism sees this world in its entirety as just one of an immense range of real and existing alternative possibilities. Each world is a concrete reality, of individuals with their properties and relations, complete and fully determinate. Actuality is no more than the immediacy to him or her of the world of the speaker. Each world is actual to itself. Our world is actual only in being our world. The foremost defender of this view is David Lewis, in his *Counterfactuals*, ch. 4, and more recently and fully in *On the Plurality of Worlds*. He comments in the latter how his early presentations of these views met with incredulous stares, but few cogent objections. Between the two books, plenty of objections appeared.

The problems we diagnosed in modal Platonism were all a consequence of its treating all worlds as on a par. If each constitutes a concrete reality, then no object can be present in more than one world—objects may have counterparts, *doppelgängern* in other worlds, but cannot be identical with them. The problem is then to find and identify their counterparts. Resort to haecceities, that is, individual essences, strains belief and suggests some sort of magic; use of similarities threatens to limit alternatives in an unnatural way. The crucial point is that we are interested in what Edmund would be like were he completely different, not in some counterpart of him. Lewis presents his counterpart theory in 'Counterpart Theory and Quantified Modal Logic', reprinted in Michael Loux's collection, *The Possible and the Actual*.

Treating each world as a self-subsistent reality also jars with our belief that our world is unique. Our world is actual, other worlds merely possible. The suggestion that to Edmund's counterparts, their world is actual and we but a hazy possibility contradicts our sense of what is real. In addition, it introduces gratuitous epistemological problems, in suggesting that reflection on possibility requires some special kind of telescope through which to observe other possible worlds while at the same time denying that such a method is possible. Possibilities suddenly become undetectable.

Another problem for extreme realism can be mentioned: there are many modal logics. A large number are doubtless of purely formal interest, and do not correspond to any real modal conception. But it is arguable that more than one articulate valid modal structures. Behind our discussions lay an equation between 'necessary' and 'true in every possible world'. This is known as the *S5* conception, corresponding to the strongest of C. I. Lewis's five modal systems. (See e.g. G. Hughes and M. Cresswell, *An Introduction to Modal Logic.*) It is often thought to give the proper analysis of metaphysical possibility and necessity. At least two others are of interest. *S4*, another (C. I.) Lewis system, develops a sense of 'necessity' as 'provability' in some fairly informal sense. A slightly different system, *G*, developed more recently, is useful in analysing the formal concept of provability as found in Gödel's work on arithmetic (in which provability does not guarantee truth). There are other systems which develop concepts of what ought to be done, and of what is believed—deontic and epistemic logics. What should the modal Platonist say of all these systems? Is there a full range of concrete reality behind each of them, or only for some—if so, which?

The Platonist puts his picture forward because he believes it the only one which can secure proper objectivity for modal judgements. The alternatives to Platonism set out to show either that objectivity is a myth, or that it can be obtained more cheaply. A useful collection of papers on this theme has already been mentioned—Loux's *The Possible and the Actual.* Reductionist programmes are there presented by Cresswell, Adams, Mondadori, and Morton. Armstrong's combinatorial theory of possibility is, perhaps, the most sophisticated and best worked out reductionist theory to date. Moderate realist solutions, like my own, are given by Stalnaker and Plantinga. Possible worlds are ways the world might have been—real, but not constituting concrete realities. They are abstract possibilities, the result of abstraction, but mind-independent and objective. Of course, this view needs further elaboration and defence, beyond what I have said here, but nevertheless, I believe it is the most promising account.

Philosophical reflection in the past twenty-five years or so on possible worlds and modal logic has been profoundly influenced by Saul Kripke's formal work in which the notion of possible worlds was clearly elaborated to give a satisfactory formal semantics for modal logic. Until that time, scepticism about modal discourse was paramount, led by W. V. O. Quine. His most famous attack on it can be found in 'Three Grades of Modal Involvement', reprinted in his *Ways of Paradox and Other Essays*. Acceptable modal logic was *de dicto* (the second grade, which could be reduced to the first) and could be handled in non-modal predicate logic (the classical paradigm). The case against Quine was put by Ruth Barcan Marcus. A recent retrospective can be found in her 'A Backwards Look at Quine's Animadversions on Modalities', in *Perspectives on Quine*, edited by R. Gibson and R. Barrett. A clear account of how care about scope distinctions in Russell's theory of descriptions avoids the puzzles about illicit substitutions is given by A. F. Smullyan in 'Modality and Description', reprinted in L. Linsky's still useful collection, *Reference and Modality*.

Kripke's paper 'Semantical Considerations on Modal Logic I', also reprinted in Linsky's *Reference and Modality*, produced a sea-change, first among formal logicians, who started to appreciate what an effective tool for logical analysis was provided by the modal logics (for example, in Stalnaker's and Lewis's analyses of conditionals), and followed up by his *Naming and Necessity*, first given as lectures in 1970 and published as an article in 1972, which showed the philosophical effectiveness of modal notions. He also argues strongly for moderate realism about possible worlds, both in the original lectures and in the introduction added for the 1980 edition. It was in this work that Kripke spelled out the examples which separate the modal notions of necessity, possibility, and contingency from the epistemic notions of apriority and aposteriority. The distinction is also emphasized (without examples) in Aaron Sloman's ' "Necessary", "A Priori" and "Analytic" '. The extension to the idea that every proposition has both contingent and necessitive a priori equivalents, and so on, was made by Leslie Tharp in the mid-1970s, but was not published until after his death, in 'Three Theorems of Metaphysics'.

5 Plato's Beard: On What There Is and What There Isn't

How is language possible? How is it possible, from a finite and learnable stock of basic vocabulary in a language, to form indefinitely many novel utterances, new propositions expressing thoughts which have not previously been framed? For it is possible. Although the vocabulary of a language is very large, as a glance at a dictionary can reveal, it is small compared with the immensity of sentences which make up the books in the libraries of the world. Few of these sentences are identical. Few of the sentences we read are ones we have seen before. How is it possible for the reader to understand them? How is it possible for their authors to conceive and compose them?

The answer is obvious: but its implications are powerful. We can learn a language because its vocabulary and its grammatical rules are relatively small—each can be contained in a small number of volumes; a multi-volume dictionary like the *Oxford English Dictionary* contains far more than the vocabulary of most individual speakers—and even that is contained in some ten or twelve volumes, a tiny part of the whole library that contains it. The grammatical rules permit the creation of indefinitely many sentences out of this vocabulary. To understand these new sentences, the meanings of the individual words are put together according to the structure given by the grammar. In other words, just as the sentence is literally composed of the words in it, so too the meaning of the sentence, the proposition, is—in some way—'composed' of the meanings of the words in it. The thought starts from the obvious: we understand novel sentences because we understand how their meaning results from the meanings of the constituent words. The implication is not so obvious, and what it says is not so clear: the meanings of the individual words combine together in some way to compose the meaning of the whole sentence, the proposition expressed by it.

The principle involved is sometimes called the 'compositionality principle', sometimes 'Frege's principle' after the great German philosopher of mathematics and of language of the late nineteenth century, Gottlob Frege. The two terms cover rather different applications of the idea. But the underlying motivation is the same. Somehow we must explain the 'creativity' of language, the way in which a child, hearing a small finite number of utterances, develops an ability to produce and understand an indefinite number of propositions which were not among the data on which the ability was based. The explanation is both the most plausible and simple which will bridge this gap, and accords with introspective experience, what it feels like to be a speaker of a language and follow a conversation— a set of utterances of one's own and others. The data and the novel products are broken down into meaningful components, and a connection between the meanings of whole and parts is postulated. But what is that connection?

Those who call the idea a 'compositionality' principle are likely to interpret this connection in rather literal terms. I mentioned in Chapter 1 how Russell took propositions, the meanings of sentences and the objects of belief, to have particulars and universals as constituents, so that, for example, the proposition that Socrates is wise literally has Socrates and wisdom as constituents. The meaning of 'Socrates' was, for him, the philosopher Socrates himself; and the meaning of 'is wise', the universal or property, wisdom; thus the meaning of the sentence, 'Socrates is wise' was composed of Socrates and wisdom just as the sentence is composed of its subject and predicate. A more sophisticated view points instead to a functional dependency of the meaning of the complex expression on the meaning of its parts. Take an analogy: 4 is the result of squaring 2, $4 = 2^2$, but 4 does not literally contain 2 as a constituent (nor does it contain the squaring function, either). Rather, 4 results from applying the squaring function to 2. So too, for a philosopher like Frege, for the connection between the meaning of a sentence and the meanings of its parts. The picture is complicated by the fact that Frege distinguished separate components to an expression's meaning. But the principle is preserved: the meaning of a complex expression such as a sentence results from the meanings of its parts and can be calculated from them. So an understanding of the parts and the method of dependency explains the understanding of the whole.

The reason for developing this background is to provide a context for a particular puzzle. Consider the propositions: 'King Lear did not exist', 'There is no greatest prime number', 'The image you can see is not real'. They are often called 'negative existential propositions', and many of them seem to be true. But how can that be? In order to understand these propositions, their meanings must be composed of (or depend upon) the meanings of their parts. Yet if they are true, then there is no real object corresponding to the expressions 'King Lear', 'the greatest prime number', 'the image you can see'. So these expressions must lack meaning—they are empty terms. Compositionality then implies that the whole will lack meaning too. It seems that propositions of the form 'X does not exist', 'There is no X', 'X is not real' must either be false or meaningless. Either X exists, in which case they are false in denying X's existence; or X does not exist, in which case 'X' has no meaning, and so propositions containing that expression lack meaning too.

Willard van Orman Quine called one solution to this problem, 'Plato's Beard'. Plato inherited it from the great thinker of the fifth century BC, Parmenides. In the 'Way of Truth' in his poem *On Nature*, Parmenides had written, 'It cannot be said or thought that "it is not"'. What is, is, and what is not, is not, and cannot even be thought not to be. Plato's reaction is found in several places in his writings, but most notably in his dialogue, the *Parmenides*. What is not must in some sense be, for we are ascribing some character to it. As Quine put it, 'Nonbeing must in some sense be, otherwise what is it that there is not?'

Descriptions

Quine, and Russell before him, had recoiled at the liberality of this suggestion. A firm sense of reality must reject the idea that whatever can be spoken of, or even thought about, must in some sense be. What does not exist really does not exist, and arguments claiming to show that it really does exist after all must be fallacious. How is that fallacy to be diagnosed?

Russell's diagnosis led to his theory of descriptions, and, as I remarked in Chapter 4, provided a vital spur to the whole movement of analytical philosophy in the twentieth century. Let us rehearse the problem. Meaningful sentences depend for their meaning on meaningful parts; but if X does not exist, expressions seeming to refer to X cannot have meaning, and so nothing meaningful can be said about X, not even that it does not exist. Russell's answer was to distinguish logical form from grammatical form. Grammatically, 'King Lear did not exist' is a subject-predicate proposition, predicating non-existence of its subject, King Lear. Similarly, 'King Lear had three daughters' is a subject-predicate proposition, predicating the having of three daughters of him. Neither of these propositions can be meaningful, if their logical form follows their grammatical form. Since they clearly are meaningful, the proposition must be analysed in a different manner from a logical point of view from what its grammatical form would indicate. Russell started a whole movement in philosophy by providing such an analysis of descriptions. He and others moved on to dealing with other puzzles by a similar analytical method.

Take a descriptive phrase, whether a definite description, such as 'the father of Goneril and Regan' or an indefinite one, such as 'a mountain of solid gold'. Neither exists, so they cannot get their meaning by denoting anything, and so cannot contribute a meaning to propositions of which they are a part. None the less, they can belong to meaningful propositions. Russell's solution was to provide a logical analysis of propositions of which they formed a grammatical constituent, but an analysis which showed them not to be a logical constituent. For example, take the second description, in a proposition such as 'A mountain of solid gold does not exist'. Rather than concede, as Plato does, that there is in some sense a mountain of solid gold whose existence we then deny, Russell claims that the logical analysis of the proposition does not give it the obvious subject-predicate form. Logically, what it says is that there is nothing which is a mountain of solid gold, and what that means is, the property of being a mountain of solid gold is not instantiated.

Russell is here drawing on an insight of Frege's, namely, that the quantifiers are second-level or second-order predicates. Recall the distinction I drew in Chapter 2 between first-order and second-order languages. First-order languages contain individual variables—variables ranging over individual objects—and schematic letters for predicates applying to those objects. Second-order languages contain in addition (first-order) predicate variables—variables ranging over predicates (or properties) of individuals (as in 'Napoleon had every quality of a great general')—and schematic letters for predicates applying to first-order properties. Typical properties of a first-order property like 'being a mountain' are: being instantiated, being universally instantiated, being essential, being true of Parmenides and so on. The first two of these are (standard) quantifiers. Quantifiers say how widely a predicate is distributed. The existential quantifier, 'for some' or 'there is/are', says that a predicate is true of at least one thing. The universal quantifier, 'for all' or 'for each/every', says that a predicate is true of everything. First-order logic, although it does not admit first-order (i.e. predicate) variables or second-order schematic letters, includes this limited second-order vocabulary, namely, the existential and universal quantifiers. Similarly, second-order logic admits limited third-order vocabulary, namely, quantification over first-order variables, which say that second-order predicates are at least once, or universally, instantiated.

Which second-order predicates should one be allowed to add to a first-order language? That is, while stopping short of moving to a full second-order theory, in which every second-order predicate is allowed, what second-order expressibility is it reasonable to permit in a first-order language? Classical first-order logic allows only the existential and universal quantifiers, that is, the second-order properties of being instantiated at least once and of being universally instantiated—and any predicates definable in terms of these, for example, not being instantiated at all (since negation is included) or being instantiated exactly twice (if identity is allowed). Many other second-order properties are not so definable—for example, being finite or being true of most things. Adding quantifiers corresponding to such predicates produces an extension of first-order logic. Recall the observation in Chapter 2 that classical first-order consequence is compact: logic with the quantifier 'for only finitely many' is not compact. For compactness says that what follows from any set of premisses must follow from a finite subset of them. Let A be 'for only finitely many x, Fx'. Then A is compatible with every finite subset of the set of premisses, '0 is F, 1 is F, ...' and so on, for every n, but not with the whole set. Hence 'not-A' follows from '0 is F, 1 is F, ...' but not from any finite subset of those propositions. So the consequence relation generated by adding the quantifier 'for only finitely many' to first-order logic is not compact.

Frege's observation that the quantifiers are second-order (or as it is usually expressed in discussions of Frege, 'second-level') gave formal expression to a claim of Kant's (and arguably, Aristotle's) which we considered in Chapter 1. When Kant said that existence was not a property, what he meant was, according to Frege, that existence is not a first-order property—it is not a property of individuals. Existence is a property of properties, namely, that the property has an instance. Coming back to Russell, 'A golden mountain does not exist' denies this property of the first-order predicate 'being a golden mountain'; this predicate does not have an instance. In a sense, the proposition is of subject-predicate form; however, its subject is not a phrase purporting (and failing) to refer to a golden mountain (a non-existent individual). Rather, its subject is 'the property of being a golden mountain'. Its logical form is 'The property of being a golden mountain has no instances'.

What of a proposition like 'A mountain of solid gold has been discovered'? This, says Russell, is also of a form different from its grammatical form—but its grammatical predicate is still a first-level predicate. The indefinite description is not its subject, however. The true logical form is: 'There is something which is a mountain of solid gold and has been discovered', that is, 'For some x, x is a mountain of solid gold and x has been discovered'. Once again, the apparent subject disguises a predicative phrase, and the proposition is actually a quantified proposition, falsely attributing the property of having an instance to the complex predicate 'being a mountain of solid gold and having been discovered'.

When Russell moves on to considering definite descriptions, he analyses them essentially no differently. The only difference lies in the implication of uniqueness given by the definite article. Thus, 'The father of Goneril and Regan did not exist' has the logical form, 'The property of being uniquely father of Goneril and Regan had no instances', that is, 'It is false that for some x, x and x alone fathered Goneril and Regan'. This is true, for the story of King Lear is a myth. It follows for Russell that to say anything positive of Lear is false. For example, 'The father of Goneril and Regan went mad' is false, for its true form is 'For some x, x and x alone fathered Goneril and Regan and x went mad'.

One might jib at this conclusion, for in the play, Lear does go mad. This suggests that one should prefix a fiction operator, 'In the fiction', to such propositions. 'In the fiction, Lear went mad', that is, 'In the fiction, there is one and only one father of Goneril and Regan and he went mad' will then, it seems, come out true; whereas 'In the fiction, Lear murdered Duncan' will be correctly shown as false.

This is a shrewd move, and in essentials correct. However, it will not work as stated. For one thing, it is as yet far too vague. It invites the reader to cast around for any appropriate fiction in an unconstrained way. Who knows that there may not be some fiction which will make 'Lear murdered Duncan' true? What is needed—and this is the precise nub of the question—is a clear indication of the fictional domain in which such propositions should be evaluated. That is what we will obtain when we move on later to consider an alternative to Russell's analysis. Russell's analysis cannot be saved by the vague appeal to a fiction operator.

There are in fact two significant aspects of Russell's theory which cause difficulty, and we have here met the first of them. To begin with, however, we should be clear that Russell's account of descriptions is intended to apply to all descriptions, not only those for which there is no corresponding object. Russell rightly perceived that whether a sentence has meaning is an a priori matter, and should not be dependent on the existence of certain objects. Whether it is true or false can be an empirical matter, but not its meaningfulness. So 'the father of Goneril and Regan' and 'the father of Emily and Charlotte Brontë', are alike 'incomplete expressions', expressions which lack meaning in their own right, and whose presence in sentences indicates a contribution to meaning by their parts but not via a meaning for the whole. The first problem with Russell's theory comes out in this way: 'The father of Emily and Charlotte Brontë was Irish' is correctly given the value true by its Russellian analysis—the Brontë sisters had one and only one father and he was Irish; 'The father of Emily and Charlotte Brontë predeceased them' is correctly recognized as false by its Russellian analysis. But on Russell's account, every simple proposition apparently predicating something of an empty description is false. No distinction is made between, say, 'The father of Goneril and Regan went mad'—which is arguably true—and 'The father of Goneril and Regan was king of Denmark', which certainly is false. Russell's theory says they are both false—indeed, everything (simply and positively) predicated of this description is false.

This does not cover complex predications, for example, 'did not exist', 'was not king of Denmark', 'was thought by Shakespeare to be king of Britain', 'might have been Charlotte Brontë's father'. Propositions predicating such expressions of descriptions can be analysed in two different ways, as we saw in Chapter 4, depending on whether the description is taken to have wide or narrow scope—what Russell calls primary and secondary occurrences of the descriptions, respectively. That is, however, by the by. Russell's theory makes an exciting methodological move, in distinguishing logical from grammatical form. But it cannot be right in its details, for it gets the truth-values wrong. Any theory which says that every positive statement, without distinction, about objects which don't exist is false, has to be wrong. It is an improvement on a theory which says they are all meaningless. But the right theory will draw a distinction between true propositions, like 'The father of Goneril and Regan went mad' and false ones, like 'The greatest prime number is even'.

The other problem with Russell's theory concerns names. As so far presented, it is a theory of descriptions. But the puzzle of Plato's Beard applies to every referring expression which fails to refer. Propositions such as 'Satan does not exist', 'Pegasus was captured by Bellerophon', 'Hamlet had an Oedipus complex' are still under threat: the first must be false or meaningless, and the others simply meaningless—unless the theory can be extended. This is what Russell did. Genuine names are only those which are guaranteed a reference, and so evade the problem— names like 'nine' or, according to Russell's epistemology, 'this' and 'that' as applied to the immediate objects of sensation. Other names are not genuine, but must be disguised descriptions. Names like 'Pegasus'—'the winged horse sprung from the blood of Medusa', 'Cicero'—'the author of *De Lege Manilia*' and 'Everest'—'the tallest mountain on Earth', cannot get their meaning by naming something (for not all do, and those that do are not guaranteed a reference a priori) but contribute to the meaning of propositions expressed by sentences of which they are part by being short for descriptive phrases analysed according to the theory of descriptions.

Although his response to the puzzle of Plato's Beard is different, Frege makes a very similar move here. Frege's example is 'Nausicaa found Odysseus naked on the beach'. Russell's theory of meaning was straightforward: names meant objects and predicates had universals as their meaning. Frege's was more subtle: although names signified objects (unless they were empty) this did not exhaust their meaning; they had in addition a sense. 'Cicero' signifies Cicero; but its sense is given by a description or other means of recognition—the author of *De*

Lege Manilia, perhaps; 'Nausicaa' is an empty name, it signifies nothing, but it has a sense—the daughter of King Alcinous of Kerkyra. We understand 'Nausicaa found Odysseus naked on the beach' by calculating its sense from the senses of the component expressions—it depends functionally upon them. Frege applied the functional dependency thesis to both signification ('reference'—*Bedeutung* in the original German) and sense. But 'Nausicaa' lacks significance, and so the whole sentence lacks signification, which Frege identified with the sentence's truth-value. Hence the sentence has sense—we can understand it, but lacks truth-value—it makes no significant assertion.

Frege's theory differs from Russell's in many ways: distinguishing sense from signification, claiming that sentences containing empty names lack truth-value, and so on. The common element to note is the association with each name of a descriptive manner of identification, or of some means of recognition. F. H. Bradley, a near contemporary of Frege's, spelled the point out, as I mentioned before: if there were no criterion of reidentification of the referent of a name, the name could not get to stand for it at all. That, he said, was what was wrong with Mill's connotationless account of names; the same point is a problem for Kripke's account, which I mentioned in Chapter 4. (Kripke answers it with a theory about how a name and its reference is passed from one occasion of utterance to another.)

None the less, the association of names with descriptions (for Russell) or sense (for Frege) has its own difficulty. We can spell out the meaning of 'King Lear' as 'the eponymous hero of Shakespeare's play', 'Shakespeare' as 'the famous playwright born at Stratford', 'Stratford' as 'the market town on the River Avon ten miles down river from Warwick', and so on. Nongenuine names, names whose reference is not guaranteed a priori, must for Russell be cashed out in descriptive terms, based ultimately on genuine names. It is a reductionist enterprise, returning the reference relation to an atomic level—'logically proper names'. Russell claims, by a transcendental argument, that there must be such a level; at the same time he candidly admitted to difficulty in identifying any genuine names. As we

saw in Chapter 1, logical atomism was committed to the existence of atomic propositions containing genuine names that
simply could not be found.

Free Logic

A better response to that difficulty may come from adopting a
non-foundationalist epistemology. The first difficulty is still with
us, however, in responding to Plato's Beard. We need our theory
to draw a distinction between, say, 'King Lear went mad' and
'King Lear was King Lear' on the one hand and 'King Lear was
Hamlet' and 'King Lear murdered Duncan' on the other.
Russell's theory does not—it says all are false; nor does Frege's
theory—all come out lacking a truth-value.

Actually, I am using the phrase 'Plato's Beard' in a somewhat
different sense from Quine's. For me, it denotes the puzzle:
how can sentences with empty names have meaning? For Quine,
it denotes a particular response to that puzzle: that empty names,
while they must denote nothing existent, nevertheless denote
something—everything has being, though only some beings
actually exist. The most famous exponent of this view in recent
times has been Bertrand Russell himself. 'Being is that which
belongs to every conceivable, to every possible object of thought',
he wrote in 1903. The theory of descriptions was his way out of
this extravagance.

Russell's extravagant position was certainly formed under the
influence of the contemporary German philosopher, Alexius
Meinong. But it was not Meinong's position. Many objects were,
Meinong said, 'beyond being and non-being'. He did not believe, as his view is often reported, that besides what exists,
everything else 'subsists'. For him, concrete objects exist; abstract objects subsist; and beyond that, every term denotes an
object for which the question of being should not arise. The
principle at the heart of the doctrine was his Principle of Independence, of so-being from being. That is, whether an object
has certain properties is independent of whether it has being
and of what kind. Pegasus is a winged horse, even though it

doesn't exist; the golden mountain is made of gold, even though there isn't one; the horse which is not a horse is a horse, and not a horse, and there is no such thing. As Meinong put it, in an aggressively paradoxical way: 'There are objects such that there are no such objects'.

For all that the Meinong scholars may protest that this view is different from the early Russell's, it is equally extravagant. It starts off by recognizing our intuition: King Lear went mad but he did not murder Duncan. But it threatens to go far beyond those intuitions, admitting what Quine calls an 'ontological slum' and others, 'Meinong's jungle'. Consider the horse which is not a horse. It is both a horse and not a horse. Is this not a contradiction? Meinong agrees—the Principle of Non-Contradiction applies only to possible objects. These objects are impossible— that is why the horse which is not a horse does not exist, or even subsist.

In Chapter 4, I argued for moderate realism about possible worlds—that there are such worlds, they are real, but abstract; other possible worlds differ from this world in that this world is concrete, while they are but abstract possibilities. In Chapter 3, I proposed that the semantics for conditionals requires us to admit 'impossible worlds' besides possible ones, worlds in which contradictions are true. For example, to evaluate the conditional, 'If Pegasus were a horse which was not a horse, then . . .', we need to consider a world in which Pegasus is an impossible object, a horse which is not a horse. Is this position not the same as Meinong's, and equally extravagant? Am I committed to rejecting the Principle of Non-Contradiction for some classes of object?

There is a crucial difference between the two positions, between the position I embraced about the semantics of modality and the ontology of Meinong and the early Russell. Where I say, 'there might have been a winged horse, but there isn't', Meinong and Russell say, 'there is a winged horse but it does not exist'. When I say, 'consider a situation ('impossible world') in which Pegasus is a horse which is not a horse', I am not admitting that there is such an impossible horse. Clearly there is not, and the Principle of Non-Contradiction says so. The distinction concerns the range of the quantifiers. When we say, 'for some' or 'for all', are we quantifying over what there actually is, or over what there might (or might not) have been? Russell in 1903 quantified over 'every conceivable' thing; Meinong quantified over 'objects such that there are no such objects'. I do not.

For this reason, neither Meinong's nor the early Russell's theories are free logics. 'Free logic' is shorthand for 'logic free of existence assumptions'. There are two existence assumptions built into classical predicate logic, the orthodoxy we considered in Chapter 2. One is that the domain of the quantifiers is non-empty; the other that every term denotes. The first has the consequence that 'For some x, either x is F or x is not F' is a (classical) logical truth (for every F); the second that for every term a, 'a is F' is a logical consequence of 'For every x, x is F'. Not every free logic rejects the first of these. Those that do are known as 'universally free logics'. If the domain is empty, then there is no value of x for which either 'x is F' or 'x is not F' is true. If the domain is non-empty, then there must be a value of x denoting something in the domain, and either F will be true of it or not.

Free logics no more quantify over what does not exist than does classical logic. Their freedom concerns the classical assumption that every term, that is, every individual constant, or name, or description, or functional expression (unless analysed away), denotes something which exists. It is usual to classify free logics into three sorts: positive, negative, and neuter. Positive free logics are those which hold that some propositions containing empty terms (that is, terms denoting something which does not exist) are true; negative free logics hold that all such atomic propositions are false; and neuter free logics, that all such propositions lack truth-value. Actually, this classification is unhelpful, and entirely superficial. It distinguishes free logics which are in important respects similar, and lumps together free logics which are essentially different. For example, the method of supervaluations, which we will consider in the next section, renders some propositions containing empty terms true, yet its metaphysical assumption—or at least, the metaphysics of free logics making use of supervaluations—has much more in common with negative and neuter free logics.

The most important philosophical difference between free logics concerns their semantics for 'empty terms'. So far I have equivocally described empty terms as ones 'denoting something which does not exist'. This covers two possibilities: that such terms literally do refer to things which do not exist; and that such terms refer to nothing—that is, do not refer at all. I shall call the first type of free logic, 'outer domain free logic', and the second, 'irreferential free logic'. The distinguishing features of outer domain free logic are that every term is taken to refer to something, but that the domain of objects to which terms refer is divided into an inner domain and an outer domain. The inner domain is as in classical logic (except that we may allow it to be empty—if we wish our logic to be universally free): it consists of real existing objects, Cicero, Red Rum, my desk, the planet Pluto, and so on. The outer domain consists of the references of 'empty' terms, Pegasus, King Lear, the golden mountain, the round square, and so on. The outer domain may not be empty—for every term must refer, so the minimal domain possible is a singleton outer domain and empty inner domain. (Of course, this is not how things actually are. But recall from Chapter 2 how it is necessary to allow the domain to vary in order to avoid overgeneration of logical truths and logical consequence.)

Thus far, outer domain free logic sounds exactly like Meinong's theory—an inner domain of real objects (whether existent or subsistent is a mere matter of terminology) and an outer domain of the most impossibilist extravagance. The crucial difference is what was mentioned above: the quantifiers in free logic range only over the inner domain. While 'Pegasus is a winged horse' is true, it does not follow that there is a winged horse, for 'there is' means 'there exists' and Pegasus is not one of the existents—it is not in the inner domain. The inference 'a is F, so for some x, x is F' fails. The term a may denote something in the outer domain, while the quantifier 'for some' ranges only over the inner domain. If the inner domain may be empty, we obtain a universally free logic: 'for some x, x is F or x is not F' is not logically true, for it is false if the inner domain is empty. Whether this is so or not, the distinctive inference distinguishing classical logic from free logic fails: 'for every x, x is F' is true if every object in the inner domain is F; none the less, 'a is F' may be false, since a may denote something in the outer domain of which F may not be true. For example, 'No horse has wings' (that is, 'For every horse, it does not have wings') is true, but 'Pegasus does not have wings' is false. Universal specification (or elimination, or instantiation, as it is variously called) is invalid in free logic in the form 'for every x, x is F, so a is F', for each term a.

Instead, the free logic form of the inference requires an extra premiss, namely, 'a exists'. 'a is F' follows from 'for every x, x is F' and 'a exists'. For if 'a exists' is true then the reference of a is in the inner domain, and every object in the inner domain is F, since 'for every x, x is F' is true. In other words, this latter formula means 'for every x which exists, x is F'. The quantifier ranges only over existents. Similarly, existential generalization (or introduction) requires the same additional premiss, and has the form 'a is F and a exists; so for some x, x is F'. In classical logic the second premiss is not needed. But in free logic, a might otherwise denote a non-existent.

Do not think that it follows that 'exists' is a (first-order) property in free logic. 'a exists' means that the reference of 'a' lies in the inner domain. Hence 'a exists' means that there is something (in the inner domain) which is a, that is, for some x, x is a (since 'for some x' means 'for some x in the inner domain', i.e. 'for some x which exists'). In other words, 'a exists' is true if the first-order predicate, 'being identical with a', has an instance (which exists). In general, 'for some x, x is F', means that the property, being F, has an instance, that is, an instance in the inner domain, the domain of what exists.

We noted that Meinong's theory was contradictory—this was Russell's major objection to it. Allowing that 'the horse which is not a horse' is a legitimate term, denoting an impossible object, and that the descriptive elements in such a name must truly hold of what it refers to, it follows that the horse which is not a horse is both a horse and not a horse. In the context of *Ex Falso Quodlibet*, this trivializes the theory. Every proposition must be true. The inconsistency affecting impossible objects permeates to all objects, even the existents. One might seek to avert this danger by adopting a relevant or paraconsistent logic in which *EFQ* is invalid. But free logic, as usually developed, is an extension of classical logic, and *EFQ* is accepted. Is free logic similarly inconsistent and trivial, at least free logic in its outer domain version, where 'the horse which is not a horse' and such-like terms are taken to denote elements of the (outer) domain? It is not; and the reason lies in the restriction on the quantifiers, so that they range only over existents.

The inconsistency can be seen to threaten (and be resisted) as follows: the inconsistency will result from being forced to admit that the *F* (or an *F*) is *F*, for an inconsistent predicate *F*. For suppose we assert that anything which is an *F* is *F*, that is, for every *x*, if *x* is an *F* then *x* is *F*. (Call this, following Meinong, the Principle of So-Being—PSB, for short.) Then, provided an *F* exists, it follows by universal specification from PSB that if an *F* is an *F*, then an *F* is *F*, whence, if it is universally true that an *F* is an *F*, we have the unwanted conclusion, that an *F* is *F*. That is, the unwanted conclusion (threatening inconsistency) follows from the reasonable assumption PSB (that anything which is an *F* is *F*) only on the two premises, that an *F* exists and that an *F* is an *F*.

For example, it follows that the horse which is not a horse is both a horse and not a horse only if the horse which is not a horse both exists and is self-identical. We can avoid the inconsistency, therefore, by the fact that there is no such horse—indeed, the derivation of the contradiction tells us, by the usual *reductio ad absurdum* move (if we had not realized it already) that there is no horse which is not a horse. This example is transparent; but there might be a predicate *F* which was not obviously inconsistent, but where the assumption that the *F* was *F* entailed a contradiction. The natural response is that there can be no such *F*.

Inconsistency is avoided by the crucial difference between (outer domain) free logic and Meinongianism—that the quantifiers range only over the existents. To say that anything which is an *F* is *F*, is to say that any existent which is an *F* is *F*. It does not follow that non-existent *F*s are never *F*; some are and some are not. If inconsistency threatens, they are not.

Supervaluations

None the less, there is something unsatisfactory about outer domain free logic, and that is its bivalence. It is not simply a positive free logic, that is, that some proposition containing an empty name is true; rather, every proposition containing an empty name is either true or false. That is, outer domain free logic forces us to choose, for every proposition concerning a non-existent, whether it is true or false. Of course, even classical logic requires us to admit, for propositions concerning existents, bivalence as well, even in cases where we cannot make the decision. For example, 'Oswald shot Kennedy' is either true or false; so too is 'Every even number greater than 2 is the sum of two primes' (it is Goldbach's Conjecture, a famous unsolved conjecture of arithmetic). The realist response is to reply that these are indeed true or false regardless of our ability to decide. (We will consider in Chapter 8 the anti-realist rejection of Bivalence.) This response has a plausibility for existents which it lacks for non-existents, fictional and mythical characters and beyond. Consider 'King Lear could whistle', 'Pegasus stood sixteen hands tall', 'The horse which is not a horse is a horse'. The first two might set one searching Shakespeare or the ancient myth and legends for an answer; but if one seriously believes Lear and Pegasus are mythic creatures, one must be prepared for there being no answer—if they once existed, there is a fact of the matter, which doubtless we will never know; if not, then there is none, and the proposition is neither true nor false. About the horse which is not a horse, we have just noted that it cannot be both a horse and not a horse and so is plausibly neither.

What these considerations should bring out is that outer domain free logic really avoids the issue. When we say a name is empty, that it refers to nothing, we do not mean that it refers, but to something which does not exist; we mean that it does not refer at all. There really is nothing to which it refers. It is irreferential. It is this thought which is taken up by irreferential free logic. There is a domain of existents, over which the quantifiers range; there may or may not be an outer domain of non-existents; and names may refer or not. Propositions containing names which do refer (whether to existents or not) are evaluated in the usual way. The question is: how to evaluate propositions containing names some of which are truly empty.

Actually, the desiderata are clear: we do not want all propositions about non-existents to be false (negative free logic) as in Russell's account; nor truth-valueless (neuter free logic) as in Frege's theory; nor do we want every such proposition to be required to have a value, as in outer domain free logic. Some are true, for example, 'Lear went mad'; some are false, for example, 'Lear murdered Duncan'; and some lack truth-value altogether, for example, 'Lear could whistle'.

The question as far as logic is concerned is whether these desiderata can be achieved and at the same time preserve a logic, that is, compatibly with an acceptable account of logical truth and logical consequence. Consider Addition, the inference from a proposition A to one of the form 'A or B'. A may be either true or false, or lack a truth-value. How is the truth-value of 'A or B' related to those of A and B? We must preserve the classical values: if both A and B are true, or one is true, the other false, 'A or B' is true; and if A and B are false, 'A or B' is false. What if either A or B lacks truth-value? There are two options open to us. We can either interpret lack of truth-value as a kind of plague which infects everything it touches—so that if either A or B lacks a value, so does 'A or B'; or we can reason that if say, A is true, then 'A or B' is true regardless of the contribution from B (and symmetrically for B), so that 'A or B' lacks a value only if both A and B do. The first option corresponds to what are called Kleene's weak matrices (the matrices are a 3-by-3 display, like a truth-table, portraying the 'value' of 'A or B'—and other combinations—dependent on the 'values' of A and B; where the 'value' is either truth, or falsity, or lack of truth-value); the second to Kleene's strong matrices. On the weak matrices, 'A or B' lacks value if either A or B does, and otherwise obtains its value classically; on the strong matrices,

'*A* or *B*' is true if *A* is true or *B* is true, and lacks value only when *A* and *B* both lack value, or one is false and the other lacks value.

Let us work with the strong matrices, for the problem which ensues also affects the weak matrices and more besides. The classical account of consequence says that one proposition is a consequence of others provided no interpretation leads from truth to falsity. But this will permit the inference from '*a* is *F*' to '*a* exists', which we do not want. For that would rule out empty names. Whenever '*a* is *F*' is true, '*a* exists' is true; when '*a* is *F*' lacks a value (i.e. when *a* is empty), '*a* exists' is false. Thus we need to extend the classical account of consequence to cover the case of lack of truth-value. To exclude the inference of '*a* exists' from '*a* is *F*', we need to rule out the move from lack of value to falsity as invalid. That is, we will say that one proposition is a consequence of others if no interpretation leads from propositions none of which are false to one which is false. Unfortunately, this revised criterion invalidates inferences which we will wish to class as valid. Consider, for example, the move from '*a* is *F* and *a* is not-*F*' to '*b* is *G*'—and remember that free logic (as presently developed) is an extension of classical logic, in which any proposition is said to follow from a contradiction. Suppose *b* exists and is not *G*. If *a* is non-empty, the premiss and conclusion are both false; while if *a* is empty, the premiss lacks value (for negation exchanges truth and falsity and leaves lack of value alone, and conjunction, 'and', matches 'or' in being truth-valueless if both conjuncts lack value) while the conclusion is still false. Thus the inference leads from lack of value to falsity, and so will be deemed invalid by the revised account of consequence.

We appear to be caught with our pants down. If we extend the criterion of logical consequence to rule out the move from lack of value to falsity we will invalidate *EFQ* (which might be independently desirable, as we noted in Chapter 2, but is not part of our brief in setting up a free logic), while if we do not, we will make it appear that every term denotes by validating the inference from '*a* is *F*' to '*a* exists' (and so to 'for some *x*, *x* is *F*').

One remedy, which will allow us a free logic preserving the classical inferences such as *EFQ*, restricting existential generalization (and similar quantifier inferences) in the way we explored in the last section, but assigning no value to atomic predications of the form '*a* is *F*' when *a* is empty, is to adopt the method of supervaluations. Actually, van Fraassen's idea in introducing the method was to defend classical logic as it stood, and show that the restrictions of free logic were unnecessary. However, we will see that this was a result of his not taking the method seriously enough.

Consider the Law of Excluded Middle, '*A* or not-*A*'. We noted before that if *A* and *B* both lack a truth-value, then we have no grounds for assigning a value to '*A* or *B*'—we need one or other to be true to be sure the whole is true, and both to be false to be sure the disjunction is false. Similarly, if *A* lacks a value, we have no ground on which to assign a value to 'not-*A*'. So if *A* contains an empty name, and so lacks value, so does '*A* or not-*A*'. Why then do we believe that '*A* or not-*A*' is a logical truth? The reason seems to be that if *A* did have a value, then one or other of *A* and 'not-*A*' would be true, and so the whole disjunction would be true.

This is how the method of supervaluations starts. We take a partial valuation—an assignment of truth-values such as we presently have which assigns truth to some propositions, falsity to others, and no value to the rest. Consider all ways of extending this partial valuation to a total valuation, by arbitrarily assigning values (consistent with the truth-conditions—e.g. if *A* is arbitrarily made true, then so is '*A* or *B*') to those propositions which previously had no value. Call these the classical extensions of the original partial valuation. Then the supervaluation over the original partial valuation is defined as follows: a proposition is true according to the supervaluation if it is true in all classical extensions of the original partial valuation; false according to the supervaluation if it is false in all classical extensions; and has no value in the supervaluation if it takes different values in different classical extensions. Thus the supervaluation is still a partial valuation—some propositions have no 'super-value'. But the supervaluation does extend the original partial valuation.

For example, consider 'A or not-A', where A contains an empty name (that is, a name assigned no reference by the original valuation). Then 'A or not-A' has no value in that valuation. But in every classical extension, A does take a value, and 'not-A' the opposite value. Hence, in all classical extensions of the original partial valuation, either A is true or 'not-A' is true, and so 'A or not-A' is true. Hence 'A or not-A' takes the super-value true. Similarly, 'A and not-A', which has no value in the original valuation (since A has none), takes the value false in the supervaluation.

We can now define logical consequence and logical truth. A proposition is a logical consequence of other propositions if there is no (partial) interpretation (or valuation) every classical extension of which makes all the premisses true and the conclusion false. A proposition is a logical truth if there is no (partial) interpretation every classical extension of which makes it false. That is, the logical truths are those which are false on no supervaluation over any interpretation. Every instance of 'A or not-A' is logically true by this definition: any partial valuation either assigns a value to A or it doesn't. If it does, then 'A or not-A' will be true in that valuation, and so true in every classical extension of it; if not, 'A or not-A' will be true in each classical extension, and so true in the supervaluation. Hence the Law of Excluded Middle comes out true on the supervaluation over every partial valuation, that is, however the non-logical terms are interpreted. Similarly, every proposition of the form 'A and not-A' comes out false on every classical extension of every partial valuation, and consequently *EFQ* is validated, since there will be no classical extension of any partial valuation making 'A and not-A' true and whatever proposition is taken as conclusion, false.

The idea is simple; one has to be careful with the details, however. For without some constraints we will still invalidate some inferences we wish to make valid, and validate some principles we wish to relinquish. Van Fraassen takes account of the former (by 'arbitrary' constraints, that is, constraints specifically designed to ensure that the resulting consequence relation is completely classical); he need not, for the same reason, take any steps about the latter. Consider, for example, the Law of Identity, 'a is a' for any term a. If a denotes, this is true; if a fails to denote, it lacks a value in each partial valuation, and so, since we have made no special provision, can take either truth or falsity in each classical extension, and so lacks value in each supervaluation, too. But we were persuaded earlier that, even though the names 'King Lear', 'Pegasus', and so on are empty, the propositions 'King Lear is King Lear', 'Pegasus is Pegasus', and so on are true. The Law of Identity is a logical truth. Van Fraassen arbitrarily requires that 'a is a' be true in each classical extension. Another example is the Principle of the Indiscernibility of Identicals, which we encountered in Chapter 4. It says that if a is b and a is F, then b is F. If a and b are non-denoting under some interpretation, then there is so far nothing to prevent a classical extension making 'a is b' and 'a is F' true and 'b is F' false. This is far from what a classical extension is intended to reflect. Again, van Fraassen imposes a constraint on classical extensions to prevent it.

The questionable principles which the above definition validates, are the classical forms of Universal Specification and Existential Generalization, from 'everything is F' to 'a is F' and from 'a is F' to 'something is F' respectively, for every term a. For suppose 'a is F' is false on a classical extension of some partial valuation. Then the denotation of a lies outside the interpretation of F—something is not F. So 'everything is F' is false under this extension of the partial valuation. Conversely, if 'a is F' is true on a classical extension, a must denote something in the interpretation of F, and so 'something is F' is true on this extension. The classical forms of the inferences cannot be invalidated. Yet these two inferences are at the heart of free logic. Can the situation be redeemed?

The most promising solution is to combine the method of supervaluations with the idea of an outer domain. We do not consider all classical extensions, where truth-values are arbitrarily assigned to those propositions lacking truth-value in the partial valuation. Instead, we consider all ways of assigning a denotation to the empty terms, and the total valuations which will result from that. However, the denotations of the empty terms are chosen not from the domain of the partial valuation, but from arbitrary extensions of that domain by the addition of an outer domain. So we say that a free extension of a partial valuation comprises an extension of the domain by the addition of a (non-empty) outer domain, together with an extension of the interpretation of the predicate letters to the outer domain and the resulting total valuation resulting from these extensions. A supervaluation is defined as before, but substituting 'free extension' for 'classical extension'. Then the Law of Identity is validated, since whatever a is assigned to—whether by the original partial valuation or by the free extensions—it will always be assigned the same reference as itself; the Indiscernibility of Identicals comes out valid in the free extensions, for if a and b, empty names in the original partial valuation, are assigned the same denotation in a free extension, and if 'a is F' comes out true, so too must 'b is F'. Lastly, Universal Specification and Existential Generalization turn out invalid in their classical form and valid in their free form, with the extra premiss, 'a exists'. For suppose 'a is F' is true in some free extension. If 'a exists' is true, the denotation of a must lie in the domain of the original valuation, so 'a is F' and consequently 'something is F' must have been true on that valuation, and so the latter is true on the extension; while if 'a exists' is false on the free extension, the denotation of a lies in the outer domain compatibly with nothing in the inner domain being F. Thus 'something is F' can be false when 'a is F' is true, but not when both 'a is F' and 'a exists' are true, as required. A similar analysis shows that 'a is F' can be false when 'everything is F' is true, but not when both it and 'a exists' are true.

We have therefore achieved a clear semantic account of the logical behaviour of empty names, one which does not commit us to the actual existence of objects corresponding to them. Indeed, we can now see how to deal systematically with the question of fiction: we populate the outer domain with the intended fictitious and non-existent objects. (This is only a partial solution, however. It does not deal with the fictional ascription of fictitious properties to real objects.) All the apparatus is in place to deal with both names referring to things which don't

exist (e.g. 'King Lear' and 'Nausicaa') and for irreferential names
(e.g. 'phlogiston', 'the emperor's new clothes', 'the man who
wasn't there—whom I met upon the stair'). In particular, we
now have a clear and acceptable account of logical consequence—that there be no partial valuation every free extension
of which makes all the premises true and the conclusion false—
which validates inferential principles consonant with the semantic
picture we have drawn.

Summary and Guide to Further Reading

As philosophy emerged as an identifiable subject, the enigmatic
thinker Parmenides bequeathed us a puzzle: how can we talk
meaningfully about what does not exist? For if it does not exist,
how can we refer to it? What is it which does not exist? Parmenides' and Plato's response to this puzzle was to refuse to
deny being of anything—whatever we can think about must in
some sense have being. The fragmentary remains of Parmenides' 'Way of Truth', and the whole of Plato's dialogue, the
Parmenides (whose main speaker is, unusually, given the name
'Parmenides'—it's usually 'Socrates' who dominates Plato's dialogues) are collected and discussed in F. M. Cornford's *Plato and
Parmenides*.

Willard van Orman Quine created the delightful image of
'Plato's Beard' to describe Plato's uninhibited response to
Parmenides' puzzle; I have appropriated the epithet to allude to
the puzzle itself. Quine launched an unbridled attack on such
Platonist extravagance in a classic paper, 'On What There Is',
reprinted in his *From a Logical Point of View*. Quine is the
foremost advocate of a solution originally proposed by Bertrand
Russell in another classic paper, 'On Denoting', first published
in 1905 and reprinted in his *Logic and Knowledge*, edited by
R. C. Marsh. Russell had earlier held a view much like Plato's;
but in 'On Denoting' he rejected it. The solution proceeds in
two stages: descriptive phrases, though they appear to get their
meaning by referring to an object, are shown not to do so, but
are 'incomplete symbols' which do not correspond to a unitary
component of the logical analysis of the proposition. Propositions

containing such descriptions therefore retain their meaning even if no object corresponds to the grammatical description. Secondly, other singular terms are distinguished into a class of genuine names, which do depend on the existence of objects they denote for their meaning, and disguised descriptions, nongenuine names, whose analysis follows the theory of descriptions. Russell experienced subsequent metaphysical difficulty in identifying objects and their names as secure enough in our a priori knowledge of their existence to provide the atomic level of elementary propositions and logically proper names (recall Chapter 1, and see his 'The Philosophy of Logical Atomism', also in *Logic and Knowledge*, especially lectures 2 and 6); Quine tried to show that, logically, names and singular terms can be dispensed with entirely.

For independent reasons, Gottlob Frege had drawn a distinction between the signification (*Bedeutung*) of an expression and its sense (*Sinn*)—see his 'Über Sinn und Bedeutung', translated as 'On Sense and Reference' (or 'On Sense and Meaning') in *Translations from the Philosophical Writings of Gottlob Frege* by P. Geach and M. Black. Like Russell, he believed the meaning of a proposition resulted from the meanings of its parts (though functionally, rather than as a literal combination, as for Russell), a principle which he expounded—both as applied to signification and to sense—so forcefully that it is often called 'Frege's principle'. The distinction of two elements to meaning can also be applied to the problem of Plato's Beard, so that an expression can be empty, that is, lack signification, while at the same time being meaningful, that is, having sense. Frege discusses this in a paper unpublished in his lifetime, but now available in translation as 'Further Remarks on Sense and Meaning' in his *Posthumous Writings*, ed. H. Hermes *et al.*, tr. P. Long and R. White. (As the reader will have noticed, the translation of Frege's term *Bedeutung* causes some difficulty: I have used 'signification'; Geach and others have variously used 'reference' and 'meaning'; Russell translates *Sinn* as 'meaning' and *Bedeutung* as 'denotation'; all coloured by one's evaluation of what his theory actually says.)

With Frege's idea that a proposition might be meaningful

but contain empty names, we are getting closer to an account matching our intuitions. But it is not clearly consonant with classical logic, which embraces principles, in particular, Universal Specification and Existential Generalization, which require that every term denotes. Three reactions are possible: the Russellian, that every genuine name denotes an existent, and 'non-denoting names' must be eliminated; Plato's, taken up in modern times by Alexius Meinong, that every name really is a name and really does denote, albeit denoting objects 'beyond being and non-being'; and free logic, which revises classical logic, and permits non-denoting (empty) terms. Meinong's account, despite a bad press (largely through the attacks by Russell, attacks more against his own earlier theory than Meinong's), is a brave attempt and much can be learned from it, even if Russell is right that ultimately it collapses in inconsistency. Karel Lambert's *Meinong and the Principle of Independence* is a modern, non-scholarly, discussion.

Lambert is himself, however, an originator and advocate of free logic, logic free of existence assumptions. I have not followed the traditional distinction between positive, negative, and neuter free logic, but contrasted, rather, outer domain free logics with irreferential ones. This characterization threatens to be anachronistic, for free logics (like modal logic before them) were initially presented as syntactic systems with no clear semantics, and my distinction is semantic. None the less, I believe that logics are now more commonly, and should be, approached semantically. Outer domain free logics share with classical logic, Meinong, and Plato the belief that empty names are empty in name only, that they all denote something, albeit something which does not exist. They differ in that the quantifiers do not range over these non-existents, but only over an inner domain. Irreferential free logics take seriously the idea that empty names really do not denote. However, the response of neuter free logic (if there ever was such a response) to this situation, that all propositions containing at least one empty name lack truth-value, is unsatisfactory. Some propositions about the non-existent are true: e.g. 'Pegasus never existed', 'King Lear had three daughters', 'Either Bellerophon had a happy childhood or he did not'; others are false: e.g. 'Nausicaa really existed', 'Deep down, Hamlet was fond of his uncle', 'Pegasus was both a grey and a dun'; and some cannot be given a truth-value (and not simply through our lack of information): e.g. 'Pegasus was a grey', 'Lear could whistle', and so on.

The real problem for irreferential free logic is to spell out how the truth-conditions of complex propositions with empty names are to be given. Adopting Kleene's weak or strong matrices makes it difficult to define satisfactory notions of logical consequence and logical truth. Using van Fraassen's method of supervaluations threatens to undermine the whole endeavour of free logic, by validating Universal Specification and Existential Generalization in their classical forms. Van Fraassen's paper, 'Singular Terms, Truthvalue Gaps and Free Logic' is reprinted in *Philosophical Applications of Free Logic*, edited by Karel Lambert, along with many of the most important papers on free logic. Peter Woodruff's idea of combining supervaluations with outer domain techniques is unpublished, but briefly mentioned in Ermanno Bencivenga's contribution, 'Free Logics', to the *Handbook of Philosophical Logic*, iii, edited by D. Gabbay and F. Guenthner, one of the more approachable papers in that excellent, but usually highly technical, four-volume survey.

This combination of supervaluations with outer domain ideas shows what the truth-values of propositions with empty names would be if the names were not empty, and how the truth-conditions of complex propositions can be articulated in this situation of partial valuations. But has it penetrated to the heart of Parmenides' puzzle? 'Another, that it is not, and must needs not be—this, I tell thee, is a path that is utterly undiscernible; for thou couldst not know that which is not—for that is impossible—nor utter it.' Have we answered Parmenides by calmly reassuring ourselves that we can?

6 Well, I'll be Hanged!
The Semantic Paradoxes

IN Cervantes' novel, Don Quixote at one point leaves his man-servant Sancho Panza as governor of the island of Barataria. Sancho Panza is presented with many problems as governor. His first morning brought this one: he was told that it was the governor's task to preside in court, and the first case arose from a law concerning the use of a bridge leading from one parish to another. The landowner had made a decree:

Whoever passes over this bridge from one side to the other, must first take an oath whence he comes and what business he is going about. If he swear true, let him pass, but if he tell a lie, he shall die for it upon the gallows, without any remission.

This law served well enough for many years, until one day a man stood before the bridge and declared:

By the oath I have taken, I swear I am going to die upon that gallows which stands yonder, and that this is my business, and no other.

The bridge-keepers were set in a quandary by this; and so had appealed to the governor for a ruling. For if they let the man cross the bridge, he would have sworn falsely and lied, and so should have been hanged. Whereas if they hanged him, he would have sworn truly, and so should have been allowed to pass over the bridge.

Sancho Panza takes some time to appreciate the problem here. For the law concerning the bridge works well enough in most circumstances, ensuring that only those who truthfully reveal their business will be allowed to pass from one parish to the other. Surely the landowner had found a sensible way of ensuring that rogues and vagabonds could not cross his land without being caught. However, when faced with one particular case the law cannot cope, and ties itself in knots. If someone comes to the bridge and says that his business is to die on the gallows, then whatever is done to him will be declared wrong by the landowner's decree: to let him go free will mean he has lied, and so should be hanged; to hang him will mean he spoke truly, and so should go free.

Sancho Panza's first reaction is to find a way of both hanging him and letting him cross the bridge; he says: 'They should let pass that part of the man that swore the truth, and hang that part that swore a lie; thus the conditions of the passage will be literally fulfilled.' But when it is pointed out that cutting the man in half will kill him anyway, and so make it impossible for any part of him to go free, Sancho Panza summons up a precept of Don Quixote's, that when justice happens to be doubtful, incline to the side of mercy. So he says they should let the man pass freely. This is in effect to set the law aside, and declare it inoperable in this case. In other words, the law should have been more carefully framed in the first place, and was unsatisfactory. Let us look at some more cases to see if such a solution is generally applicable.

One of the most famous cases of such paradoxes was related by Bertrand Russell. It concerns the barber of Tombstone. The seemingly unremarkable fact about Tombstone, says Russell, is that the barber there shaves all and only those men who do not shave themselves. For surely, those men who shave themselves clearly do not need the barber's services; and who but the barber should shave everyone else?

But think a moment: who shaves the barber? If he shaves himself, then it's not true that he shaves only those who don't shave themselves; while if he doesn't shave himself—if he has a beard, or is shaved by his wife—then it is not true that he shaves all those who don't shave themselves.

The obvious conclusion is that the barber is a woman! For if not, then the description of the barber of Tombstone is just incorrect. It gives an inconsistent specification of him. Perhaps he shaves all and only other men in Tombstone who don't shave themselves. But there can be no man in Tombstone who shaves all and only those men who do not shave themselves.

What the stories about Barataria and Tombstone give us are paradoxes. A paradox arises when an unacceptable conclusion is supported by a plausible argument from apparently acceptable premisses. The conclusion that the man at the bridge in Barataria should be both hanged and let free, and the conclusion that the barber of Tombstone must both shave and not shave himself, are clearly unacceptable conclusions, which none the less apparently follow validly from what seem at first sight acceptable premisses, namely, that a law governing rights of passage over the bridge has been enacted, and that a description of the barber of Tombstone has been given. In each of these cases, we reject the premiss: the law was unacceptable, and needed revision; the description of the barber was incorrect, and needed revision.

But other cases, we shall find, do not allow such an easy rejection of the premiss. And if it cannot be rejected, then we may be forced to accept that the conclusion really is true after all, unless we can show that it doesn't really follow from the premisses. So three different reactions to the paradoxes are possible: to show that the reasoning is fallacious; or that the premisses are not all true after all; or that the conclusion can in fact be accepted. Let us look at some of these tougher examples of paradox.

Perhaps the most famous of the harder cases concerns Epimenides, the Cretan. Epimenides was embarrassed by his compatriots; they always lied, he believed. So he said, 'All Cretans are liars.'

But he was a Cretan himself: was he telling the truth? If he was, then he himself was lying, since that is what he said, and so not telling the truth. In other words, if we suppose he was telling the truth, we must conclude that he was both telling the truth and not telling the truth. But that is impossible. So that supposition that he was telling the truth must be wrong, that is, he was not telling the truth.

We have followed the so-called *reductio ad absurdum* mode of inference: assume something, derive a contradiction (or absurdity) from it, and so be forced to conclude that the assumption cannot hold, that is, it is false. Here, we have shown that

Epimenides was lying. For if he was telling the truth, then the truth is he was lying. That's a contradiction. So he must have been lying.

But if he was lying, then, given that every other Cretan had indeed lied—that is, Epimenides' basic pessimism was well founded—then he was indeed telling the truth, for again, that is what he said. So he was not lying, but telling the truth. But that's puzzling. For we have already shown that he was lying; and now we've shown that, if he was lying, he was telling the truth. Hence Epimenides was, it seems, both lying and telling the truth.

To repeat the argument: if one supposes Epimenides was telling the truth, it follows that he was lying and so not telling the truth, whence by *reductio and absurdum*, he cannot have been telling the truth, that is, he was lying. But then it follows that, since he said that he and others were liars, and we have supposed the others were indeed liars, that he was telling the truth. It seems to follow that Epimenides was both lying and telling the truth.

That conclusion is surely unacceptable, so we have a paradox again—an unacceptable conclusion derived from seemingly reasonable premises. But it is not so easy to get out of this paradox as it was for the previous ones: we cannot simply infer that Epimenides couldn't have existed, or if he did, that at least he never said that all Cretans are liars, for we are told by, for example, Paul in the Epistle to Titus (and by earlier fragmentary sources) that he did. Nor can we escape the problem by saying that Epimenides must have got it wrong, that is, that his remark was false. For that was part of the paradox: if it was false, then he was lying, and so, given that all the other Cretan claims had been false, Epimenides had it right, and was telling the truth.

The same problem arises, magnified this time, in the Psalmist's misanthropic remark: 'I said in my haste, All men are liars' (Psalm 116). If his pessimism was justified, then if what he said was false and he too was lying, then what he said was true; and if what he said was true, then he too was lying, and so it wasn't true. So what he said was both true and false—if indeed all men are liars. He certainly did speak in haste.

Bertrand Russell tells a delightful story about G. E. Moore:

He had a kind of exquisite purity. I have never but once succeeded in making him tell a lie, and that was by a subterfuge. 'Moore', I said, 'do you always speak the truth?' 'No,' he replied. I believe this to be the only lie he had ever told.

But is Russell being disingenuous here? If Moore had indeed never lied then this statement must be a lie. Yet, if it is a lie that he sometimes lies, it must itself be true. So it cannot be his only lie.

The Truth Hierarchy

Perhaps the simplest case where such paradox arises is the Liar

The proposition expressed by this very sentence is false.

The proposition says of itself that it is false. Suppose it were true; then it would be false—for that is what it says—and so it cannot be true. That is, if it is true, then it is false. But if it is false, it must be true, for it says that it is false. That is, if it is false then it is true. So, if it must be either true or false, it will follow that it is both.

We might think, therefore, that we could avoid this particular paradox by inferring that the proposition is neither true nor false. Perhaps some propositions are neither true nor false. For example, 'The present provost of St Andrews is a good cyclist' could be said to be neither true nor false, since St Andrews has no provost any more.

But this way out cannot deal with all the paradoxes. Consider the proposition:

This very proposition is not true.

Once again, suppose it were true; then things would be as it says they are, that is, it would not be true. So if it is true, then it is not true. But if we suppose it is not true, it must be true, for that is what it says. So if it is not true then it is true. But surely it must either be true or not true, in which case it must be both true and not true.

We haven't used the Law of Bivalence, that every proposition is either true or false, in that proof. But we have used the Law of Excluded Middle, that every proposition or its contradictory is true, in particular, that every proposition is either true or not true.

There are several ways of denying Excluded Middle. We will explore one of them. We might agree that every meaningful sentence expresses a proposition which is either true or not true. But if a sentence is meaningless, then it really is meaningless, and so will not express a true proposition even if things are as it appears to say they are. In the present case, it appears to say that the proposition it expresses is not true. Being meaningless, it does not express a true proposition. But that does not entitle us to infer that, since it says that it does not express a true proposition, it does express a true proposition after all.

What we really need in order for this to be a convincing solution, is a proper account of meaningfulness relative to which it is clear that the sentence, 'This proposition is not true', is meaningless, and why. For that sentence certainly appears to be meaningful—we know what it means, namely, that the proposition it expresses is not true. Moreover, if it is meaningless, then it certainly cannot express a true proposition. So presumably we can say it does not express a true proposition. Why can we not use that sentence itself to say it does not express a true proposition? This is puzzling. It is sometimes termed 'the revenge problem'. The claim is that the proposition, 'This proposition is not true', is not true; yet that is exactly what is says—so what is wrong with it? The answer has to be, therefore, that it is meaningless for that very sentence to attempt to say that it does not express a true proposition. But if so, why? What is the general account of meaning which will convincingly show that this sentence is meaningless? We are presented with a negative argument: if it were meaningful, we would land in paradox. But what positive account of meaning can we give which can explain its meaninglessness?

Here is a further paradox (the Strengthened Liar) which emphasizes this point:

This very sentence either expresses a false proposition or is meaningless.

If the proposition expressed were true, it would be false or the
sentence would be meaningless, and so it would not be true. So
it cannot be true. If it were false, it would be neither false nor
would the sentence be meaningless, and thus it would be true;
so it cannot be false. If the sentence were meaningless, the
proposition would appear to say just that, that it is meaningless
(or expresses a false proposition), so it would seem to be true—
and so the sentence would not be meaningless. So it doesn't
seem to be meaningless either.

What account of meaningfulness can we give which will both
show that these paradoxical sentences are meaningless—and
why—and produce a generally acceptable account of the
meaningfulness of non-paradoxical sentences?

One idea is that what is present in all these cases of paradox
is self-reference. We have sentences, or Cretans, or travellers,
referring to themselves. When we put forward the sentence,
'The proposition expressed by this very sentence is false', we
should, it is urged, explain which sentence. But when we do, we
will find that explanation to be circular. We start to say, for
example, '... this sentence ...', and are interrupted by the
peremptory question, 'Which sentence?'; '... this sentence ...',
we repeat, and again are asked immediately, 'Which sentence?',
and so on.

This account of meaning fails the second condition we laid
down at the end of the previous paragraph. For it rules out
apparently acceptable non-paradoxical sentences as meaningless,
but gives no defence for doing so, other than its possible success
in banning paradoxical sentences. That won't do—of course
Epimenides can refer to himself, if he wants to tell someone
what his name is, or that he is hungry and wants some food.
And even sentences can legitimately refer to themselves, for
instance the sticker on the back of a car: 'If you can read this,
you are too close.'

So it cannot be self-reference alone that is at fault. Rather,
what seems to cause the problems in the paradoxes is the
combination of self-reference with falsity, where being false—
or something like that—is predicated of the proposition expressed by the very sentence itself, or speaking truly or falsely

of the speaker himself, and so on. Actually, it is going to be quite difficult to explain what is covered by the clause 'and so on', to ensure that all the cases that lead to paradox are covered. Here is a perhaps unexpected example. Consider the argument:

$1 = 1$
Hence this argument is invalid.

(It's a one-premiss argument: the premiss is the necessary truth that $1 = 1$; the conclusion is that the argument itself is invalid.) That argument is actually a self-referential paradox, though it doesn't mention truth or falsity. For we can argue: if the argument is valid, then it has a true premiss and a false conclusion. But all arguments with true premisses and false conclusions are invalid (for validity guarantees that if the premiss is true then so is the conclusion). So the argument is, if valid, invalid. Hence it must be invalid. But in showing it to be invalid, we had to rely on the fact that '$1 = 1$' is true; i.e. we deduced the fact that it is invalid from the claim that $1 = 1$. But that is just what the argument says one can do. So it must be valid. Therefore it is both valid and invalid!

Validity relates to arguments much as truth relates to propositions. Hence, we must beware of applying and denying validity to self-referential arguments. And doubtless other concepts too. We will need, therefore, if this line of solution is to work, to characterize, in general terms, semantic concepts, concepts to do with truth, meaning, validity, and so on.

Most sentences do not mention truth or falsity (or validity, or semantic concepts in general) at all. Let us call these the basic sentences. Other sentences predicate truth or falsity (and so on) of the propositions expressed by the basic sentences; call these sentences 'sentences of level 1'. Yet other sentences will predicate truth and falsity of the propositions expressed by level-1 sentences; these are level-2 sentences. And so on, with sentences possible of every level. The construction is due to Alfred Tarski. He called the levels separate and distinct languages, so that level 1 acts as the meta-language for level 0, level 2 the meta-language for level 1, and so on. We can call it 'Tarski's hierarchy'.

The idea for a paradox-avoiding restriction is that a sentence should only be allowed to predicate truth or falsity of the propositions expressed by sentences of level lower than its own. The paradoxical sentences break this restriction in attempting to predicate truth or falsity of the propositions expressed by themselves, that is, of sentences of their own level. Any sentence which breaks this requirement about levels is rejected as meaningless. Although the sentence, 'The proposition expressed by this very sentence is false or the sentence is meaningless', appears, if one supposes it meaningless, to express a true proposition, it is not, for it really is meaningless—or so this theory of meaning alleges—to attempt to say of the proposition expressed by the very sentence in which one is saying it, that it is false or the sentence is meaningless. Any appearance to the contrary is simply a conceptual confusion, arising from an ignorance of the complexities of predicating truth and falsity.

So we are presented by this solution to the paradoxes with a hierarchy of levels of sentences. Each sentence has a level—although often we may not know what it is. If Epimenides had realized that, if the present view is correct, his actual utterance, 'All Cretans are liars', was meaningless, he might have said, 'All Cretans up till now have been liars', instead. But not knowing in detail quite how often other Cretans had spoken of the truth or falsity of propositions, or how these remarks had built on one another, he would not have known what level attached to his own utterance.

He might find, none the less, that even his corrected remark was meaningless—if some other Cretan had at some time said, for example, that Epimenides was the only one among them who always told the truth. For then there would be (indirect) self-reference, unbeknownst to Epimenides. In medieval times, the standard such paradox portrayed Plato only asserting that whatever Aristotle says is true, while Aristotle only claims that whatever Plato says is false. (For example, suppose Aristotle mishears Plato and thinks he says, 'What Aristophanes says is true'—so Aristotle seeks to deny it. But Plato actually referred to Aristotle.) Then if Plato speaks truly, so does Aristotle—and so what Plato says is false. So what Plato says really is false, in which case so is what Aristotle says, and so Plato is speaking the truth. Again, we have self-reference—though indirectly—leading to paradox.

The present proposal would forbid this kind of circularity. Whatever the level of Plato's utterance, he can only be talking about Aristotle's utterances of lower level, and so those in turn can only be of lower level again, and cannot reflect back on Plato's remark about Aristotle.

What is puzzling, however, is that often we may be unaware of the full complexity present. Such uncertainty would trip Epimenides up, as we suggested, if another Cretan had expressed his faith in Epimenides' (unique) veracity.

So one consequence of trying to impose such an order on our attribution of truth and falsity to our propositions is that those attributions may have properties which elude our investigation. Indeed, whether what we say is meaningful or not may, accordingly, be something of which we cannot tell. Take Epimenides' case. He thought he had expressed an intelligible proposition. His hearers thought so too, and reported him as having said that all Cretans were liars. But if another Cretan had at some time said, for example, 'Epimenides always tells the truth'—himself thinking he had said something meaningful—it would turn out (according to Tarski's hierarchy) that they were both mistaken, and mistaken not about the truth of what they said, but the very meaningfulness of their remarks. Meaningfulness would be purely conjectural whenever anyone said anything. We might think they had said something meaningful, but our belief might at any time be wrong. That is a very strange consequence.

There is another disturbing feature of the present proposal. It is entirely *ad hoc*. No reason has actually been given why ascribing semantic concepts in the presence of self-reference results in meaninglessness. It appears that it leads to contradiction—we knew that; and to brand such sentences as meaningless—given that meaningless sentences do not express true nor false propositions—will avoid that contradiction. For if we are serious that, for instance, 'The proposition expressed by this sentence is not true' is meaningless, and so does not express a true proposition, then it really is meaningless, and does not say that it itself is not true—being meaningless, it says nothing (though it appears to say something). But why?

We saw in Chapter 5 that it is plausible to suppose that the meaning of a sentence results from the way it is composed of meaningful parts—that way, we can explain how we are able to understand and ourselves produce novel sentences which we have not heard or uttered before. A corollary is that if a sentence is correctly composed of meaningful parts then it is meaningful. The present proposal denies this. The generally correct technique of predicating such a phrase as 'is not true' of a term referring to a proposition, results in this particular case in meaninglessness. But that charge is *ad hoc*, failing any explanation for the lack of meaning. Simply describing the case as self-predication of falsity is no explanation.

True Contradictions

We noted that we could avoid paradox in three different ways: by denying the apparently acceptable premiss, by accepting the apparently unacceptable conclusion, or by denying that the conclusion does follow from the premiss. Clearly, the proposal we have just considered is, like the solution to Sancho Panza's problem and the Barber paradox, an attack on the premiss— denying, for example, that Epimenides had really uttered a meaningful proposition to the effect that all Cretan utterances were false. But this line of solution has failed. So let us turn to see whether a better solution may be found by grasping the nettle—by exploring the possibility of accepting that the para- doxical conclusion is in fact true in the cases we have looked at. We will find that there is another powerful paradox that forces us, in following out this line of solution, actually to revise our logic.

The present solution to the paradoxes is to claim that what the paradoxes show is just what they seem to show—that cer- tain contradictions must be accepted. Certain propositions really are paradoxical. They really are both true and false. For example, we must accept that Epimenides' utterance is both true and false, and so also for the other examples. Note that this is not in itself yet a contradiction. But a proposition is false when its negation is true. Hence both Epimenides' utterance, 'All Cretans are liars', and its contradictory, 'Not all Cretans are liars', are true. So their conjunction is true, and that is a contradiction. Note also, that we may not now infer from, for example, a proposition's being false, that it is not true. On the present proposal, it may be both.

Clearly, however, this solution will only be reasonable provided we are not forced to accept too many contradictions. Take any clear falsehood, for instance, 'Snow is black'. No account of the paradoxes can be acceptable if it entails that the proposition, 'Snow is black', is true. The problem is that if we accept the conclusion of any of the above paradoxes, we will have also, it seems, to admit that snow is black. Since 'Snow is black' is false, this will be yet another paradox. For we will now have just too many propositions both true and false, and not just a few self-referential ones.

Here is the proof. Let us take it that what Epimenides said is both true and false. Then in particular it is true, that is, all Cretans are liars; so either all Cretans are liars or snow is black. But also, by hypothesis, it is false, and so not all Cretans are liars. Hence, given that either all Cretans are liars or snow is black, and that not all Cretans are liars, we must accept that snow is black.

How can we escape from this new paradox, that snow is black, engendered by attempting to stomach the conclusions of the paradoxes? We cannot accept that snow is black. So if we are seriously to accept that what Epimenides said is both true and false, that is, that both all Cretans are liars and not all Cretans are liars, as the original paradox seems to show, then we must find grounds for rejecting the validity of the argument deriving the conclusion that snow is black from the claim that both all Cretans are liars and not all Cretans are liars.

We saw in Chapter 2 that this type of inference, from a proposition and its contradictory to any other proposition whatever, has been rejected on other grounds by a number of logicians. Its name is *Ex Falso Quodlibet*—from the false (or a contradiction), anything follows. For example, one consequence of admitting the validity of this mode of inference will be that anyone who mistakenly holds contradictory beliefs will be committed to the truth of any proposition whatever. But clearly, someone may believe that Cicero wrote *De Lege Manilia* but that Tully did not—not realizing they were the same person—without thereby being committed to believing that snow is black. Moreover, we must accept that he is logically committed to the logical consequences of his beliefs, since that is how we bring him to change his beliefs.

If this mode of inference is indeed invalid, what makes it look so plausible? I argued in Chapter 2 that the reason is that 'or' is ambiguous. In one sense, 'or' permits the move from A to 'A or B', for example, from 'All Cretans are liars' to 'All Cretans are liars or snow is black'. But it is quite another sense of 'or' which allows one to move from 'A or B' and 'not-A' to B, namely the sense of 'or' in which 'A or B' means 'if not-A then B'. For example, 'All Cretans are liars or snow is black' can mean 'If not all Cretans are liars then snow is black', and clearly from this, given that not all Cretans are liars, it follows immediately that snow is black. But 'All Cretans are liars' does not imply that if not all Cretans are liars then snow is black—it implies no such thing. So the argument commits a fallacy of equivocation—the middle proposition, 'Either all Cretans are liars or snow is black', exhibits an equivocation or ambiguity over the sense of 'or'. Taken in one sense, the proposition follows from the premiss that all Cretans are liars, but then it does not imply the conclusion (even given the additional 'information' that not all Cretans are liars). Taken in the other sense, it implies the conclusion, that snow is black (given the other conjunct of the premiss, that not all Cretans are liars), but it does not then follow from the premiss.

However, even if we can find a way out of that first problem, by rejecting the soundness of *Ex Falso Quodlibet*, we are not yet home and dry. For there is another paradox which arises if we allow such self-referential truth-predications. Consider the proposition:

If this (conditional) proposition is true then snow is black

where the phrase 'this (conditional) proposition' refers to the whole conditional. Recall that the present proposal is not to reject such a proposition as meaningless—as the hierarchy approach would do—but to try to stomach the consequences, such as that Epimenides' statement is both true and false, of admitting the possibility of self-referential predication of truth and falsity. Consider, however, the following argument about the above conditional.

Suppose that it is true. Then it has a true antecedent (the first clause), and so, by the mode of argument called *modus ponendo ponens* (if *A*, and if *A* then *B*, then *B*), it must have a true consequent (the second clause). That is, if the conditional is true, then snow is black. But that is just what the conditional says. In other words, we have shown that the conditional is true. But then, given that the conditional is true, it has a true antecedent, and so we must conclude, by *modus ponendo ponens*, as before, but now no longer on the assumption that the conditional is true (for we have shown that it is), that its consequent is true. That is, snow is black. We have shown first that the conditional is true, and secondly that it immediately follows from the fact that it is true that snow is black. This form of paradox is known as Curry's paradox, after the logician Haskell B. Curry, who discovered it around 1940.

Hence, if we intend to stomach the paradoxes, we must reject not only the argument that shows that if any proposition is both true and false, then snow is black, but also the argument that the above conditional is true, and hence, once again, that snow is black. So the present solution will require considerable revision to our logic. (Incidentally, note the similarity between this last paradox and the earlier paradox about the argument, '1 = 1, so this argument is invalid': an argument is valid if and only if the matching conditional is necessarily true. The argument '1 = 1, so this argument is invalid' becomes the proposition 'If 1 = 1 then this (conditional) proposition is false', which contraposes— roughly—into 'If this proposition is true then $1 \neq 1$', or, just as bad, 'If this proposition is true then snow is black'.)

One logical principle which lies behind the argument about the conditional and which has been called into question, is that two applications of an assumption in an argument can be replaced by one. The move is sometimes called 'Contraction', or 'Absorption'. For, having assumed the conditional was true, we applied that assumption twice—once as the conditional premiss of *modus ponendo ponens*, secondly, as the antecedent of that conditional premiss—to infer that snow was black. But we recorded that assumption only once when we concluded that if the conditional was true then snow is black. If we were to make explicit the double use of the assumption, we would obtain

If the conditional is true then if the conditional is true then snow is black,

which is not the conditional. Hence the argument no longer goes through.

However, is it possible to block the derivation of Curry's paradox without rejecting Contraction entirely? For to do the latter would have the unforeseen consequence that the earlier arguments, like Eubulides', presently being construed as proofs that some contradictions are true, would fail. They proceed by *reductio*; for example, if the Strengthened Liar is true, then it is not true, and so not true; but since it is not true, it must be true; so it is both true and not true, a contradiction. Now, *reductio* is closely linked to contraction. Its basic form is that of *consequentia mirabilis*, 'if *A* then not-*A*; so not-*A*'. 'Not-*A*' in turn is equivalent to 'if *A* then absurdity' ('$0 = 1$' or some other unacceptable proposition—'snow is black', perhaps). So *consequentia mirabilis* expands into, 'If *A* then if *A* then $0 = 1$; so if *A* then $0 = 1$', and that is an instance of contraction. In other words, we have a dilemma: if we accept the validity of Contraction, Curry's paradox will lead to triviality—that every proposition is true; but if we reject it, then whatever rationale we give for its rejection will probably mean rejecting *reductio* and *consequentia mirabilis* as well—and then none of the paradox arguments will work, and there will be no reason (at least from consideration of the semantic paradoxes) for supposing that any contradictions are true. This is a strange and unexpected result for the proposal to accept the verdict of the semantic paradoxes at face value.

In the end, the idea that some contradictions are true does not work. For Curry's paradox shows that unless one is willing drastically to revise one's logic, one's theory of truth will result in every proposition, however absurd, being accounted true. On the other hand, if one does proceed to adjust one's logic to the new situation, the original paradoxical 'proofs' of the existence of true contradictions will fail. Moreover, the famous proofs of the uncountability of the real numbers and of Gödel's theorem, which are closely modelled on the reasoning in the paradoxes, will no longer go through. (Cantor's diagonal argument, to show that all the infinite decimals between 0 and 1, say, cannot be written down even in a single never-ending list, was the basis of a whole new mathematics of so-called 'transfinite' numbers at the end of the nineteenth century, which we will look at in Chapter 8. Gödel's proof in 1931 of the incompleteness of arithmetic—we discussed it in Chapter 2—that the truths of arithmetic cannot be completely captured in an effective set of axioms, sparked off research into effective computability which eventually led to the theory of the digital computer.) Most importantly, however, the charge of being *ad hoc*, which we earlier applied to the attempt to brand the paradoxical sentences as meaningless, will apply here too. For we have given no other reason for rejecting *reductio ad absurdum* and the underlying principle of Contraction than that they make the acceptance of the existence of true contradictions impossible. Contrast the situation with that for the inference of B from 'A and not-A'. There we explained the error in the inference by pointing to an ambiguity in the sense of 'or', which, had it been noticed in its own right, would have independently shown the inference invalid. No similar explanation seems available in the present case.

Semantic Closure

Trying to accept the verdict of the paradox argument was a bright, and bold, idea; but it fails. Trying to regiment language into a hierarchy of object and meta-languages was equally bold; but it is counter-intuitive. As a third possibility, let us see how far we can get by retaining semantic closure—our language contains its own truth-predicate—while avoiding paradox by separating the conditions for truth from those for falsity, as the advocates of true contradictions do. That is, let us return to the idea of rejecting Bivalence, but try to avoid succumbing to the Strengthened Liar.

The idea was put forward in its most intriguing form by Saul Kripke in the mid-1970s. It caught the imagination of the times, and led to a great deal of formal work. The proposal is, in essence, simple enough; the technical details of following it through can be omitted here (though, of course, they are essential for its proper articulation). What we do is to mimic Tarski's hierarchy, except that we actually expand our language each time, collecting up as we go. The 'meta-language' each time contains the object language as a part, as in a homophonic Tarskian theory, that is, where p in 'S is true if and only if p' is replaced by the very proposition designated by what replaces S. The success of the method depends on two facts: first, that we eventually reach a point where the expansion in effect fails—where the 'meta-language' actually contains no further truth-attributions than the 'object language' it sought to expand; that is, we reach semantic closure. Secondly, that the truth-predicate is a partial valuation (recall this notion from Chapter 5), and so the paradoxical propositions lack a value in this so-called 'fixed point', the point where the expansion stops. Kripke's reply to Tarski is, therefore, that we can attain semantic closure while maintaining consistency, if we are careful.

How is the fixed point constructed, and how do we know it exists? Let us start at the bottom, with a language, like our own, but in which the truth-predicate is so far uninterpreted. The interpretation to be arrived at is a partial one, so we need to treat truth and falsity separately—falsity is not simply non-truth. The interpretation of the truth-predicate, T, say, is to be a pair $\langle S_1, S_2 \rangle$, S_1 containing those propositions which are true, S_2 those which are false. So when we start, S_1 and S_2 are empty. We now, at the first stage, add to S_1 all the truths of our language ('Snow is white', 'Cicero denounced Catiline', and so on) and to S_2 all the falsehoods ('Snow is black', 'Caesar died peacefully in his bed', and so on). The interpretation is partial, for some propositions will lack a value—for instance, ' "Snow is white" is true'—for at this stage of evaluation, the truth-predicate was uninterpreted. So we need some way of evaluating compounds of propositions one part of which lacks value. We noted three methods in Chapter 5, namely, Kleene's strong and weak matrices, and van Fraassen's supervaluations. Any of these will do; Kripke in fact used the weak matrices.

We have now changed the interpretation of the truth-predicate. So when we repeat the procedure, we will expand S_1 and S_2. At this, the second stage, S_1 will contain all it contained before, but more besides—what results from the further interpretation of T at the first stage. For example, ' "Snow is white" is true' will now go into S_1, for 'Snow is white' was in it at stage 1. We will thus successively expand S_1 and S_2 as we apply the procedure again and again.

The procedure of constructing the fixed point will in fact go by transfinite induction. The notion of iteration into the transfinite is something we will not meet until Chapter 8, when we look at the concept of infinity. But in principle, the idea is simple. We started with a base case—the interpretation of T was empty. We then proceed recursively, or successively, to construct partial valuations, one for each finite level. The first transfinite level comes from collecting up the interpretations of each of S_1 and S_2 at each finite level. Once that has been done, we can start again (as we will see Cantor do, in his construction of accumulation points, in Chapter 8). The procedure has three components—the base case, the case of successors, and the collecting-up at limit points. It threatens to go on forever.

But it cannot go on forever. That is the result on which Kripke's construction relies. At some point, the reinterpretation of T fails to add anything. It is a special case of a famous result about fixed points of normal functions on the ordinals. A normal function is one which is monotonic, increasing, and continuous. Let us say that $\langle S_1, S_2 \rangle \leqq \langle S_1', S_2' \rangle$ if and only if $S_1 \subseteq S_1'$ and $S_2 \subseteq S_2'$, that is, S_1 is included in S_1' and S_2 in S_2', that is, everything in S_1 is in S_1' and perhaps more besides, and the same for S_2. Then $\langle S_1', S_2' \rangle$ is more inclusive—it interprets more—than $\langle S_1, S_2 \rangle$ does. Let the operation of expanding $\langle S_1, S_2 \rangle$ by taking the truths and falsehoods of the language in which T is interpreted by $\langle S_1, S_2 \rangle$ be represented by ϕ; so $\phi\langle S_1, S_2 \rangle$ will expand $\langle S_1, S_2 \rangle$—it will repeat all the interpretations contained in $\langle S_1, S_2 \rangle$ but with possibly more besides. Thus $\langle S_1, S_2 \rangle \leqq \phi\langle S_1, S_2 \rangle$. This means that ϕ is increasing. Moreover, if $\langle S_1, S_2 \rangle \leqq \langle S_1', S_2' \rangle$, then $\phi\langle S_1, S_2 \rangle \leqq \phi\langle S_1', S_2' \rangle$; the result of applying ϕ to a more inclusive interpretation will be at least as inclusive. This shows the ϕ is monotonic. Lastly, we have decided to collect up at the limit points all that went before: if $\langle S_1, S_2 \rangle$ is a limit point, $\phi\langle S_1, S_2 \rangle$ results from collecting up the results of applying ϕ to less inclusive interpretations. We say that ϕ is continuous.

Any monotonic, increasing and continuous function has fixed points, indeed, it has arbitrarily large fixed points—given any fixed point, there is a greater. Moreover, it has a minimal fixed point. At each fixed point, $\phi\langle S_1, S_2 \rangle = \langle S_1, S_2 \rangle$. That is, the language with T interpreted by the choice of $\langle S_1, S_2 \rangle$ is semantically closed. The interpretation of the truth-predicate by $\langle S_1, S_2 \rangle$ is as inclusive as one can get. Adding all the truths to S_1, falsehoods to S_2, with T so interpreted, gives nothing new. The construction of T is complete.

But the interpretation is still partial—$\langle S_1, S_2 \rangle$ at the fixed point gives a partial valuation. For the construction is designed to preserve consistency. At no point is a proposition assigned to both S_1 and S_2. We start consistently, with S_1 and S_2 empty. At each successive stage, we add to S_1 those propositions which are true according to the interpretation of T constructed at the previous stage—that is, by hypothesis (induction hypothesis), consistent, and the same for S_2 and what is false. At limit stages we simply collect up what is already present, and so consistent. So S_1, S_2 remain forever disjoint.

Indeed, this can help us picture the situation. Obviously, we cannot continue to add propositions to S_1 and S_2 forever—at some point we would run out. (This may seem wrong—there are infinitely many propositions, so why can we not continue forever? The reason is that we are iterating the process into the transfinite, and so there must come a point at which the iteration exhausts the set of propositions. This notion of 'iteration into the transfinite', introduced by Cantor, and its philosophical implications, will be discussed in Chapter 8.) The interesting fact is that we reach a fixed point long before we have added all the propositions—even all the propositions we consistently can—to S_1 and S_2.

The fact that S_1 and S_2 are always disjoint means that there is a group of propositions which remain uninterpreted. These we can call 'ungrounded'. They include the Liar and its kin, and also the Truth-teller, 'This proposition is true'. One intuition tells us that there is no ground on which to assign this a value; another intuition tells us that it can take either. The construction respects both intuitions. The Truth-teller has no value in the minimal fixed point. But after the construction of the fixed point we could give it an arbitrary value—true, say. Then we repeat the process of construction of T, reaching a higher fixed point. In the new fixed point, the Truth-teller is true. But the Liar still lacks a value.

Whatever solution we give to the semantic paradoxes, something must give. What is it on Kripke's construction? Moreover, how does he cope with the Strengthened Liar, and the revenge problem? They fall to the same point—the vestige of the Tarski hierarchy. They cannot be expressed in the language in question. Since 'This proposition is not true' lacks a value, we cannot say in the language of the construction that it is not true—that it lacks a value. All the discussion, definition, and construction above belonged to a meta-language. Predicates like 'paradoxical' and 'ungrounded' also belong to this meta-language, not to the semantically closed fixed point. All that the fixed point can do is contain a truth-predicate whose interpretation is in some sense complete. It cannot suffice for all the semantic work which we require.

It is for this reason that Tarski's T-scheme is also a casualty. A and 'it is true that A' will have the same value in the fixed point. But 'A if and only if it is true that A' will not be valid— for if A lacks value, so does 'it is true that A', and consequently the biconditional will lack value—obviously so, on either Kleene scheme, and on the supervaluation scheme too, since it can have different values in different classical extensions.

Kripke's idea for semantic closure is a bold one. The cost is, however, high. It includes revision of Tarski's T-scheme; the continuation of the Tarski hierarchy for a great deal of our semantic discussion; and a schizophrenic outfacing of the revenge problem by maintaining that 'the Liar is not true' lacks value (in the fixed point) but is true (in the meta-language). The reader must weigh these costs, and decide whether they are too high.

Summary and Guide to Further Reading

What are the semantic paradoxes? We can really only characterize them by reference to proposed solutions and explanations. For example, the prediction paradox does not at first glance look like a semantic paradox. It comes in a number of forms, under many names, The Hangman, The Unexpected Egg, The Senior Sneak Week, The Unexpected Examination, and The Surprise Quiz. Here is one version:

A schoolmaster tells his class that on one day the following week there will be a test, but which day it will fall on will be a surprise. The class reason, however, that it cannot fall on Friday, for on Friday morning, knowing it had not happened on Monday to Thursday, they would know it must be held that day, and so it would not be a surprise. But if it cannot fall on Friday, for the same reason it cannot be held on Thursday, for if it were, the class, knowing on Thursday morning that it had not happened on Monday to Wednesday, and having realized it cannot wait until Friday, would know it must happen on Thursday; and so it would not be a surprise. And so on. Hence, they reason, the test cannot both be held and be a surprise. Accordingly, when the test is held on, say, Tuesday, it is a great surprise.

There is certainly a paradox here. The situation is familiar, and its description seems correct. There will be a surprise test. So what is wrong with the reasoning which suggests it is impossible? One explanation is that the schoolmaster's proposition has the form:

There will be a test, but you will not know on the basis of this statement on which day the test will be held

Hence his statement is self-referential. Moreover, it involves the concept of knowledge, which entails truth, and so implicitly involves semantic concepts. For the following example shows that semantic paradox arises in such a case by use of the concept of knowledge:

No one knows this proposition.

Suppose this proposition were false. If it were false that no one knew it, someone would know it. But knowledge entails truth (that is, if something is false, one could only have thought one knew it—one did not really know it), and so the proposition would be true, given that someone knows it. That is, if the proposition were false, it would be true. Hence it cannot be false. So it must be true. Therefore we know it is true (for we have just proved it). So someone knows it. Hence it is false. So it is both true and false!

The paradox of the Unexpected Examination (and its variants) can be found discussed in very many places. Perhaps the best is that of R. Montague and D. Kaplan, 'A Paradox Regained', reprinted in R. Montague, *Formal Philosophy*; see also Mark Sainsbury's *Paradoxes*, ch. 4.

Semantic paradoxes can arise in many unexpected places. If the analysis above is correct, the Prediction or Unexpected Examination Paradox is yet another case of semantic paradox. A paradox arises where a plausible argument leads from apparently acceptable premises to an unacceptable conclusion. We have looked at a number of these paradoxes associated with semantic notions such as truth, meaning, validity, and knowledge. Examples were Epimenides the Cretan's claim that all Cretans were liars, and propositions such as 'This proposition is not true', and 'If this proposition is true then snow is black'. These pose a real problem which the story of the barber did not. There simply is no barber who shaves all and only those who do not shave themselves.

Useful discussions of the semantic paradoxes can be found in Susan Haack, *Philosophy of Logics*; and Sainsbury, *Paradoxes*, chs. 5–6. The story about Sancho Panza comes from M. de Cervantes, *Don Quixote* (written in 1614), pt. 2 ch. 45. It was a familiar story in medieval times.

We have explored three lines of solution. One imposes a

hierarchy on all predications of truth and other semantic notions, and rules out breaches of these requirements as resulting in meaningless utterances. It thus threatens to rule out many more than just the self-referential sentences that lead to contradiction. Moreover, it seems that every predication of semantic notions must have a level, even if the speaker is ignorant of it. Hence, whether or not a particular utterance is meaningful may turn out to be unknown to both speaker and hearer.

The namely-rider solution is canvassed in G. Ryle, 'Heterologicality', reprinted in his *Collected Papers*, ii. Similar ideas are used by Dorothy Grover to extend her prosentential theory of truth to the semantic paradoxes in her 'Inheritors and Paradox' and 'Berry's Paradox', reprinted in her *A Prosentential Theory of Truth* (mentioned in Chapter 1). The hierarchy solution is probably the most widely accepted solution at present. Its classic form was given by Alfred Tarski—see e.g. his 'The Semantic Conception of Truth', in H. Feigl and W. Sellars (eds.), *Readings in Philosophical Analysis*. The problems with the argument '$1 = 1$, so this argument is invalid' were noticed in the fourteenth century (their example was 'God exists, so this argument is invalid'). See e.g. Albert of Saxony, *Perutilis Logica* (written in the early 1350s), tr. in N. Kretzmann *et al.*, *The Cambridge Translations of Medieval Philosophical Texts*, i, 360–1; and also the discussion by an anonymous author (often referred to as Pseudo-Scotus, because his writings, though dating from the 1340s, some 50 years after John Duns Scotus, were later published along with Scotus' genuine works) described in, for example, I. Boh, 'Consequences', in N. Kretzmann *et al.*, *The Cambridge History of Later Medieval Philosophy*, ch. 15.

The second attempt grasped the nettle of the contradictory conclusion, claiming that certain paradoxical utterances really are both true and false. It was left, however, with the task of drastically revising the principles of logic, so we would not be forced thereby to admit that every proposition, for example, 'Snow is black', is true. Moreover, this revision was found finally to undercut the very ground for supposing we should endorse true contradictions. The idea that there are true contradictions, shown not only by the semantic paradoxes, but by many other puzzling cases, e.g. Zeno's paradoxes of space and motion and the metaphysics of change, is enthusiastically urged in Graham Priest's *In Contradiction*. Priest there succeeds in retaining *reductio* by rejecting contraction. So he avoids Curry's paradox while maintaining that the Liar, for example, is indeed both true and false. The proposal was criticized (and Priest replied) in 'Can Contradictions be True?' by Timothy Smiley, at an *Aristotelian Society* symposium in 1993. Curry's paradox was first discovered, and presented, by H. B. Curry in the context of set theory. It is elegantly explained as giving rise to a semantic paradox in P. Geach, 'On *Insolubilia*', reprinted in his *Logic Matters*.

The most influential treatment of the semantic paradoxes in recent years has been Saul Kripke's famous paper, 'Outline of a Theory of Truth'. It is reprinted, with other important papers developing similar or related lines of thought, in R. L. Martin, *Recent Essays on Truth and the Liar Paradox*. We saw that the idea was to retain semantic closure—as intuition demands—by taking seriously what is needed for a truth-value gap approach, to deny a truth-value to the Liar and its variants. We start a construction of a truth-predicate by assigning an initial empty interpretation and slowly refining it, expanding it, in a way which maintains consistency. That is, some propositions are made true, some false, and others neither. One might think that this exercise would continue indefinitely. But the nature of the construction is such that sooner or later the expansion will cease. There will be no more to add. In one sense, the construction will be complete—repeating it will add no more. But at the same time, the interpretation will be incomplete—it will be partial. The Liar paradox will not be given a value—it will be assigned neither to the set of truths nor to that of falsehoods.

It is an elegant solution. The cost is a certain schizophrenia: on the one hand, we proclaim that we have a semantically closed language, one containing its own truth-predicate; while on the other hand, we must resort to a meta-language to describe it, and to say, for example, that the Liar proposition is not true.

We have examined only a small number of the many attempts at solution which have at some time been suggested.

Nevertheless, they are representative of the different ways in which one may respond to these paradoxes. But as each attempt looks less attractive the further it is taken, another thought may occur. Could it not be that the semantic concepts which we use are inherently contradictory, and that our only mistake lies, not in misapplying those concepts in some way, but in adopting these concepts in the first place? Such a suggestion is similar in many ways to the first line of approach we examined, in that it entails that there is something inherently wrong in the self-referential application of semantic concepts. But it recalls the second in that its adoption would lead us to revise, not now our logic, but the truth principle, Tarski's T-scheme, which underpins our application of logic to the paradoxes. It is our choice whether to keep our old familiar semantic concepts, and continue to live with the semantic paradoxes; or whether to search for a brave new world of stability, from which the savagery of contradiction is banished.

7 Bald Men Forever: The Sorites Paradox

One must criticise [the New Academy] for employing an exceedingly captious kind of argument, of a sort that is usually by no means approved in philosophy—the method of proceeding by minute steps of gradual addition or withdrawal. They call this class of arguments *sorites* because by adding a single grain at a time they make a heap . . . No faculty of knowing absolute limits has been bestowed upon us by the nature of things to enable us to fix exactly how far to go in any matter; and this is so not only in the case of a heap of wheat from which the name is derived, but in no matter whatsoever—if we are asked by gradual stages, is such and such a person a rich man or a poor man, famous or undistinguished, are yonder objects many or few, great or small, long or short, broad or narrow, we do not know at what point in the addition or subtraction to give a definite answer. (Cicero, *Academica*, tr. H. Rackham, bk. 2. 49 and 92)

THE Sorites Paradox is usually attributed to Aristotle's contemporary, Eubulides, the Megarian philosopher who we noted in the previous chapter is also credited with inventing the purest form of the Liar paradox. The argument proceeds little by little to take us from truth to falsehood. For example, two are few, and three are few, and whatever number we have which is few, adding one more does not take us from few to many. So, by 9,998 steps, we reach the absurd conclusion that 10,000 are few. Or working by subtraction, a man with 10,000 hairs on his head is not bald, and removing only 1 hair cannot make him bald, so by 9,999 steps we find that a man with only one hair on his head (or even none!) is not bald. One stone does not make a heap, and adding only one stone to what is not yet a heap cannot make a heap. So heaps don't exist. Thus we have the paradoxes of the Bald Man and of the Heap, attributed to Eubulides.

The epithet 'sorites' is in fact a pun; in Greek it means 'heap'. It names not only one of the famous applications of the form of argument, concluding that either (by addition) 10,000 stones do not make a heap, or (by subtraction) that 1 stone does make a heap, but also the method of argument itself. For it proceeds by adding steps, steps which defy us to question them. If three are few, then surely four are few; given that four are few, it must follow that five are few; and so we go on, adding a heap of steps of the form 'if n are F then $n + 1$ are F' in the additive form, or 'if n are F then $n - 1$ are F' in the subtractive form. The argument is itself a heap, or sorites, of steps of *modus ponens*:

$F(0)$	$G(10,000)$
if $F(0)$ then $F(1)$	if $G(10,000)$ then $G(9,999)$
So $F(1)$	So $G(9,999)$
if $F(1)$ then $F(2)$	if $G(9,999)$ then $G(9,998)$
So $F(2)$	So $G(9,998)$
if ...	if ...
...	...
... so $F(10,000)$	... so $G(0)$.

Of course, whether one starts or stops at 0 and 10,000 is arbitrary. The point is to move by gradual steps, which are too small to affect the applicability of the predicate, F or G, from a case where the predicate clearly applies to one where it does not, thus engendering a contradiction. A man 1 m. tall is short; if a man 1 m. tall is short then a man 1 m. and 1 mm. (or one-thousandth of a millimetre, if necessary) is also short; and so on, picking an increase in height each time which cannot plausibly make a difference, to conclude that all men are short, even one 2 m., or 3 m. tall.

The classic form of the argument proceeds by a heap of applications of *modus ponens*. It needn't; the vital move can be achieved in one step of induction. For each major premiss of the *modus ponens* has the same form: 'if n are F so are $n + 1$'. Mathematical induction (see Chapter 2) takes us in one bound from $F(0)$ and 'for every n, if $F(n)$ then $F(n + 1)$' to 'for every n, $F(n)$' (or from $F(k)$ to 'for every n greater than k, $F(n)$'). Adding or subtracting one hair cannot make a difference to baldness; so since a man with no hair on his head is bald, it follows that all men are bald. Adding one stone to what is not a heap cannot create a heap; since one stone is not a heap, there are no heaps.

In whatever form, the challenge of the sorites argument is to identify a cut-off point. Two are few; 10,000 are not. Where does the cut-off point come? Is there a number, n, such that n are few but $n + 1$ are many? Is there a number of hairs such that a man with that number of hairs on his head is not bald, but with one less would be bald? Is there a number of stones which marks the cut-off point between what is a heap of stones and what is not? On the one hand, it seems absurd, and impossible, to point to a particular number as marking the dividing line; on the other, if there is no dividing line, the insidiousness of the sorites argument infers that 10,000 are few (or one is many), that hairless men are not bald, and so on.

Vagueness

The sorites argument gets its purchase from the fact that certain of our concepts are vague. As Cicero says, we cannot give a definite answer to when a poor man becomes rich, a short walk a long one, a narrow road a broad one, a hirsute man bald, and so on. Other concepts are precise. One cannot employ sorites reasoning against a concept like '1 m. 80 cm. tall' or 'uncle'. These concepts do not have grey areas of application, as 'rich', 'tall', 'bald', and so on do.

Max Black cautions us to distinguish vagueness from both ambiguity and generality. A word like 'bank' (money bank vs. river bank) or 'gag' (to stop a person's mouth vs. a joke) is ambiguous. It has two (or more) distinct meanings. That does not make it vague. Again, a word like 'chair' covers many possibilities—armchairs, dining chairs, dentist's chairs, Charles Rennie Mackintosh chairs, and so on—but is not in that regard vague. In fact, it is also vague; and what makes it vague is not its generality but the existence of borderline cases, a penumbra of cases where we are unsure if it correctly applies. It can be difficult to draw a line between what is a chair and what is not. That is where vagueness comes in; and where the sorites threatens.

We should also distinguish vagueness from another aspect of these expressions. What is large for a mouse is not large for an elephant—a large mouse is very much smaller than a small elephant. Such adjectives as 'large', 'few', 'tall', 'good', 'beautiful', are called 'attributive'. Few hairs on a man's head can be very many more in number than many people at an election meeting; a beautiful dancer may not be beautiful *simpliciter*; a tall man is shorter than a short lamppost. Again, this facet of these terms is distinct from the vagueness that characterizes many of them.

Frege and Russell thought that vagueness was undesirable, indeed, that it led to incoherence, and so must be removed from proper scientific, and logical, discourse. The incoherence can be given three forms. One derives from the sorites, extending a term with a vague boundary beyond it. Another derives from the Tarski T-scheme of Chapter 1: if we deny truth-value to attributions in the penumbra, the T-scheme will land us in contradiction. For suppose we wish to say, 'Fifteen are few' is neither true nor false. By the T-scheme, ' "Fifteen are few" is not true' is equivalent to 'Fifteen are not few', and ' "Fifteen are few" is not false' is equivalent to 'Fifteen are few'. So ' "Fifteen are few" is neither true nor false' is equivalent to 'Fifteen are both few and not few'. This is a contradiction. Thirdly, to call a range of application a penumbra means that it is not wrong to apply it there: it is wrong to say 10,000 are few (because false) and it is wrong (because nonsense) to say Beethoven is few; but it is not wrong to say fifteen are few. However, for the same reason it is not wrong to say fifteen are not few. Hence, it seems, there is nothing wrong with saying fifteen are both few and not few, again a contradiction.

One reaction to such arguments is to conclude that vagueness is a source of incoherence, and so should be removed. Note that there are two distinct claims here. First, there is the claim that a language containing vague expressions will be liable to incoherence and inconsistency; secondly, there is the presupposition that that incoherence can be eradicated. The above arguments only support the first of these claims. The latter assumes that any vague predicate can be replaced by (one or more) precise ones, and that in turn presupposes that the world itself is not vague, that the vagueness in certain terms in natural language resides in the term itself, not in what it refers to. The claim is that there are no vague objects.

For suppose there were. Indeed, suppose there are two vague objects, Everest and Gaurisanker (perhaps it is indeterminate quite where a mountain begins and ends) and it is indeterminate whether Everest and Gaurisanker are identical (for it is indeterminate whether their penumbras are the same). So Everest has the property of being indeterminately Gaurisanker. But Gaurisanker does not have that property—it is clear that Gaurisanker is Gaurisanker. Hence by the Indiscernibility of Identicals, Everest is not Gaurisanker (they have distinct properties). This contradicts the assumption that their identity was vague, which was a consequence of supposing there were such vague objects. So—it seems—there are no vague objects.

The early Wittgenstein took an even tougher line on this. He claimed that there are no vague expressions—'What we mean must be sharp', he said. Where Frege and Russell despaired of natural language for its incoherence and sought an ideal language, Wittgenstein argued that our language must, despite appearances, be already ideal. It does not appear to be. But it works; and no language which was incoherent in the way Frege and Russell said it was could work. 'It would be odd,' Wittgenstein wrote, 'if the human race had been speaking all this time without ever putting together a genuine proposition.' One way or another, whether by reform, or by proper recognition of what we already have, language must be precise, and vagueness is unacceptable.

Suppose then, that we have replaced 'bald', 'heap', and so on by precise terms, or are convinced that despite appearances, they are sharp. That means that the sorites is blocked by there being a sharp cut-off between correct application of each predicate and its misapplication. For example, suppose a bald man is henceforth to be one with fewer than 5,000 hairs on his head; a heap of wheat will require, say, 350 grains as a (precise) minimum; and 100 will be many (say, people at a political rally), ninety-nine not. The attributions of baldness and so on will now be precise, and have well-defined truth-value. What has been lost is our ability to know, in general, whether we have used them correctly. We are not usually aware, down to the exact number, how many hairs are on a particular head; we are not usually aware exactly how tall someone is, to the nearest millimetre. The present view replaces—or identifies—vagueness with ignorance. The problem was thought to be that a language containing (real) vagueness was incoherent; we must now ask whether a language without vagueness would be usable at all.

We have not yet addressed what we will find is the most taxing of all sorites examples, namely, colour predicates. In this example, we are presented with a linear array of colour patches, stretching from, at one end (the left, say), clear reds to, at the other, clear greens. If we cover all but two adjacent patches, we cannot discriminate them—they are too alike in colour and shade (for example, suppose they are temporarily removed from the array: we suppose that we could not, looking only at these two patches, decide which should be placed nearer the red end, which the green). Reflection on our experience with colours should convince us that this is possible. It may be necessary for there to be very many patches, so that each is different, and discriminably different, from a patch next but one, or next but ten, away from it, but indiscriminable from its closer neighbours. The point is that colours form a continuous display, and what is needed is a sufficient stretching of a normal spectrum of shades.

The set-up is ripe for the application of the sorites. The steps no longer work by the earlier quantification—the patches do not have intrinsic numbers (it is naïve to suppose all the colours, even between red and green, are a simple function of wavelength—red can be produced by many combinations of wavelength), but the principle is unaltered. The leftmost patch is clearly red. Its neighbour is indiscriminable from it, so how can we deny that it too is red; and so on. The first patch is red; and any patch indiscriminable from a red patch must itself be red. Hence, by many applications of *modus ponens*, or by induction, every patch in the display is red. But that is false. Those on the extreme right are clearly green, and not red at all.

According to the doctrine of vagueness as ignorance, the

sorites is blocked by the fact that at some point in the series there is a sharp cut-off. For some pair of (indiscriminable) adjacent patches, the left-hand one is red and the right-hand one is not. This doctrine, therefore, blocks the sorites by denying the major premiss (or one major premiss), that is, that a patch indiscriminable from a red patch is red. The thought that should give us pause is this: what is the fact of which we are supposedly ignorant? It is certainly true—or at least, we have no reason to doubt—that there is a difference in the light-reflecting quality of the adjacent patches. Suppose we designed instruments— they probably exist—for measuring this difference. We can take it that the difference is one that no perceiver, however fine his powers of discrimination, can detect—we have designed the sequence of patches accordingly. What should we do with the information gleaned from the instruments? Can they tell us what colour the patches are—that one of them is red and the other not?

There seems every reason to believe that they cannot do this, and this is because words like 'red' are observational predicates. 'Red' gets its meaning from being applied to and withheld from, objects of perception. The ground of our judgements of the correctness of applications of 'red' is observational. It is an interesting fact that some of our observational judgements are based on recognition of features of which we are not consciously aware. Subjects may be exposed subliminally to visual stimulation (in the famous cases of advertising, now banned, or in psychological experiments) which, while not evoking conscious awareness—even denial—of perception, can be shown to influence subsequent behaviour. So it is conceivable that we discover that individuals judge colour patches to be different in shade while admitting that they cannot see any difference. But that is here, *ex hypothesi*, not the case. The adjacent patches in question have been designed not to elicit such discriminations. Observational predicates are attributable on the basis of observation, and observation fails to discriminate between these adjacent patches. If one patch is red, and 'red' is an observational predicate, an observationally indistinguishable patch is also red.

Of course, the proponent of precisification, of replacing our vague terms by exact scientific ones, or the theorist who claims our terms must, despite appearances, be exact, is happy to allow this point. So much the worse for (an observational concept of) 'red', he will say. But there is no cure here for the sorites. First, it will rob us of the ability to apply terms 'just by looking'. We will need to carry meters and gauges around, to know when to apply 'red' and 'tall', just as we already do for 'radioactive' and 'poisonous'. But even if we were willing to stomach this impracticability, a second point is decisive: the sorites will reappear for distinctions beneath the level of discrimination of the meters and gauges, and our ability to measure with them.

We have vague terms in our language for a very good reason, namely, that our recognitional capacities, however enhanced by instrumentation, cannot make indefinitely fine discriminations. We can introduce precise terms into the language, for example, 'over 1 m. 85': we recognize that, in certain cases, we may be unsure—ignorant—whether the term correctly applies or not. Depending what hangs on it, we may employ more or less stringent techniques of measurement. But these terms rest on the back of vague terms, terms which have positive cases, negative cases, and in between a range of cases where we are unsure of their correct application, an uncertainty which depends not on ignorance of the facts, but on the true vagueness of the term.

Analysis of the Sorites

If we accept that vagueness is endemic to our language, must we surrender to the sorites and incoherence, or was there a fault in the arguments which we overlooked? The drive to precisification depended on three arguments, one of which was the sorites, whose devastating conclusion we accepted perhaps too readily. Let us look first at the other two arguments, starting with the last one, that it is not wrong to deny both a term and its contrary of items in the penumbra.

What we need is a distinction, and it is often described as that between internal and external negation. However, that terminology alludes to a scope distinction which is not present. None the less, it is a distinction we need more generally in other cases where scope is not operative. Consider the sentence, 'Virtue is but'; it is not well formed, and does not express a proposition. One way to say this is to reply, 'Virtue is not but'. Of course, in one sense, if 'Virtue is but' is nonsense, so too is 'Virtue is not but'. In another, 'not' serves as an 'external' negation, to express in what is sometimes called the material mode of speech (following Carnap)—'Virtue is not but'—what in the formal mode would be expressed as ' "Virtue is but" is not significant'.

The same point applies, though as regards vagueness, not significance, to 'Fifteen are not few'. As an 'internal' negation, 'Fifteen are not few' means that fifteen are many; as an external negation, it means that it is not correct to say that fifteen are few. The mistake in the earlier argument comes, therefore, when we said 'for the same reason it is not wrong to say fifteen are not few'. The sense in which it is not wrong to say fifteen are not few is 'external'—'few' does not correctly apply to fifteen. But the sense in which it is not wrong to say fifteen are few is 'internal'—'many', that is 'not few' does not apply to fifteen. So the conclusion that fifteen are both few and not few equivocates—they are few because it would be wrong to say they were many (internal negation) and they're not few because it would be wrong to say they were few (external negation). If this is confusing, try it in the formal mode of speech. The sense in which fifteen are not few is that 'Fifteen are few' is penumbral. So we cannot infer that fifteen are many—the 'not' in 'Fifteen are not few' is not the normal denial of their being few, but the material mode expression of the vagueness of 'Fifteen are few'.

This distinction also clears up the second argument, the one using the T-scheme, and serves additionally to resolve a problem we have postponed from Chapters 5 and 6. The problem is whether the minimalist theory of truth which I supported at the end of Chapter 1 is compatible with the denials of Bivalence in Chapters 5 and 6, in particular, with not identifying Bivalence with Excluded Middle. Is there not a quick argument from Excluded Middle (that 'A or not-A' is always true, whatever A is) to Bivalence (that every proposition is true or false, that is, A is true or false, whatever A is) using the T-scheme? From

'*A* or not-*A*', we derive '*A* is true or "not-*A*" is true' by the T-scheme, and so '*A* is true or *A* is false' by the equivalence between ' "not-*A*" is true' and '*A* is false'.

If *A* does not express a proposition, then there is no problem. Excluded Middle applies only to propositions, and so sentences which do not express propositions can coherently be said to express neither true nor false propositions. But in Chapter 5 we considered expressions containing empty names, and wished both to concede their significance (that they expressed propositions) and to deny truth-value of them. So too in Chapter 6, in truth-value gap approaches such as Kripke's. And again here; we wish to accept that attributions of vague terms to items in the penumbra do not result in propositions with clear truth-value, while accepting that a proposition is expressed. For example, 'Fifteen are few' expresses a proposition which is neither true nor false. But when we say ' "Fifteen are few" is not true' is equivalent to 'Fifteen are not few', 'not' here is external negation; and when we say ' "Fifteen are few" is not false' is equivalent to 'Fifteen are few', we have collapsed internal and external negation. Here are the successive steps, with 'NOT' for external negation, and 'not' for internal negation:

> 'Fifteen are few' is neither true nor false
> so 'Fifteen are few' is not true and 'Fifteen are few' is not false
> so fifteen are NOT few and 'Fifteen are not few' is not true
> so fifteen are NOT few and fifteen are NOT not few.

The contradiction only ensues on identifying 'NOT not few' with 'few', whereas it simply means 'NOT many', that is, it is not correct to say fifteen are many. To say 'Fifteen are neither few nor not few' looks contradictory, until we realize that it expresses the fact that fifteen falls in the penumbra. Neither of the attributions 'few' nor 'many' properly applies to fifteen. Fifteen are NOT few and NOT many.

What has to give in the quick argument to Bivalence, therefore, is what we noted at the end of Chapter 6: that the T-scheme can no longer be stated as an equivalence, but that *A* and 'it is true that *A*' will have the same value, or both lack value together. Otherwise we will identify 'not-A' with both 'it is true that not-A' (i.e. 'A is false') and 'it is not true that A' (i.e. 'A is false or truth-valueless'). That is, we would allow 'not-A' to equivocate between internal and external negation.

Thus neither the second nor the third argument succeeds in showing that the acceptance of vague terms leads to inconsistency and incoherence. What, however, of the first argument, the sorites itself? First, a minor quibble, then a more substantial point.

The sorites gets its force from the major premiss, for example, that removing one stone from a heap does not stop it being a heap, or removing one hair from a hirsute man does not make him bald. However, the explanation of this may not be so much a tolerance, as it is often called, in the terms 'heap' and 'bald', that they refer to anything sufficiently similar to anything they refer to, and so do not refer to a specific and exact number of stones or hairs, as that the number of stones or hairs is simply irrelevant to their application, that 'heap' and 'bald' do not refer to a number of stones or hairs at all. We judge whether a collection of stones is a heap not by reference to even an approximate number of stones in the pile, but by virtue of their configuration. It is the disposition and layout of the stones which is relevant, not their number. Of course, there is a connection— a contingent and accidental connection—between their number and their configuration. Recall the game of 'pick-a-stick'. Taking one straw from a heap can result in the total collapse of the heap. Once the straws are spread over the table, there is no heap. None the less, there may still be enough straws to build a new heap. What makes it a heap is their configuration, not their number.

Plucking hairs from the scalp is different, but the point is the same. It is the overall distribution of hairs on the head which distinguishes the bald from the not bald. An insufficient number of hairs will not usually permit a sufficient covering of the scalp to avoid the charge of baldness; but even 10,000 hairs, if they are all clustered round the base leaving the top bare, will not avoid it.

I call this a minor quibble, for I do not think it defuses the sorites challenge. But it should be borne in mind, for allowing the sorites to be sloppily presented may obscure for us its true solution. Great care is needed in identifying the crucial fallacy in the argument.

A more major point is this: the major premiss of the sorites reads, 'for every n, if n is F then $n + 1$ is F'. It is supported by the claim that if it were false, there would be a sharp cut-off, a pair k and $k + 1$ such that k is F and $k + 1$ is not F, a cut-off which is counter-intuitive—between few and many, between small and large, short and tall, and so on. Our examination of conditionals in Chapter 3 should have alerted us to the fallacy here. It assumes that conditionals are truth-functional, and as we saw in that chapter, this component of the classical view of logic is implausible and nowadays widely rejected. (Apart from a few recidivists, the logical world is roughly evenly divided between apologists—usually invoking the name of 'Grice'—and radicals, ranging from Stalnaker through to those who claim conditionals do not even express propositions.) Recall the slow argument for the truth-functionality of conditionals from Chapter 3. First, a counterexample shows the conditional false: given A and not-B, it follows that 'if A then B' is false. Secondly, if A is false, or if B is true, then 'A and not-B' is false, and so 'if A then B' is true. (This second step can be spelled out, slowly, by *Ex Falso Quodlibet*, Simplification, and Conditionality.) That is, the claim that conditionals are truth-functional says that not only is a counterexample sufficient for the falsity of the conditional, it is also necessary—in other words, if there is no counterexample ('A and not-B' is false) then the conditional is true. That is exactly the move made by the sorites (as presently formulated): if the conditional ('if n is F then $n + 1$ is F') is false, then there must be a counterexample, where n is F and $n + 1$ is not. If we accept this move in the sorites, then we admit the necessity of a counterexample to the falsity of the conditional, in which case we are committed to treating conditionals truth-functionally.

How can a conditional be false without a counterexample? This is the classical challenge, which leads to truth-functionality. The reply is that the truth of a conditional requires more than simply a favourable distribution of truth-values. It requires a connection of some sort between antecedent and consequent.

If that connection is lacking, even if the actual truth-values do not yield a counterexample, the conditional is false. This is as true on, for example, the similarity and probability theories, as on any relevantist account. If A is false, but an 'A and not-B'-world is closer than any 'A and B'-world, the conditional is false (on Stalnaker's account), even though the counterexample is only possible, not actual. Again, if $p(B/A)$ is low, even though $p(B)$ is greater than $p(A)$, the conditional is false (or improbable)—let A be 'you are dealt an ace' and B be 'you are dealt a heart'. $p(B/A) = \frac{1}{4}$; you may none the less receive the ace of hearts.

However, the similarity and probability theories still entail a sharp cut-off. The reason is that, as we noted in Chapter 3, they identify the value of a conditional with true antecedent with the value of its consequent. If A is true, then on both those theories 'if A then B' is true if and only if B is. Now $A(0)$ is true; and the succession of applications of *modus ponens* makes $A(n + 1)$ true whenever $A(n)$ and 'if $A(n)$ then $A(n + 1)$' are true. Take the smallest k for which 'if $A(k)$ then $A(k + 1)$' is false. ('Small' may be vague; but 'smallest' is sharp.) Then $A(k)$ is true, and so, by the above reasoning, $A(k + 1)$ must be false. That is, the similarity and probability theories entail a sharp cut-off. Only by rejecting the idea (as in Chapter 3 I argued we should) that 'if A then B' is true whenever A and B are both true, can one resist the step from the falsity of the conditional to the existence of a sharp cut-off.

If one accepts this point, then it does not follow that if there is no sharp cut-off, each of the conditionals is true. All the sorites needs is a starting point (usually uncontentious) and a uniform sequence of conditionals. To obtain the latter, it trades on a reluctance actually to deny the conditional—for a variety of reasons, as we have seen. First, there is the sensitivity to context. One cannot actually deny that if 10,000 is many, then one fewer is still many, for in general, without a specific context, this is true. Secondly, there is the irrelevance of the numbers involved. One cannot deny that if a man with only 3,000 hairs on his head is bald, so too is one with 3,001—for one envisages the distribution as similar, and the extra hair is unnoticeable.

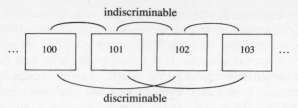

indiscriminable

... | 100 | 101 | 102 | 103 | ...

discriminable

FIG. 7.1

But it is the distribution which counts, not the number. Thirdly, one is in a weak position to deny that if *n* stones don't make a heap neither do *n* + 1 if one cannot exhibit a heap of *n* + 1 stones no proper subset of which can make a heap, especially if, as the second point emphasizes, the number of stones is only accidentally (and so probably contingently on the size and shape of the stones) related to their heap-building quality. Finally, yet another equivocation is employed to help the sorites along.

Take our series of colour patches, shading indiscriminately from red to green. Studying an adjacent pair in isolation, we cannot discriminate one from the other. None the less we can certainly discriminate the leftmost patch (red) from the rightmost (green). It follows that the patches can be discriminated. Let us say that if two patches considered in isolation are indiscriminable, they are first-order indiscriminable (for short, indiscriminable). If there is a third patch from which one can be discriminated but the other cannot, they are second-order discriminable. Here is an argument to show that the patches of our series, while first-order indiscriminable, are second-order discriminable. Start with the simplest case: adjacent patches are (first-order) indiscriminable, but each patch can be discriminated (first-order) from the next but one patch (in each direction)—see Fig. 7.1. So patches 100 and 101 are (in isolation) indiscriminable, as are 101 and 102, and so on. But 100 and 102 are (taken in isolation, i.e. first-order) discriminable, as are 101 and 103 and so on. Then each adjacent pair is (second-order) discriminable. For example, take pair 101 and 102. 101 is indiscriminable from 100 while 102 can be discriminated from it. Hence we have a means,

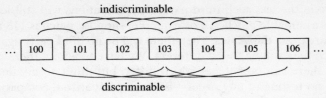

FIG. 7.2

namely, comparison with 100, to discriminate 101 from 102; and so on for each adjacent pair.

The change in shade over the series may be finer and more subtle, however. Suppose that not only may each patch not be (first-order) discriminated from its immediate neighbours, but also from the next-but-one patch too—see Fig. 7.2. So, for example, patch 103 cannot be discriminated from 101, 102, 104, or 105, but it can be (in isolation) discriminated from 100 and 106. Then 103 can be discriminated, at second-order, from 102, by for example, comparison with patch 100. For 102 cannot be discriminated from 100, while *ex hypothesi*, 103 can.

Again, the shading may be finer and more subtle than this. None the less, there are only finitely many patches, and certainly red and green can be discriminated at first-order. So there must be a maximal value to the length of indiscriminable chains—two in our first example (100 and 101; 101 and 102; and so on), three in our second (100, 101, and 102; 101, 102, and 103; and so on)—chains no members of which may be distinguished from others in the chain by isolated inspection. Suppose it is twenty, say. Then patches 119 and 120 can be discriminated at second-order by the fact that 119 is not first-order discriminable from 100, while patch 120 is; and so on for each pair of patches.

If we think about our practice with colour discriminations, we will recognize that such 'third-party' or second-order comparisons are an integral part of our ability to make colour-judgements. Not only colour-judgements, too. We perform similar comparisons in order to discriminate the heights of different people—indeed, use of a ruler is effectively that very 'third-party'.

None the less such third-party discriminations will still leave indiscriminable patches. For example, suppose patches 118 and 119 are exact duplicates. Then there will be no third party against which they will be found different. We have to admit, therefore, that there can be patches which differ, but differ so minimally that no testing of any order—isolated comparison, comparison against a third-party which is first-order discriminable from one but not the other, third-party testing against a patch only second-order discriminable from one but not from the other, and so on—which can discriminate them. Even with higher and higher orders of comparisons, certain differences may be so small as to elude our powers of discrimination. That is when the sorites can re-enter. It is not yet defeated.

Fuzzy Logic

The picture we have so far is this: between the clear positive cases of application of certain concepts and equally clear negative cases (e.g. of 'tall' or 'red' or 'few') there is a fuzzy area, a penumbra of borderline cases. In the borderline cases we are unsure whether the concept applies or not. This has prompted the development of a theory of fuzzy sets, and a companion 'fuzzy logic'. I think we can show it is mistaken, and not the right route to follow—the right route being to take further the idea of indiscriminability. But it is instructive to consider the theory of fuzziness first. It has, it seems, made an important contribution to the theory of expert systems. It does not, however, provide a satisfactory resolution of the sorites paradox.

Naïve set theory treats of the extensions of concepts within a given universe of discourse or domain—for each well-defined concept there is a set of things in the universe of discourse which fall under it. Paradoxes similar to those we looked at in Chapter 6 place a limit on the applicability of such notions outwith a specified domain (we'll look at a couple in Chapter 8). Provided we steer clear of fairly well understood paradoxical cases (e.g. the set of all sets which are not members of themselves) we can give a coherent theory of extensions. But the theory assumes that concepts are precise and exact. It must be clear and determinate whether or not a particular object belongs to a particular set. Orthodox sets are precise and exact. There is the set of things which belong to it, and the complement (within the universe of discourse) of those which do not.

Fuzzy sets divide their universe of application into three parts, the positive, the negative, and a (usually graduated) borderline. We can think of orthodox sets as mappings or functions from a concept to the values 'true' and 'false' (or 1 and 0, perhaps). An object x belongs to an orthodox set A if the 'value' of 'x belongs to A'—let's write it '$A(x)$'—is 1, and does not belong if $A(x)$ is 0. For all objects in the universe of discourse, U, it must be determinate that $A(x)$ is 1 or 0. Orthodox sets can, therefore, be seen as a limiting case of fuzzy sets. For a theory of fuzzy sets, take a set of values, V. V might consist of the two values 'true' and 'false' alone (the limit case), or of three values, 0, 1 and $\frac{1}{2}$, say, or of all real numbers between 0 and 1, [0,1]—and even more elaborate sets of values are possible. A fuzzy set, A, is a mapping defined over U, the universe of discourse, which assigns to every object x in U, a value $A(x)$ from V. Consider the predicate 'tall', for example. We could assign to 'tall' the function $(x-1)^2$ from people's height (in metres) to the real interval [0,1]. Thus someone 2 m. tall would be tall to degree 1, unquestionably tall; someone 1 m. tall would be tall to degree 0, that is, not tall at all. In between, a person of height 1.8 m. (about 6 feet) would be tall to degree 0.64, that is, quite tall. Each of our sorites predicates, 'tall', 'red', 'few', and so on, can be seen as defining not an orthodox set, but a fuzzy set, distinguishing clear positive case (value 1), clear negative cases (value 0) and a range of unclear or fuzzy cases in between, with intermediate values.

Besides fuzzy predicates, which define fuzzy sets, there are also fuzzy quantifiers and fuzzy modifiers. For example, there is no exact number or proportion of As which must be Bs, for most As to be Bs (one could redefine it to be half the As plus 1; but that would be an orthodox precisifying move). 'Most' and 'few' are fuzzy quantifiers. 'Usually' is a fuzzy modifier. If we say 'Usually, few people in the audience have red hair,' there is a vagueness introduced not only by the fuzzy predicate 'red-haired' and the fuzzy quantifier 'few', but also by the phrase 'usually'—most performances follow this pattern, but no exact proportion. Fuzzy logic and fuzzy arithmetic are an attempt to mark out a systematic theory of these quantifiers and modifiers. Frege, in his dismissal of vagueness, claimed that mathematicians deal only with exact and precise notions. This is not true: for example, a theorem of (orthodox) number theory states that 'round numbers are very rare'. A round number is one which is the product of a considerable number of comparatively small factors. Thus 'round' is a fuzzy predicate of numbers, 'rare' is a fuzzy quantifier, and 'very' is a fuzzy modifier. None the less, one can give a precise proof of their connection.

Fuzzy logic and the theory of fuzzy sets do not help with the sorites, however. First, note the strangeness on a fuzzy theory of requiring that precise values be assigned to the degree to which an object is tall or red. Actually, although this often appears in presentations of the idea, it is not essential. One can take any set in place of V as the set of values—they can be linguistic values, for example, 'a bit', 'not very', and so on. This looks rather more plausible as a model for our practice—we can't say 'This patch has degree of redness $\frac{\pi}{4}$' or 'This person is tall to degree 0.81'. Degrees are fuzzy. An ordinal scale is all that is needed. But this is a symptom of a larger difficulty. The smoothness and continuity of [0,1] as the set of values masks a quite implausible discreteness in the assignments. What is to be the borderline? One suggestion is all members, x, of U for which $A(x)$ lies between 0 and 1; another is all those for which $A(x)$ lies between certain non-extremal values α and β, i.e. $0 < \alpha < \beta < 1$. But whatever values are picked, the consequence is an implausible sharp cut-off between the positive and negative values and the borderline. Not only indeed, is such a cut-off implausible—consider the colour patches, starting with clear reds at the left; there is no first patch which is not clearly red—but such a sharp cut-off, not now between A and not-A, but between A and not-A and the borderline, will be equally unobservable, clashing with the recognition (against the precisifiers) that our practice treats certain predicates as observational.

This fuzziness to the borderline of the borderline is usually called the phenomenon of 'higher-order vagueness'. Not only is there a borderline of 'quite tall' between tall and not-tall, the boundary between tall and quite tall is itself blurred. There is no least height to which 'tall' applies or greatest height to which it doesn't, whatever the qualification introduced to modify it. There is no way in which the functional basis of fuzzy set theory can accommodate this. It cannot be done by varying the range of the function (the set of values, V). It is endemic to the fact that the domain of the function (the set of heights) is a linear ordering of points. We will see that the solution comes from changing the conception of the members of the set, not from introducing a fuzziness by talking of their degree of membership.

There are logical problems, too. Consider the form of the sorites, either proceeding by successive steps of *modus ponens*, or by an induction (perhaps followed by the extraction of an instance—'. . . so all the patches are red, and so this green patch is red'). The major premises have the form 'if $A(n)$ then $A(n + 1)$'. When n belongs to the borderline, the truth of $A(n)$ is slightly greater than that of $A(n + 1)$—that is, n is A to a higher degree than is $n + 1$. So it is natural to say that each conditional is slightly less than wholly true. Each conditional is true to degree δ, where δ is close to, but less than 1, just as $n + 1$ is A to degree γ, where γ lies between 0 and 1 and is slightly less than (perhaps δ less than) the degree to which n is A.

We start with $A(0)$, which is true to degree 1 (*ex hypothesi*). We then apply a succession of steps of *modus ponens*, to reach, say,

$$\frac{A(0), \text{if } A(0) \text{ then } A(1), \text{if } A(1) \text{ then } A(2), \ldots, \text{if } A(k-1) \text{ then } A(k)}{\text{So } A(k)}$$

$A(0)$ is wholly true; each of the other premises is close to truth—as close as we like, by making the differences between n and $n + 1$ as small as necessary. But $A(k)$ is very small (or 0). So we have a choice: we can either make the joint truth of the premises 0, or we can deny that the inference is valid. The latter requires denying the validity of *modus ponens*. That is the true cost of fuzzy logic, for we will see that it cannot take the first option. The reason is the link with the theory of fuzzy sets.

Naïve set theory consists for the most part of an account of the combination of and relationships between sets. Given two sets, A and B, we can form their union, $A \cup B$, the set whose members are those objects in either A or in B; their intersection, $A \cap B$, whose members are those things common to A and B; and their difference, $A - B$, those things in A but not in B. Note that $A \cup B = B \cup A$, $A \cap B = B \cap A$, but obviously $A - B \neq B - A$. The complement of A, written A', is $U - A$, those things in the universe of discourse not in A. Fuzzy set theory seeks to define analogous operations on fuzzy sets. If A and B are fuzzy sets, their intersection, $A \cap B$, is defined by a membership function $f_{A \cap B}$ from $A \cap B$ to V, related to the membership functions defining A and B separately. How should $f_{A \cap B}$ be defined? Let us suppose, for simplicity, that $V = [0,1]$, the real interval, as before. There are three plausible proposals for the definition of $f_{A \cap B}$. The first is, that the operations $\cap$, $\cup$, and so on should behave in the same way as the analogous operations on probability functions. Recall that $p(A \text{ and } B) = p(A).p(B/A)$, where A and B are propositions; $p(A \text{ or } B) = p(A) + p(B)$, provided A and B are independent, this is, A entails not-B. That identifies the first problem: the probabilistic equations do not determine $p(A \text{ and } B)$ or $p(A \text{ or } B)$, they only constrain them. To follow the probabilistic model would not permit a uniform account of union, intersection, and so on for fuzzy sets. The second problem concerns the borderline. $p(A \text{ and not-}A) = 0$, for all A. But if A is fuzzy, there will be a fuzzy overlap between A and not-A, where something is both A and not-A to some degree. The degree distributions do not function like probabilistic distributions.

Another proposal is that $f_{A \cap B} = f_A.f_B$, the product of the separate defining functions. This will give the right answer for *modus ponens* (keep it valid) but the wrong answer for sets. Consider $A \cap A$. Clearly, the intersection of a set with itself should be unchanged: $A \cap A = A$. But $f_{A \cap A} = f_{A \cdot A} = f_A^2$ by this second account and in general $f_A \neq f_A^2$. So we cannot define intersection by the product. This is unfortunate, for this proposal would make the premiss of the above *modus ponens* inference tend to zero (as intuitively it should) the more conditionals it contained. If the degree of truth of 'if $A(n)$ then $A(n + 1)$' is, say, $\delta < 1$, then for any $\varepsilon > 0$ however small, there is a number k such that $\delta^k < \varepsilon$. That is, the degree of truth of a conjunction of enough not quite true premises will be nearly zero. If we could take the product of degrees of truth of the premises of the *modus ponens*, we could keep the *modus ponens* step valid, that is, the degree of truth of its premises would be less than that of its conclusion, and still explain why green is not red.

The same goes for the inductive form of the sorites, where the premises are $A(0)$ and 'for every n, if $A(n)$ then $A(n + 1)$'. A universal quantification 'for every n', is essentially a long conjunction, so the truth of this premiss would be practically zero, just like the conclusion. But conjunction cannot work by the product—on pain of not giving an adequate set theory. The only plausible proposal for $f_{A \cap B}$ for fuzzy set theory is Min (f_A, f_B), that is, that $f_{A \cap B}$ takes the value of the least of f_A and f_B. Then $f_{A \cup B} = \text{Max}(f_A, f_B)$, and $f_{A'} = 1 - f_A$. Fuzzy set theory now proceeds apace; but *modus ponens* is the casualty. The degree of truth of its premises (in the sorites) is greater than that of its conclusion. If the value of each conditional, 'if $A(n)$ then $A(n + 1)$' is at least δ (and that of $A(0)$ is 1), then the degree of truth of all the premises is still δ, that is, Min $(1, \delta)$, but that of the conclusion is (close to) zero. Similarly for induction: the degree of truth of 'for every n, if $A(n)$ then $A(n + 1)$' is δ, close to 1, but that of $A(k)$ is zero, for large enough k.

Of course, as should be clear from previous chapters, no rule of inference, even *modus ponens*, is unquestionably correct. We have ourselves challenged *ex falso quodlibet*, Disjunctive Syllogism (and so, implicitly, *modus ponens* or detachment for material, that is, truth-functional, implication), Existential Generalization and so on. But fuzzy logic does not provide a clear logical rationale for its rejection. Suppose we had no conditional, and consequently no sorites paradox. What would the objection be to introducing a new connective (the conditional 'implies') by the rule that one could assert 'A implies B' whenever one could derive B from A? For then *modus ponens* would be valid for 'implies'; that is, whenever both 'A implies

grid of discriminations

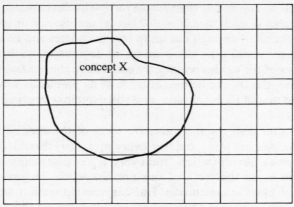

F ɪ G. 7.3

B' and *A* were assertible, one would be justified in asserting *B* (for *A* has been asserted, and the fact that '*A* implies *B*' is assertible shows that we can derive *B* from it). But that would land us immediately in the sorites paradox. To object to the introduction of such a connective simply on the ground that it leads to paradox would be entirely *ad hoc*. There would be no explanation or diagnosis of the problem. Yet the claim by fuzzy logic that *modus ponens* is invalid is no different.

This rather lengthy analysis of the treatment of the sorites in fuzzy logic confirms the initial point. Fuzzy logic and fuzzy set theory do not give the correct account of vague predicates. A different account of the nature of predicates like 'tall', 'red', and 'few' must be given, better respecting the fuzziness of their borderlines.

Tolerance

What fuzziness suggests is that the grid which we place over reality does not correspond precisely to our concepts. There is a certain thickness in our ability to discriminate, but our concepts are not definable in terms of it (see Fig. 7.3). This picture has led to the development of the notion of 'rough set', whose members, rather than membership relation, are fuzzy. What the sorites shows us is that many of our concepts pick out rough sets, sets that do not correspond to clearly distinguishable classes of elements. Take a universe of discourse, U, and a relation, R, over it. U might be a set of coloured patches, or of men, or of numbers. R is a tolerance relation, that is, it groups together elements of U which cannot be discriminated. R must be reflexive (each element is indiscriminable from itself) and symmetric (if one element is indiscriminable from another, the latter is indiscriminable from the former). For each element x in U, let $[x]_R$ be the set of members of U related by R to x (i.e. indiscriminable from x). For example, R might be 'having the same number of hairs' over the universe of men, so that R divides the universe of discourse up into equivalence classes—an exhaustive and exclusive covering of the universe. In this case, R is also transitive, so that it is an equivalence relation, which familiarly provides a set of elementary classes in U whereby each member of U belongs to one and only one equivalence class.

However, there is no special reason why the elementary classes should be disjoint, providing they cover U. For example, if U is the set of integers, R might relate any number x to those numbers differing from x by at most 5. Then R divides U into as many elementary classes as there are integers, each containing 11 members. Recall also our example of colour patches: the relation of indiscriminability—even when modified by third-party discriminability—breaks the series up into a succession of overlapping sets, probably with varying numbers of members. The picture we gave (Fig. 7.3) of the elementary classes over a domain showed disjoint equivalence classes. In the case of colour patches (or of numbers), the picture is more like that in Fig. 7.4. In a two-dimensional array, one would have overlapping circles or ellipses: see Fig. 7.5. Let R be a tolerance relation, and $[x]_R$ for all x in U be the elementary sets in U. Then the elementary sets cover U, but do not necessarily divide it into disjoint classes.

A subset X of U is definable if X is the union of a set of elementary sets in U; otherwise it is not definable. The rough sets are those which are not so definable. A rough set, X, can

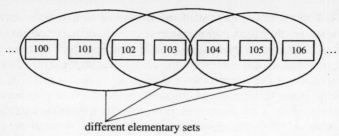

different elementary sets

FIG. 7.4

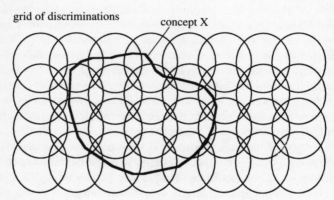

grid of discriminations   concept X

FIG. 7.5

only be approximated by elementary sets. The upper approximation of X is the union of elementary sets of U each of which contains a member of X; its lower approximation is the union of all elementary sets of U wholly contained in X. The lower approximation of 'red' consists of those objects which are definitely red. The upper approximation contains things which are arguably not red. Red itself is a rough set. That is the lesson of the sorites. There are elementary sets on the borderline of 'red' which contain elements which, on the one hand, cannot be discriminated, and, on the other, fall on opposite sides of the divide between red and not-red.

In the case of colour predicates, the elementary sets are shades. Michael Dummett and others have argued that the notion of shade is incoherent—at least if, as seems at first plausible, it has three properties:

1. discriminably different objects have different shades:
2. objects not discriminably different have the same shade; and
3. no object has more than one shade.

The third clause needs clarifying: no object has more than one shade at a given point on its surface, at a given time, to a particular observer, in normal—or at least, constant—lighting conditions. In fact, however, it is the third clause which must be given up. For indiscriminability is non-transitive, as we saw. It is a tolerance relation, and tolerance relations divide their domain into overlapping elementary classes.

It follows that we must deny the major premiss of the sorites. It is false that adding 1, or moving from one patch of colour to the one to its right, cannot take us from 'few' to 'many', from 'bald' to 'not bald', from 'red' to 'yellow'. Yet, that does not mean that concepts have sharp edges, that there is a sharp cut-off. The edge is blurred by the fact that it runs through classes of indiscriminable elements. Sorites predicates mark out rough sets. Near their borderlines, sorites predicates are only approximated by elementary sets. But rough sets cannot be defined by elementary sets—they fall short of the union of all elementary sets containing any of their members, their upper approximation. The upper approximation contains objects which do not fall under the concept, yet contains nothing which does not belong to the same elementary class as something which does fall under it—that is, nothing for which there is not something indiscriminable from it which falls under the concept.

It seemed earlier that we must deny this, on pain of making predicates like 'red' non-observational. The idea was that observational predicates must extend to everything indiscriminable from what they extend to. That thought is indeed what drives the sorites—and so it is incoherent. Observational predicates must work differently from how we might initially suppose. Here is a suggestion: observational predicates (and others too, but concentrate on the observational for now) work by locating paradigms, and by contrasting paradigms of contraries. 'Few' and 'many' are a pair, as are 'large' and 'small', 'tall' and 'short'. Colour predicates constitute a whole system of contrasting paradigms: 'red', 'blue', 'green', 'yellow', 'brown', and so on. If one looks at a colour array—set out two-dimensionally, say on the surface of a cylinder as it often is—one sees a continuous variation of colour. If one were to map indiscriminability classes on to that surface, one would obtain an overlapping set of patches—distinct shades. The two lessons of the sorites are, first, that the shades overlap, second, that the main colour descriptions are not definable by shades—there is no set of shades whose union maps out any of those colours. For those indiscriminability classes have sharp borders, which the colours lack.

A final point about higher-order vagueness. The upper and lower approximations of a concept, on this model, have sharp edges. But earlier we argued that the borderline of a concept must itself be fuzzy. Can rough sets have rough borderlines? Shifting attention from a concept to its borderline involves a change of focus, to speak metaphorically. But that metaphor contains the answer. There are different tolerance relations for different contexts and purposes. If all I want to know is whether someone is short or tall, my measuring stick can be quite crude. If asked whether he is quite tall, or hardly tall at all, or really tall, I have to be more accurate. If asked more precise questions about his height, I have to refine my methods and my discriminations still further. Higher-order vagueness can be modelled in the language of rough sets, and consists in varying the size of the tolerance mesh.

Summary and Guide to Further Reading

The sorites takes the form of a succession of applications of *modus ponens*, or of an induction, leading us from a clear example of application of a concept, say 'child', by a succession of barely discernible moves—anyone who is a child after n heartbeats, will be a child after $n + 1$ heartbeats—to a clear example of incorrect application—nonagenarians are children, everyone is a child.

An exemplary survey of the sorites argument in the ancient world was given by Jonathan Barnes, 'Medicine, Experience and Logic'.

We noted in Chapter 6 that in response to a paradox one can deny one or more premisses, reject the inferential move itself, or seek to find the conclusion palatable after all. The third option is no more available here than it was in the case of Curry's paradox—the conclusion trivializes the concepts involved, and must be rejected.

Fuzzy logic rejects the inferential move—it claims that the sorites shows that *modus ponens* is not universally valid. The combined premisses, though each less than wholly true, are close in degree to truth, both individually and jointly—for in conjunction, the minimum of the conjoined degrees must be taken, properly to define the intersection in fuzzy set theory. But the conclusion is false. *Modus ponens* is seen as permitting the degree of truth of the premisses to fall—not greatly, but enough for its validity to be impugned. Sufficiently many reductions, by accumulating a heap of applications of *modus ponens*, leads eventually to the falsity of the conclusion, that 10,000 are few, or that a green patch is red. The classic presentation is by J. Goguen, 'The Logic of Inexact Concepts', building on Zadeh's original idea of 1965. A useful collection of Zadeh's papers is found in *Fuzzy Sets and Applications*, ed. R. Yager.

But this reaction to the sorites is *ad hoc*—no general theory of the conditional and its behaviour in inference is forthcoming—and coupled to the other drawbacks of the fuzzy set-theoretic approach, suggests we have not here found the real cause of the sorites phenomenon. Other diagnoses focus on the major premiss, the propositions of the form 'if $A(n)$ then $A(n + 1)$', or in its most virulent form, 'if a is F and b is indiscriminable from a then b is F'. Certain concepts appear to be vague, and drawing an exact boundary to them is impossible. In addition to clear positive and negative cases there is a penumbra, a borderline region. The sorites insidiously extends the predicate across this boundary, by daring us to draw a line, to identify a cut-off point beyond our powers of discrimination.

Frege and Russell believed this showed that our everyday

language was incoherent, needing to be replaced by an ideal language of precise and exact concepts. J. van Heijenoort surveys Frege's arguments in 'Frege and Vagueness' in his *Selected Essays*. But van Heijenoort does not distinguish carefully enough between vagueness and distinct though similar phenomena of ambiguity, generality, and so on, distinctions brought out by Max Black in his paper, 'Vagueness'. This accusation of incoherence against vague concepts was repeated in the 1970s by Michael Dummett in 'Wang's Paradox', in a special issue of *Synthese* (1975) containing other papers on vagueness by e.g. Fine, Wright, and Zadeh. Wang's paradox applies the sorites to the concept 'small number', to conclude that all numbers are small. Crispin Wright has extended this argument to a full-scale attack on a common account of the idea that language is rule-governed: see his 'Further Reflections on the Sorites Paradox'.

If vague concepts really are incoherent, one valiant approach is to deny that our language contains any such predicates. Perhaps the sorites results from simple ignorance—there is always a sharp cut-off point, it is only that we do not know where it comes. Some number is small and its immediate successor large, some number of stones is insufficient to form a heap and one more suffices, and so on. Tim Williamson gave an able defence of such a solution in 'Vagueness and Ignorance'. An alternative, which we did not look at in the chapter, is to use the technique of supervaluations from Chapter 5: construe vague predicates not as ones with fuzzy borderlines and no cut-off, but as having a cut-off somewhere but in no particular place. There is no particular number where the major premiss of the sorites fails, but in any application of the concept, some number must be chosen. The logic of vagueness then results from taking the supervaluation over all classical extensions, in each of which a particular, but arbitrary, cut-off is taken. (See e.g. K. Fine in *Synthese* (1975).)

But these are 'make do and mend' attempts to repair where no conclusive proof of defectiveness has been given. The real question is whether a coherent account of vague but observational concepts can be given. There is a reason why concepts whose application depends on observation should have vague boundaries—observation cannot discern an indefinitely sharp boundary. Our concepts must be ones we can use and apply.

The strongest argument for incoherence in vague concepts is the sorites. But the sorites gets much of its dramatic force by illegitimate moves. The foremost of these is the claim that the major premiss, 'if $A(n)$ then $A(n + 1)$' can only be false if there is a sharp cut-off, that is, a number k such that '$A(k)$' is true and '$A(k + 1)$' false. That, however, depends on taking the conditional to be material and truth-functional, a theory of the conditional which we saw in Chapter 3 cannot be maintained. It also relies on rhetoric: How many hairs does a man need? How can these coloured patches, viewed in isolation, be distinguished? How many, forget the context, are few?

Recognizing these features serves not to dispel the sorites, rather, to clarify the essential point. Take a universe of discourse. Then our powers of observation, and our battery of concepts, can make discriminations between the elements—but not indefinitely. We are left with 'elementary classes', groups of elements between which we cannot, or at least, for the moment, do not discriminate. These elementary classes cover the domain, that is, every element of the domain belongs to at least one, and possibly more than one, class of indiscriminable elements. On to the domain we impose a set of concepts marked out by paradigms—groups of elements seen as perfect examples, contrasted with others which constitute negative examples. Between them there is not a continuum of cases, rather, an indefinitely large group many of which are indistinguishable. Wherever a line is drawn, it will pass through an elementary set, for these overlap. Consider, for example, Dummett's image of the hand of the clock, which moves imperceptibly round the dial. After two seconds, its position appears unchanged; after four seconds its position appears no different from that after two seconds, but perceptibly different from that at the start. There are finitely many discriminable positions for the hand. But these 'positions' overlap—its position after two seconds belongs both to the elementary class defined on the hour and to that defined on the four-second moment—and vice versa, those positions both belong to the elementary class defined on the two-second instant. Is this incoherent? It is puzzling, perhaps paradoxical. But here is a paradox whose conclusion we can stomach, namely, that different positions, or shades, and other observational notions, different indiscriminability classes can, indeed must, embrace identical elements of the domain. Indiscriminability is not transitive.

This theory, the theory of rough sets, was initiated by Zdzisław Pawlak. Its application to vagueness can be read in Ewa Orłowska's paper, 'Semantics of Vague Concepts'. A full account of rough sets was published in Z. Pawlak, *Rough Sets*. Pawlak's tolerance relation is an equivalence relation; it is loosened up to allow overlapping elementary classes by Orłowska. The idea of locating vague concepts by reference to paradigms was very effectively defended in Mark Sainsbury's inaugural lecture, 'Concepts Without Boundaries'.

8 Whose Line Is It Anyway? The Constructivist Challenge

IN the first chapter, I characterized the Correspondence Theory of Truth as being both ontologically and epistemologically realist. It is ontologically realist in asserting the existence of a range of abstract objects, facts, whose existence is additional to, and not reducible to, the existence of their constituent entities. Not only are there black bears, diseases, lines of longitude, and violin concertos, there are in addition facts about those bears, diseases, and so on. What makes propositions about these things true and false are not the things themselves, but the facts about them. It is not the bear which makes 'The bear is black' true, but the fact that the bear is black.

I went on to claim that one could give a satisfactory theory of truth—meeting Tarski's formal and material constraints—without the ontological commitment to facts. But the philosophical move behind the correspondence theory is a common one, arising from its epistemological realism. The latter consists in the belief in objective truth-values, that is, that propositions are true or false independently of our ability to discover which they are. Truth, on the realist picture, is epistemically unconstrained. Propositions have truth-values without regard to the possibility of our finding them out. There can, in principle, be truths that we have no way of knowing.

The link with ontological realism is an attempt to explain that independence. What is it, independent of us, that makes true propositions true? The objectivity is grounded on objects, namely, facts. The problem is admittedly shifted, from the objective truth-values of propositions, to the objective existence of facts. The hope is, none the less, that an acceptable account of the latter will be more readily forthcoming. It is sometimes suggested that the existence of facts is a truism, which no one would deny. What then becomes distinctive of realism is its particular conception of facts and of their relation to propositions. 'Hard' facts are distinguished from 'soft' facts, so that realism about some area of discourse is the claim that truth there consists in a substantive correlation with hard facts; global realism that this is the case for all (*bona fide*) propositions. Certainly, one can proceed in this way; and everyday forms of speech (e.g. 'Is that a fact?') support it. To my mind, however, it is clearer and more economical not to waste the word 'fact' on truisms, with the consequential need to carve off a subclass of 'hard facts'. Basing a theory on self-subsistent, ontologically autonomous objects (in this case, facts) has historically been the standard way to underpin a belief in objectivity about some area of discourse.

Minimalism, if some form of it is possible, shows that this thought is confused. It ascribes objective truth-values without any additional range of objects. The proposition that, for example, *a* is related by *R* to *b* is true if and only if *a* is related by *R* to *b*; and so on, for each form of proposition. '*S* is true if and only if *p*' is a schema which holds whenever what replaces *S* is a name of a proposition which replaces, or a translation of which (when meta-language and object-language differ) replaces *p*. Remember that minimalism is the thesis that there is no more to be said about truth than what is contained in the T-scheme. The be-all and end-all of truth is that the T-scheme gives the truth-condition of the proposition cited in it. That truth-condition adds nothing to the proposition; it disquotes it, and presents it barely. There is at the same time no constraint on truth, epistemic or ontological, neither a requirement that truth be discernible, nor that it rest on the existence of some range of objects. The proposition is repeated for us, bare and unchanged. No additional ontology is called for; yet neither is there any epistemic constraint on the notion of truth. Minimalism is realism without the pain.

The constructivist challenge, therefore, strikes at minimalism just as much as at more ontologically profligate theories. For constructivism sets out to show that an epistemically unconstrained notion of truth is incoherent, not in its ontological implications, but in its epistemic ones. The fault, it is claimed, lies in the objectivity of the realist notion of truth, not in its commitment to objects, if any. The challenge is to demand of the realist that he show that sense can be made of the idea that a proposition should be true even though what truth-value it has may transcend, may go beyond, our power to discover what it is. The central problem concerns the realist's commitment to the possibility of what, in the jargon, are known as 'verification-transcendent' truths, propositions whose truth we may have no means of demonstrating or verifying. The constructivist challenges the realist to defend this commitment—or to abandon his realism and adopt an epistemic, or constructivist, theory of truth.

The aim of this chapter is to try to clarify this debate. Many questions arise immediately from the bold statement of the challenge: what is an epistemic conception of truth, and how is it connected to 'construction'; why is it thought so difficult to make sense of the idea of verification-transcendent truths; and in particular, is there a particular class of truths which constitute the main battleground between the two sides? These and other questions will receive their answer in the course of considering three arguments which the constructivist marshals against the realist, what I shall call the mathematical, the logical, and the linguistic arguments.

The Infinite

The mathematical argument concerns the nature of infinity. Infinity arises in mathematics in two places. The first is in the counting numbers, or as they are usually called, the natural numbers. However far one has counted, it is always possible to count one more. There is no greatest natural number—any candidate for such a greatest number could be immediately exceeded, by adding 1. Thus there cannot be only a finite collection of natural numbers. The collection is infinite. The other context in which infinity arises is in geometry, in the study of space. A line can be indefinitely subdivided. Any interval can be further subdivided into subintervals. Once again, there is no limit to the process. However far a process of subdivision has gone, further division is possible.

Note that this indefiniteness of repetition of both processes is conceptual and ideal, but none the less essential. Suppose there are—as we are told—only 10^{80} elementary particles in the universe. We can still add to them the numbers of molecules and stars formed from them, the number of pairs and strings of particles, strings of strings, and so on. Similarly, even if physical space is 'grainy' (not admitting distinctions beyond 10^{-40} m., say), the ideal space of geometry is not so restricted; and more importantly, the 'real line', the concept of spatial extension, acts as a model for the mathematical treatment of time, velocity, mass, wavelength, and frequency, to name but a few.

However, the idea that a process (of adding 1, or of further subdividing) may be indefinitely continued introduces infinity only as potential. On this model, infinity is not something which is ever reached. Indeed, it is incoherent to suppose so; for our conception is of a process which, however many times it has been applied, may be applied again. Hence, there cannot be a point at which all possible applications have been completed. Infinity is an incompletable goal, which can never be reached.

Our concepts of the standard model of arithmetic, ω (from Chapter 2), and of the real line are, on the other hand, conceptions of the infinite as actual. ω, the set of natural numbers, is a completed totality, the result of iterating the addition of 1 infinitely many times. It contains all the natural numbers. Similarly, the real line is more than an interval; it is a collection of points, infinitely many points. The real line is actually, really, dense and continuous. Not only is there the possibility of locating points along it—they are really there. Between any two points, there is a third (denseness); and every bounded sequence of points (or intervals) has a limit—it is continuous.

These conceptions of the natural numbers and of the real line are relatively recent. For treating infinite collections as actual seemed to lead to paradox. Take the natural numbers, for example. Every natural number is either odd or even. If we think of the collection as a completed totality, it appears as the union of two subcollections—the collection of all odd and that of all even numbers. But these collections are also infinite. Is it not paradoxical that two collections should be the same size—infinite—yet one be smaller than the other? For there are, in some sense, fewer odd numbers than natural numbers, since not all natural numbers are odd.

Treating the line as an actual infinity of points also appeared to lead to paradox. Several of these are attributed to Zeno of Elea in the fifth century BC. If a racecourse consists of an actual infinity of points, a runner must complete an actual infinity of tasks before he can reach the far end—first reaching, for example, half-way, then half the remainder, and so on. Looked at another way, before reaching any point, he must first reach the half-way point to it, yet before that the half-way point to it, and so on; so he cannot even start, for before making any move, an infinite number of prior tasks are required. These puzzles have a mathematical 'solution'—the time taken to reach a point is the finite sum of progressively smaller time intervals (backwards or forwards) exactly matching the finite sum of smaller and smaller spatial intervals—but that is to miss the philosophical point. The latter hinges on the fact that an infinite collection was defined as one which, however much one has of it, there is always more to come—it is by definition incomplete. So if there actually are infinitely many tasks to complete before one has crossed some interval, then that interval cannot be crossed.

These and other puzzles about infinity and the continuum (the real line) were not solved (if 'solved' they were) until the process of arithmetization of analysis was undertaken at the end of the nineteenth century. The development of point-set topology, extending the work started by Descartes in the seventeenth century in introducing algebraic methods into geometry, led to a foundational programme whose aim was the elimination of confusion, reliance on intuition, and paradox. Consider the simple but far-reaching discovery by the Greeks of incommensurability. Take the graph of the function $y = x^2 - \frac{1}{2}$; it divides the unit interval (on the x-axis) into two segments, those values of x whose square is less than $\frac{1}{2}$, from those whose square is greater than $\frac{1}{2}$. But the point of division cannot be obtained by any process of rational division, of subdividing the line by ratios and fractions. An adequate treatment of the real line as a set of points, an actual infinity, requires the supplementation of the set of fractions by a further infinity of points obtained in this way by 'cuts', the postulation of irrational points corresponding to every possible division of the set of rational points into two classes, the first containing every rational less than any rational it contains, the second every rational greater than any rational in it.

This taming of the infinity of mathematics needed two crucial innovations, and raised a deeply puzzling question. Pressing these innovations were Richard Dedekind and Georg Cantor. The aim was to treat the infinite as much like the finite as possible. The first move was to change the definition of the infinite, so that instead of being defined as the incompletable, and seeing the Galilean paradox (that there are as many odd numbers as natural numbers) as a consequence, we define the infinite by that paradox, as any collection equinumerous with a proper subset of itself (as the odd numbers are equinumerous with the natural numbers, or the points in the interval $[0,1]$ are equinumerous with those in the interval $[\frac{1}{4},\frac{3}{4}]$, or indeed, any interval), and then ask whether all such collections are incompletable. Cantor's claim, which introduced the theory of the 'transfinite'—the tamed infinite—was that not all are incompletable. The transfinite can be treated—by the methods we use for the finite—as a completed totality, an actual infinity. For example, consider the process of taking a limit, such as the runner's progress across the stadium. The distance covered is $\sum_{n=0}^{\infty}\frac{1}{2^n}$. The symbol '$\infty$' here need not—indeed, this was the nineteenth century's essential insight—be treated as a name of a value of n. The sum is a limit; it is that number (namely, 2) which differs less and less from each partial sum, $\sum_{n=0}^{k}\frac{1}{2^n}$, as k increases. The technique is familiarly known as that of 'ε, δ' definition: $\sum_{n=0}^{\infty}\frac{1}{2^n} = \gamma$ if for any $\varepsilon > 0$ (however small) there is $\delta = \frac{1}{k}$ such that $\left| \gamma - \sum_{n=0}^{k}\frac{1}{2^n} \right| < \varepsilon$. So $\gamma = 2$.

Suppose that we have some process that we can apply repeatedly, say, to a subset of the interval [0,1] (the example which Cantor considered was the formation of the derived set of accumulation points), forming successive subsets, P, $P^{(1)}$, $P^{(2)}$, ..., $P^{(n)}$. By the analysis of limits by the 'ε, δ'-technique, we can consider the limit of this process, $P^{(\infty)}$, for each set P. It may be empty, or it may be another non-empty subset of [0,1]. If it is, we can apply the technique again, forming $P^{(\infty+1)}$. It was at this point that Cantor introduced the notation ω for the result of applying such a process once for every natural number—to the limit. So we write $P^{(\omega)}$ for the limit set, $P^{(\omega+1)}$, $P^{(\omega+2)}$, ... for the result of applying the process again and again, yielding—for suitably rich initial subsets, P—the derived sets $P^{(\omega+\omega)} = P^{(\omega.2)}$, $P^{(\omega.\omega)} = P^{(\omega^2)}$, $P^{(\omega^\omega)}$ and so on. The indices ω, $\omega.2$, ω^ω and so on were Cantor's transfinite numbers, the infinite treated as finite.

The second innovation was the completion of the real line by the irrationals, obtained by 'cuts' of the sort presented earlier. If we are to think of the real line as a continuum, we must suppose that wherever one cuts it—as the side of a square 'cuts' the diagonal, in Euclid's famous proof of incommensurability, or as the graph of cos x 'cuts' the x-axis at $\frac{\pi}{2}$, $\frac{3\pi}{2}$, and so on—there is a point on the line through which the cut passes. The line is continuous, containing a limit point to every bounded monotonic sequence, that is one every member of which is less (respectively greater) than some number, that is, bounded above (resp. below), and such that successive members are greater (resp. less) than earlier members, that is, monotonically increasing (resp. decreasing); for the sequence itself defines a cut on the continuum, which itself serves as, or serves to define, the limit, the least upper (resp. greatest lower) bound.

What, then, is the puzzling question? It comes out as follows: we now have two infinite collections, two species of actual infinity, the natural numbers, ω, treated as a complete whole; and the real line, say, the interval [0,1] again, treated as a complete whole. Each is infinite in that each is equinumerous with a proper subset of itself. On the other hand, they are also very different. ω is a discrete set in which each member (except the first) has an immediate predecessor and an immediate successor.

Technically, it is a well-ordering, that is, every subset has a least member under the ordering. The unit interval, on the other hand, is not a discrete ordering—one should not think of it as like beads on a string, pushed unbelievably close together. No member has an immediate predecessor or successor—between any two members there are infinitely many others. Indeed, between any two rationals there are infinitely many irrationals as well as rationals. The question Cantor asked was: are these two collections equinumerous?

In fact, it is not so much the question as the answer which is puzzling. For Cantor was able to prove that they are not equinumerous. What this means is that there is no pairing-off (or 1-1 onto mapping) of their members, as there is, for example, between the odd numbers and the natural numbers, or the unit interval and any segment of it. For consider any real number between 0 and 1, that is, any member of (0,1)—0 and 1 excluded. It can familiarly be represented as an infinite decimal, and, to avoid duplication (since, e.g. 0.5 = 0.4999 ...), as an infinite decimal with no infinite consecutive sequence of zeros:

$$\frac{1}{\pi} = 0.318309886 \ldots$$

$$\frac{1}{2} = 0.4999 \ldots$$

$$\frac{1}{\sqrt{2}} = 0.707106781 \ldots$$

$$\frac{13}{83} = 0.156626506 \ldots$$

Each place after the decimal point contains a digit between 0 and 9. Suppose there were a mapping from the reals to the natural numbers, that is, an exhaustive list of the members of (0,1), with a first member, a second, and so on. (The above display might be the start of such a list, showing its first four members.) Then we can 'diagonalize' out of any such list, exhibiting a real number in (0,1) which is not in the list. The 'new' real is constructed as follows. Its first decimal place is one greater than the first decimal place of the first real in the list if that digit is not 9, and 8 if it is; its second decimal place is again one greater than the second decimal place of, this time, the second real in the list if it is not 9, otherwise 8; and so on. In other words, it differs in the nth place from the nth decimal in the list.

For example, if the above display is the start of our list, then the 'diagonal' real is 0.4887.... Inspection shows that this real cannot be anywhere on the list, since it differs from any real on it in at least one place.

How should this result be interpreted? Recall Cantor's transfinite order-types, ω, $\omega + 1$, ..., $\omega.2$, ... ω^ω and so on. This series is well-ordered, extending the natural numbers into the transfinite. The mapping of the odd numbers onto the natural numbers shows the equinumerosity of ω and $\omega.2$, that is, $\omega + \omega$—for it separates out the odd numbers (as a collection of order-type ω), leaving the even numbers—another collection of type ω. That is, each of these higher order-types, $\omega + 1$, ω^2, ω^ω can be shown equinumerous with ω. Cantor interpreted his diagonal argument as showing that the reals correspond to a yet higher ordinal, one which cannot be mapped 1-1 onto ω. That is, he did not doubt that the reals could be well-ordered—presented in a list. However, such a list must inevitably be longer than ω. Any list of type ω omits some reals; so a full list must go on beyond ω, and beyond it in a radical way, a way in which, for example, ω^2 does not, for ω^2 (e.g. dividing the natural numbers into subsets sharing smallest prime divisors) can be reordered to match ω.

At this point, we have come a long way from Zeno's paradoxes and the incommensurability proof of the Greeks. We appear to have a coherent theory unifying arithmetic, analytic, and geometric methods. Mathematics has become the theory of the infinite, of the successive application of operations from the finite through into the transfinite, in the ordinal theory of limits, and of the continuum as a collection of individual elements, creating a metric of extension out of a collection of unextended points, in point-set topology. The date is, say, 1890, and the paradoxes which Weierstrass, Dedekind, Cantor, and others thought were banished forever are about to return with a vengeance.

The first of the modern paradoxes was Burali-Forti's. Consider Cantor's ordinal series. However far we have gone in the ordinal series we can always apply whatever operation is being iterated once more. The resulting ordinal is greater than the preceding ordinals. ('Greater than' here does not mean 'not equinumerous', for clearly '$\alpha + 1$' can be mapped onto α, by mapping 1 to the first element of α, and shifting successors to the right. Rather, '$\alpha + 1$' is never order-isomorphic to α, that is, it denotes an order-type of which α is a proper part—a proper initial segment.) Take the collection of all ordinals. It is well-ordered—for that is how the ordinals are constructed. So it has an order-type; that is, it is itself an ordinal, θ, say. Then we can construct $\theta + 1$, which is an ordinal greater than the set of all ordinals. That is a contradiction.

Clearly, there can, in consistency, be no collection of all ordinals. It is an absolute infinity. Cantor had claimed to tame infinity—the transfinite. But there must be an absolute infinity (subject to all the old problems), beyond the transfinite. Cantor recognized this. The problem, however, is to give a rationale, an explanation, for why there can be no collection of all ordinals. To say it cannot exist, on pain of inducing inconsistency, is to make the rejection entirely *ad hoc*. We seek an explanation, a reason why collecting some objects together, for example, all the natural numbers, appears safe and consistent, while collecting others, for instance, all the ordinals, leads to contradiction.

The most famous of the paradoxes which exploded into mathematics, essentially all in the decade 1895–1905, was Russell's paradox, published by Bertrand Russell in 1903. Russell hit on it when reflecting on Cantor's proof of the non-denumerability of the reals—that there is no list (of order-type ω) of the reals (or the reals in any interval, since the latter are equinumerous with the whole collection of reals). The proof works, we saw, by 'diagonalizing' out of any putative list, that is, using the list to construct another real which differs from every real on the list. The proof generalizes: given any set, there are more properties of things in the set than there are things in the set. For given any putative pairing of properties with things in the set, consider the property which holds of something if and only if it lacks the property with which it is paired. Take an easy case, where we consider only two things, a and b (two rocks, say) and think of properties extensionally, that is, as simply the sets of things which have them. There are then four properties, that true of neither *a* nor *b* (being seagulls, perhaps), that true of *a* (being *a*), of *b*, and of both (being rocks). We can't pair off the rocks with their possible properties—there are too many.

The crucial construction in both proofs—Cantor's and Russell's—is the diagonalization, the use of the putative 1-1 mapping to produce a number, or set, or property, which is not in the original. For Russell's paradox, take the set of all properties (or sets) and consider the property (or collection) of properties (resp. sets) which don't hold of (resp. belong to) themselves—that is, diagonalize on the identity mapping. Call it the Russell property, or Russell set. It can't hold of itself, since it is the property which holds of properties only if they don't hold of themselves. But then it must hold of itself, since it holds of all those properties which don't hold of themselves (*mutatis mutandis* for sets). That's a contradiction: the Russell property both holds and cannot hold of itself; the Russell set both belongs to and cannot belong to itself.

Intuitionism

Russell and Zermelo—who it seems had independently hit on 'Russell's paradox'—were among the leaders of the repair-work on classical set theory. Russell introduced a hierarchy of types, Zermelo a hierarchy of sets, both restricting the scale of the transfinite. But to Brouwer, and the constructivist group, the intuitionists, which he led and inspired, the paradoxes of set theory were seen as far more than a local problem in set theory which could be dealt with by logical and set-theoretic means. They undermined the whole enterprise, dating at least from Descartes, of dealing with geometric concepts algebraically, and the introduction of the infinite as actual to which that movement had led.

When dealing with finite collections, we can treat them both extensionally and intensionally. That is, as well as describing them as the extension of a concept, we can consider each member separately in turn. Take an example: suppose we assert that everyone on the plane to Fiumicino was served dinner. We might make that assertion as a general fact about passengers on Alitalia planes—treating the collection intensionally. Each member of the collection falls under a certain concept, an intension, and as such will have been served dinner. But we may also have asserted it as a result of going to each passenger in turn, and verifying that they were served dinner—as we may check the general claim in this way. This is to treat the collection extensionally. Such is possible with finite collections. But it is not possible with infinite collections. They can only be treated intensionally, as exemplifying a general concept. That is what is meant by the incompletability of an infinite collection—however many instances one has examined or enumerated, there are more to come.

The realist tries to maintain the fiction that infinite collections may none the less continue to be thought of extensionally. Even if we, with our human limitations, cannot survey them, they exist objectively—and perhaps another being, with greater powers (God) could run through them all. In Russell's famous phrase, the limitation of our powers constitutes a 'merely medical impossibility'. The realist believes that there really is a fully definite extension to concepts such as 'natural number', 'real number', and so on.

In its most hard-headed form, realism embraces the full Comprehension Principle, that every well-defined concept determines a set. Burali-Forti's and Russell's paradoxes showed that some restriction must be put on it. None the less, in the cumulative hierarchy, building sets from below in axiomatic set theory, the axioms of infinity and the power set axiom assert in particular the existence—as determinate totalities—of the extensions of the concepts 'natural number' and 'real number'.

The intuitionist denies this. What correspond to these concepts are operations or procedures—intensional notions. For example, the concept 'natural number' is constituted by a process or operation of successively adding 1. Each real number is the limit of a series of approximations, extending its decimal expansion by more and more terms. That is, both natural numbers and real numbers are obtained by a construction. There is no pre-existent objective totality of entities which we explore. Numbers are created by the successive application of an operation. Where the realist says that every potential infinity presupposes an actual infinity, the constructivist replies that every potential infinity presupposes an operation and entails that there is no objective reality. What is true is so only in virtue of our ability to apply the operation to a successful outcome, not in virtue of any correspondence with any such reality.

The picture which underpins the constructivist's approach to infinite collections is, thus, radically different from the realist's. In particular, it leads him to a very different account of existence claims. Actually, the realist tends to be equivocal on this issue. He too will often speak of 'constructions', for example, of the rationals as ordered pairs of integers, of the reals as Dedekind cuts of rationals. But he does not take the notion of construction seriously, as imposing any real constraint. So he can invoke —at least in metaphorical terms—'God' as the great constructor who can follow through such constructions to their (medically impossible) completions. In the end, his philosophical credo allows the postulation of any entity whose addition does not lead to inconsistency. That was what drove the arithmetization of analysis forward in the 1860s and 1870s; and when the paradoxes erupted, the aim of revision was to preserve as much as consistency would allow.

The constructivist, as his name reveals, takes the limitations imposed by the methods of construction seriously. Existence has no application or sense beyond what can be constructed and exhibited. An existence proof is required actually to exhibit the witness to its truth—that is, to provide a construction by which it can be calculated. A much-quoted example of such a constructive proof is that of the infinity of the primes—for any given prime, there is a greater prime. The proof shows how, from a given prime number, to construct a large one. Suppose p is prime. Consider $p! + 1$ (that is, the successor of p factorial, where p factorial is the product of p with all its predecessors— e.g. $2! = 2 \times 1 = 2$; $3! = 3 \times 2 \times 1 = 6$; $(n + 1)! = (n + 1) \times n!$). Dividing $p! + 1$ by every prime less than or equal to p leaves remainder 1. So, since every number has a prime factor, $p! + 1$ must have a prime factor larger than p. By testing every number between p and $p! + 1$ for primeness, we can find, that is,

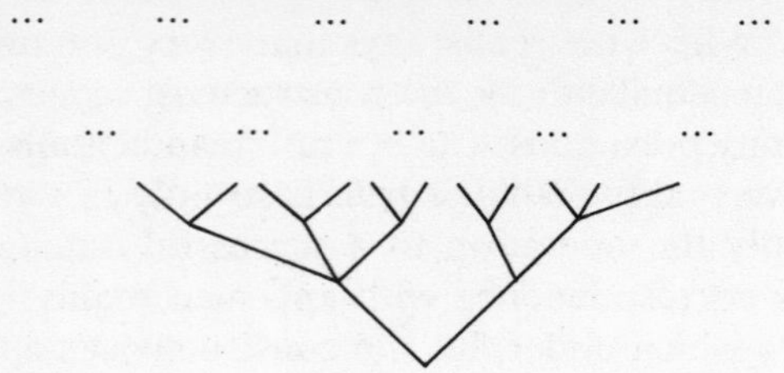

FIG. 8.1

construct, this new prime. So we have a constructive proof of the infinity of the prime numbers—of their potential infinity, that is, meaning that however many primes we have found (or constructed) there is (i.e. we can construct) another.

Contrast this proof with the proof of König's Lemma: suppose we have an infinite, finitely branching tree (see Fig. 8.1). The tree grows upwards, each node separating into a finite number of branches. König's Lemma claims that there is an infinite branch in the tree. We 'construct' it as follows. Let α_0 be the root node, and suppose α_n ($n > 0$) to have been constructed, such that α_n has infinitely many nodes above it (clearly α_0 has infinitely many nodes above it, for the tree is infinite). Then at least one immediate successor node to α_n has infinitely many nodes above it. Define $\alpha_n + 1$ to be one such node. In this way, we can proceed to 'construct' the infinite branch, α_0, α_1, α_2, ...

I have enclosed the word 'construct' in scare-quotes in this proof, for the proof is constructively unacceptable. This is a 'construction' which only the great constructor could carry out—it is not one for us. For given a node with infinitely many nodes above it, there is no constructive method of selecting an immediate successor node with the same property. We are incapable of testing or checking which of the nodes are the right ones. The constructivist will not accept König's Lemma as validly proven. Its existential claim is not backed by a legitimate construction, for there is no (real, effective) process by which the claimed branch may be constructed.

Indeed, the constructivist will reject the claim that, given a

F I G. 8.2

node with infinitely many nodes above it, but only finitely many immediate successor nodes, at least one of those immediate successors has infinitely many nodes above it. For again, that existential claim (there is at least one immediate successor node . . .) requires backing by a construction showing how, among the successor nodes, to identify one with the property. Since we have no way of verifying it—a check would require an infinite task, following out the tree to infinity—the existential claim is intuitionistically unacceptable.

This is very puzzling. How can the intuitionist maintain this position? For we know there are infinitely many nodes above α_n, and only finitely many successors, $\alpha_{n,0}$, $\alpha_{n,1}$, $\alpha_{n,2}$, $\alpha_{n,3}$, say (see Fig. 8.2). If there were only finitely many nodes above each of $\alpha_{n,0}$, ..., $\alpha_{n,3}$, then there would be only finitely many nodes above α_n—the union of all of them. So, contraposing, if there are infinitely many nodes above α_n, surely there must be infinitely many above at least one of $\alpha_{n,0}$, ..., $\alpha_{n,3}$, its immediate successors?

The step of contraposition here is intuitionistically unacceptable. We know that if each of $\alpha_{n,0}$, ..., $\alpha_{n,3}$ had finitely many successors, so too would α_n. Since it does not, it follows that not all of $\alpha_{n,0}$, ..., $\alpha_{n,3}$ has finitely many successors. The illicit step—constructively speaking—is from 'not every x, Fx' (not every immediate successor of α_n has finitely many successors) to 'for some x, not Fx' (some immediate successor of α_n has infinitely many successors). We may not pass to an existential claim in this way in the absence of a suitable construction.

In a way, we have been misled by a picture here. The diagram presented in Fig. 8.2 suggests an objective reality, an actually infinite tree sitting above α_n. So seen, it is unbelievable that there is not an infinite tree above one of its immediate successors. But that is not the right picture, which should be seen constructively. From α_n, there is an indefinite succession of finite choices to be made. But we have no method of guaranteeing that we will make the choice that will never reach an impasse—that we will not find ourselves on the finite and closed blind alley.

It is easy to think of the tree in extensional, actualist terms. We think that either the tree is (actually) infinite, or the intuitionist must claim that the tree is finite—that only a tree of finite size can be constructed. Indeed, the intuitionist does claim that actual trees, that is, completed trees, are all finite. But this tree is infinite—that is, there is a method for building it which can never be completed, an operation which will never terminate. What he resists is the actualist move from the claim that the construction above α_n will never terminate, to the claim that for one of $\alpha_{n,0}, ..., \alpha_{n,3}$ the construction above it will never terminate. There is no (finite) surefire way of choosing one of $\alpha_{n,0}, ..., \alpha_{n,3}$ which will guarantee this.

Classically, König's Lemma is equivalent to the claim that if every branch in a finitely branching tree is finite, there is an upper bound to the lengths of branches in the tree. That result is constructively provable—it's Brouwer's famous 'Fan Theorem'—but it is not constructively equivalent to König's Lemma, for the reasons given. It illustrates a frequent outcome of the intuitionistic reconstruction of mathematics and analysis: where classical analytical methods use a non-constructive method, there is often an intuitionistically acceptable alternative—albeit, the constructive result is harder to prove, requiring greater care in ensuring the availability of suitable constructions.

The failure of the proof of König's Lemma illustrates another—arguably, the central—failure of an important feature of the classical realist picture. Surely, the realist will say, either one of the immediate successors, $\alpha_{n,0}, ..., \alpha_{n,3}$, has infinitely many successors or not; but if not, the tree will be finite. So there must be a suitable successor node. Again, the picture has misled us, into thinking there is a determinate fact of the matter.

Either it is like *this*, says the classicist—pointing to some feature—or *not*. The constructivist is forced, or rather, is at pains to deny this determinacy. The tree has no reality beyond what we can, constructively, show about it. In the absence of any method for showing that these alternatives are exhaustive, we have no basis for asserting their disjunction. We do not have a construction which, applied to α_n, will show either that one immediate successor has an infinite tree above it, or none does. The mythical great constructor could perhaps carry out the (infinite) search—or 'see' the infinite tree as a whole and spot the right node. But that God's-eye viewpoint, and the actually infinite tree it 'sees', is a myth.

The Law of Excluded Middle, that for every proposition A, either A or not-A, is a central tenet of the classical, realist picture. Along with it goes the Law of Bivalence, that every proposition is true or false. (To be sure, free logic and Kripke's theory of truth appeared to deny this; but not in spirit. On either account, there is a determinate partition into the truths, the falsehoods, and the truth-valueless.) These claims are intuitionistically unacceptable. The truth of a claim requires a demonstration, a proof that it is true. That sounds more puzzling than it really is. From a classical perspective, the intuitionist seems to equate truth with proof; 'A or not-A' becomes 'Either A is provable or "not-A" is provable'; 'for some n, $A(n)$' becomes 'we can construct n and prove $A(n)$'. But these paraphrases are simply a heuristic, to help someone still entranced by the classical picture (where proof and truth come apart) to understand the constructivist's objections. For the constructivist himself, there is no such divorce. The truth of A is constituted by an appropriate construction—not a demonstration that it is true, for that is clearly regressive, but a demonstration of A. There is no reality corresponding to A beyond what can be proved.

Denying Excluded Middle and Bivalence does not entail asserting their contradictories. It is no thesis of intuitionistic logic that neither A nor not-A, for some A (as it is for free logic, or for Kripke). For we may succeed in establishing or refuting A. The intuitionistic position is more guarded. We may assert 'A or not-A' only when we are in a position to assert or deny A.

In particular, we may not introduce a blanket assertion of 'A or not-A' into a proof. Another famous non-constructive example is the proof that there are two irrational numbers a and b such that a^b is rational. For, the classicist reasons, either $\sqrt{2}^{\sqrt{2}}$ is rational, in which case we let $a = b = \sqrt{2}$; or $\sqrt{2}^{\sqrt{2}}$ is irrational, in which case we let $a = \sqrt{2}^{\sqrt{2}}$, $b = \sqrt{2}$ (whereupon $a^b = 2$, which is rational). The disjunction of alternatives here is constructively unacceptable. We have no construction whereby we can determine whether $\sqrt{2}^{\sqrt{2}}$ is rational or not. Hence we are not entitled to assert the case of Excluded Middle on which the proof rests. (Here again, there is a constructive alternative, in this case, constructively proving the same result, and allowing us to determine a and b.)

Excluded Middle is, therefore, a substantial statement intuitionistically. For example, take the statement '$x = y + z$', that a (natural) number is the sum of two others. This is decidable; that is, we have an effective procedure, given x, y, and z, of determining whether x is indeed the sum of y and z. We may assert therefore, for any x, y, and z, that either $x = y + z$ or not; for given x, y, and z, we can determine which. However, consider the claim that if x is even and greater than 2, then there are y and z which are prime and whose sum is x. Again, 'even', 'greater than 2' and 'prime' are decidable predicates: we may assert of any number that either it is even or odd, that it is greater than 2 or not, or that either it is prime or not, for there are algorithms for determining them (division by 2, subtraction of 2 and Eratosthenes' sieve, respectively). But the general claim, commonly known as Goldbach's Conjecture, that every even number greater than 2 is the sum of two primes, is not decidable. That is, we have a predicate $A(x)$ which is decidable ('x is even, greater than 2, and there are y and z which are prime such that $x = y + z$'), for we can work systematically through all pairs y, z less than x, testing whether they are prime. But 'for every x, $A(x)$' is not decidable. We have no method which is guaranteed to establish or refute this universal claim for every number x. Thus, while we may assert '$A(x)$ or not-$A(x)$' for every number x, we may not assert 'for every x, $A(x)$ or not for every x, $A(x)$', that is, we may not assert that either Goldbach's Conjecture is true

or it is not. For no one has yet shown which, and we possess no
algorithm for determining it. If it is false, one day someone may
hit on a number which refutes it; if it is true, someone may
provide a general proof that for every x, $A(x)$. But until that
time, the constructivist refrains from asserting their disjunction.

A final point, before we leave the intuitionistic reconstruction of mathematics, and turn to the other arguments for
constructivism. Constructivists often present further so-called
'weak counterexamples' to Excluded Middle, perhaps the most
surprising being that, if a is a real number (a constructive real
number), '$a = 0$' is not decidable, and so the constructivist cannot assert that all reals are either identical to 0 or not identical
to 0 (i.e. for every a, $a = 0$ or $a \neq 0$). One has to be careful here,
however, to see the point, which is essentially one of representation. Each natural number has a canonical representation.
When we concede that 'x is prime' is decidable for natural
numbers, we understand it relative to the canonical representation of those numbers. If, for example, x is characterized as '7
if Goldbach's Conjecture is true, 8 if not', then the decidability
fails. Indeed, even that number which is 7 if Goldbach's Conjecture is true, 11 if not, cannot be said to be prime, for that
depends on recognizing that the number is either 7 or 11 (both
primes), which in turn depends on Excluded Middle for
Goldbach.

'Even', 'prime', and so on are decidable for natural numbers
relative to their canonical representation, as for example, arabic
numerals. Real numbers, on the other hand, do not have a
canonical representation for the constructivist. They can be
developed as either equivalence classes of Cauchy sequences,
or in terms of Dedekind cuts (constructively, these give somewhat different theories). But Cauchy sequences (that is, sequences of rational numbers, successive terms of which, after a
certain point, differ from one another by less than a given
modulus) can be presented in many forms. Let $A(x)$ be the
Goldbach predicate (i.e. 'if x is even and greater than 2 then x
is the sum of two primes'). Then it is possible to define a real
number which is equal to 0 if and only if Goldbach's conjecture
is true. Two things follow: first, that there is no canonical

representation of this real—one cannot identify it with an infinite decimal, as one can with all the classical real numbers; secondly, that the identity of this real with 0 is no more decidable than is the truth of Goldbach's Conjecture. So we cannot assert, of all reals, that either they are 0 or not. Similarly, we cannot assert that the reals are linearly ordered (one less than the other of any pair not identical), and so on. The constructive theory of the reals is radically different from the classical.

None the less, a theory adequate for standard purposes can be developed. I do not propose here to come to a decision about the mathematical argument as it backs the constructivist challenge. The classical arithmetization of analysis led to a crisis, with the discovery of the set-theoretical paradoxes. Both classical and constructivist responses to that crisis have been proposed. The classical response retains as much as possible, indeed effectively all, of Weierstrass and Cantor's construction, within a set theory whose restrictions are philosophically puzzling. The constructivist response is far more radical, taking the philosophical issue of the actual infinite seriously, but leading not only to a much harder mathematics of the real line, but to logical revisions, in rejecting the universal validity of the Law of Excluded Middle. Let us now turn to the logical argument, which deals directly with the sense of the logical connectives.

The Logical Argument

The constructivist is an anti-realist; that is, he does not see truth as an objective characteristic of a proposition, something it has independently of us, resulting from some objective structure— say, of the natural numbers or the real line as a completed totality of objects. Rather, truth is an epistemic notion, the truth of a proposition consisting in our ability to demonstrate and verify it. Hence proof comes for the constructivist to occupy a central role. To assert a proposition as true is to have a proof of it. For the moment, we can take mathematics as he does, as the paradigm; though in the next section we will see how this model is extended to encompass empirical propositions as well.

From the classical standpoint, proof is contrasted with

semantics. Proof is thought of as a purely syntactic notion, a way of generating logical truths (theorems) by a procedure which looks only at formal properties of logical expressions, abstracted from considerations of meaning. Semantics, in contrast, is thought to imbue formulae with meaning, by correlating them with properties of various structures. As in many other areas, this point of view is entirely alien to the constructivist, and so it is unhelpful to approach constructivism with this dichotomy in mind. For the constructivist, proof is a semantic notion; it is proof which gives expressions meaning. Mathematical structures do not have any reality beyond what we can prove about them. In the finite case, this is trivial and uninteresting—proof can here consist simply in checking case by case. But in the infinite case it is crucial. The infinite is potential, consisting in the unending possibility of further generation. What is real are the procedures which generate further cases and the proofs which verify them. The constructivist could make a distinction similar to the classicist's, between formal proofs and formal systems and the informal notion of proof which they try to capture. Sometimes he does; but for the most part by 'proof' he means an intuitive, extendable, and informal notion of demonstration and verification.

It follows that the constructivist's epistemic constraint on truth turns into an epistemic conception of meaning. A realist theory of meaning is often characterized as truth-conditional, contrasted with the anti-realist linking of meaning with some epistemically constrained notion like warranted assertibility. That is because 'truth' in 'truth-conditional' is identified as realist, verification-transcendent truth, a belief in facts determining meaning without reference to our abilities to discover those facts. Arguments for an epistemic conception of meaning, that is, one which explicates meaning in terms of procedures for establishing the truth of propositions, are directed at the same goal as arguments for an epistemically constrained notion of truth, one which rejects verification-transcendence.

It is against this background that the constructivist develops an argument against the classical view, and in particular against the classical theory of negation. We have seen that the intuitionist rejects the Law of Excluded Middle, the claim that every proposition of the form 'A or not-A' is true. Some instances can be asserted, namely, those for which one has a means of either verifying or refuting A. In general, the intuitionist accepts 'A or B' only when one has a proof of A or a proof of B—or at least a method of verifying or demonstrating one of the disjuncts. The intuitionist sees that as encapsulating the meaning of 'A or B', that one who asserts 'A or B' is committed to verifying either A or B.

Why does the classicist go beyond this, and claim that 'A or not-A' is universally valid, even in the absence of any method of deciding which? It rests on a pair of inferences—indeed, either suffices. The proof method known as *reductio ad absurdum* has two forms, which the classicist sees as essentially the same. First, suppose that from A one can derive a contradiction, some proposition of the form 'B and not-B', for some formula B. Then if A were true, it would follow that a contradiction was true, which is impossible. So A cannot be true; that is, we may conclude, 'not-A'. Similarly, suppose that from 'not-A' we may derive such a contradiction, 'B and not-B'. Then 'not-A' cannot be true—so, the classicist infers, A must be true.

But this presupposes that the alternatives are exhausted by A and 'not-A', that is, that we are in a position to assert 'A or not-A'. We have already seen, however, that the intuitionist denies that. Accordingly, if 'not-A' is contradictory (that is, entails 'B and not-B', for some B) we may validly infer that 'not-A' is not true, that is, not-not-A, but we may not proceed to assert A. The intuitionist rejects both classical *reductio*, that from the derivation of contradiction from 'not-A' we may infer A, and double negation elimination, that from the assertion of 'not-not-A', we may infer A.

Indeed, these classical inferences are seen by the intuitionist as illegitimately extending the grounds for asserting, for example 'A or B' or 'for some x, $A(x)$'. For suppose we can show that supposing that 'not-(A or B)' (i.e. 'neither A nor B') is contradictory for some A and B (as we could if B were simply 'not-A' itself), or that supposing that for no x do we have $A(x)$ is contradictory (as supposing there is no infinite branch in a finitely branching tree contradicts the claim that the tree has infinitely many nodes): to infer that either A or B must be true, or that for some x, $A(x)$ must hold, is non-constructive, in that the claim is not underwritten by a demonstration of which disjunct is true, or of which object x makes $A(x)$ true. We seem to have introduced a further ground for asserting 'A or B' additional to a proof of either A or B, and a further ground for asserting 'for some x, $A(x)$' additional to the exhibition of an object x of which $A(x)$ is true.

Classical *reductio* is certainly non-constructive. The question is whether it is incoherent. That is the argument I wish to examine. If one can show that the classical account of negation, that extra feature it has over intuitionistic *reductio* (that one may assert 'not-A' when the assumption of A leads to contradiction), is incoherent in a way intuitionistic negation is not, one will have a powerful argument in favour of the intuitionistic viewpoint. The constructivist challenge will seem unanswerable. Here is the argument. It derives from a reply given by Nuel Belnap to a puzzle raised by Arthur Prior. What concerned Prior was the holism inherent in the claim that the meaning of a logical connective, like 'or' or 'for some', was determined by the inference patterns into which it validly fitted. This was to get the cart before the horse, said Prior. First establish the meaning of the connective; then, and only then, could one determine whether putative inference patterns containing it were valid or not (namely, did they threaten to take one from truth to falsity—only if we already knew what the meaning of the connective was could we know whether the premisses and conclusion were true or false). To back up these thoughts, Prior set out to show that the 'analytical validity' view was absurd—that one could not be given *carte blanche* to introduce connectives and give them meaning simply by laying down what inference patterns were valid for them. His notorious example was '*tonk*', a two-place connective, forming a proposition 'A *tonk* B' from propositions A and B (much like conjunction, disjunction, and conditionals). The rules defining '*tonk*' were as follows, said Prior: from A one was permitted to infer 'A *tonk* B'; and from 'A *tonk* B' one might infer B. (The analogy was with, say, conjunction, which an exponent of the analytical validity view might say was defined by the inferences, that from A and B one might infer 'A and B' and that from 'A and B' one could infer A, or equally B.)

So far, so good. We have a pair of rules, one of which gives the grounds for the assertion of 'A *tonk* B', the other the use in proceeding to further inferences from such an assertion—the introduction and elimination rules respectively, as they are often called. But disaster looms. For admitting the validity of these two inference patterns allows one to proceed from A to 'A *tonk* B' and from the latter to B, that is, to infer any proposition (B) from any other (A). But that is absurd. How can simply introducing a new connective entail that any pair of propositions (which in general will not contain '*tonk*') are equivalent? What Prior wants to say, is that the postulated inferences concerning '*tonk*' must be invalid—they lead to absurdity. If we were told what '*tonk*' means, we would see that one or other inference was not truth-preserving. But—and this is Prior's challenge—the exponent of the analytical validity view cannot say that, for he has no independent account of the meaning of '*tonk*' relative to which to show that the inferences are invalid. '*Tonk*' was defined as the connective for which they were valid. Prior concludes that the analytical validity view has been conclusively shown to be wrong. Meaning, even of logical connectives, must be specified independently of, and prior to, determining the validity of inference patterns.

Belnap leaped to the defence of the 'analytical validity' (confusingly, he called it the 'synthetic') view. What's missing here, he said, is any proof that there is such a connective as '*tonk*'. It is a problem for definitions generally. One cannot define a thing into existence. One must first show that there is one and only one such thing. A famous example is the 'prosum' of two fractions, $\left(\dfrac{a}{b}\right)!\left(\dfrac{c}{d}\right)$ defined as $\dfrac{a+c}{b+d}$. Consider $\left(\dfrac{2}{3}\right)!\left(\dfrac{3}{4}\right)$. It appears to be $\dfrac{5}{7}$. But $\dfrac{2}{3}=\dfrac{4}{6}$, so $\left(\dfrac{2}{3}\right)!\left(\dfrac{3}{4}\right)=\left(\dfrac{4}{6}\right)!\left(\dfrac{3}{4}\right)=\dfrac{7}{10}\neq\dfrac{5}{7}$. Definition must be representation-independent, and this one is not. The use of different representations leads to inconsistency. '!' is not here well defined. We have not shown—and cannot show—that there is such a function. So too with '*tonk*'; we have not shown that there is a unique formula which can be inferred from an arbitrary formula A and entails any other formula B. Indeed, there cannot be one, as the inconsistency shows.

A problem remains, however. What exactly should the analogy be for connectives, to the existence claim for definitions generally? What is meant by requiring that there be such a (unique) connective? After all, we are adding a connective to the language, which in one clear sense does not already exist. It cannot always be wrong to extend a language by a new connective. In fact Prior—or at least, his subsequent defenders—probably had in mind the class of truth-functions, maps from sets of truth-values to truth-values (as 'and' maps the pair 'true-true' to 'true' and so on). But this is too narrow. We saw in Chapter 4 that one can extend classical logic by a connective for necessity, 'it is necessary that . . .', which is not truth-functional; and I argued in Chapter 3 that 'if . . . then . . .' is not truth-functional.

Belnap's proposal was that the addition of a new connective by means of rules of inference defining its meaning was legitimate provided the result was a conservative extension of the original system. What this means is that if one adds a new symbol to a language, and lays down (whether by truth-tables, or by axioms, or by fiat) rules of inference involving it; and if as a result a formula B is entailed by a formula A, both in the old vocabulary, then the entailment should already have held before the extension was made. That is, a necessary condition on extending a system of inference with new connectives is that no new inferences are permitted in the old vocabulary. New inferences resulting from the extension must all involve the new vocabulary. '*Tonk*' does not satisfy this condition. For obviously, adding '*tonk*' entirely trivializes the entailment relation, so that it holds between any two formulae, including those in the old vocabulary alone.

Belnap's restriction is certainly effective. Elsewhere, I have questioned whether it is the right one (see my *Relevant Logic*, ch. 9)—it is too strong. But I wish now to consider the use which has been made of it on behalf of constructivism as a critique of classical logic, and whether, even supposing Belnap's condition is the right condition on new connectives, that shows that classical negation is illegitimate. Does classical negation break Belnap's condition? Is classical logic a conservative extension of its negation-free fragment? If it is not, then the rules of classical negation, in particular, classical *reductio* and double negation elimination, are illegitimate. They are unjustified and untrustworthy in extending the negation-free consequence relation.

Clearly, the classical rules allow us to prove formulae such as Excluded Middle, '*A* or not-*A*', which contain negation. But do they extend the negation-free fragment? The constructivists claim they do. Examples are 'If *P* then *Q*, or if *Q* then *R*' and the notorious Peirce's Law, 'If *P* then *Q*, only if *P*, only if *P*'. Take the first: it is classically valid, for if *Q* is true then the first disjunct is true (by one 'paradox of material implication'), while if *Q* is false, the second disjunct is true (by the other 'paradox'). It goes along with Excluded Middle; but it is negation-free, yet not, the constructivist urges, part of the negation-free fragment. Similarly with Peirce's Law: if *P* is true the whole is true by the first paradox of material implication (any material conditional with true consequent is true); and if *P* is false, the antecedent is false (and so the whole is true by the second 'paradox') because it has itself a true antecedent, the conditional 'if *P* then *Q*' which is true by the first 'paradox', and false consequent (*P*).

The crucial question, therefore, is whether these principles are part of the negation-free fragment—and that raises the question of how one identifies it. Extending a logic by additional connectives is a well-defined operation; but removing connectives is not. The constructivist urges that Peirce's Law is not part of the negation-free fragment because, in a particular formulation of the classical calculus, it cannot be proved without using the classical negation rules. This formulation comes in a variety of forms, but they all ultimately derive from Gerhard Gentzen's natural deduction calculus *NK* of 1934. In many ways, this is unsurprising, for Gentzen was one of the first authors to urge the analytical validity view of the logical connectives. He wrote: 'The introduction[-rule]s represent, as it were, the "definitions" of the symbols concerned, and the elimination[-rule]s are no more, in the final analysis, than the consequences of these definitions.' Taking the pairs of rules of *NK* for the connectives other than negation, pairs of introduction-rules specifying the grounds for asserting a formula and elimination rules for using such an assertion, yields the negation-free fragment of intuitionistic logic. From there, the intuitionistic negation rules (intuitionistic *reductio* and *ex falso quodlibet*) give intuitionistic logic, the classical negation rules, classical logic. But the latter rules also extend the set of validities and consequences among negation-free formulae, and so break Belnap's condition.

The problem with this argument is that it depends too much on the way the negation-free fragment of classical logic is identified—on choosing Gentzen's natural deduction formulation *NK* as the framework. Almost every other formulation gives a different answer—that is, includes Peirce's Law and the like in the negation-free fragment. For example, Gentzen's other way of presenting classical logic, his sequent calculus *LK*, allows simple proofs of these propositions without use of negation. The crucial move, in all cases, can be seen to lie in permitting the inference of 'If P then Q, or R' from 'If P then, Q or R', a move which the multiple-conclusion set-up of *LK* allows, and the single-conclusion set-up of Gentzen's natural deduction framework does not. The constructivist objects to such a move, for it introduces a disjunction in a way which does not guarantee that one disjunct is known to be the justification. For example, 'If P then, Q or P' is classically and intuitionistically acceptable; only the classicist is happy to move to 'If P then Q, or P', that is 'P or, if P then Q'—either P is true or not, in which case 'if P then Q' is true.

Multiple-conclusion natural deduction, derived from *LK*, and axiomatic formulations, reiterate the same point, as does classical semantics. Recall that for the realist, study of semantic structures comes before study of proofs. In higher-order logic it has to, for the logics are incomplete (cf. the remarks on the ω-rule in Chapter 2). Peirce's Law and the others are valid by truth-tables whether or not negation is present. Of course, the constructivist is unimpressed by appeal to such semantic arguments. But that shows where the true disagreement beyond constructivist and realist lies. Belnap's condition cannot show that classical negation is illegitimate.

The Linguistic Argument

Finally, we should turn to examine the third line of argument by which the constructivist challenges the realist, which I am calling the 'linguistic argument'. Its focus is the so-called 'manifestation challenge': what right would we have to attribute to speakers an understanding of expressions beyond what they are able to manifest in their linguistic behaviour? The form of this challenge, if it is cogent, lies in what is allowed to count as manifestation.

Recall from Chapter 5 the puzzle about language acquisition, how a child is able, on the basis of exposure to a relatively small set of linguistic data, to acquire competence in a language, the ability to produce and understand an indefinitely large class of meaningful expressions. We answered it at the time by embracing the 'compositionality' principle, of functional dependency, whereby a finite set of postulates can recursively generate a potentially infinite output. But that answered a different question from that now before us; that explains how a finite base can encompass an infinite capacity. The puzzle that is now emerging is this: how can the child or language-learner come to fix with accuracy on that particular finite base following exposure not to that finite base itself, but only to manifestations of it by other speakers? What the language-learner hears is the output, not the generator. How does it establish its own generator, one with the same output as those producing the evidence?

This puzzle taxed Chomsky and other linguists in the 1960s. They proposed a realist solution—indeed, they were self-avowed rationalists. There must be some species-specific ability possessed by humans which enables them to learn language. The difference between humans and monkeys or Martians is not a simple matter of greater or lesser native intelligence; independent of the intellectual abilities of the creature, human languages have a structure—they hypothesized—whose general character is not learned, but is 'pre-programmed', that is, results from an innate tendency for humans to behave linguistically in specific ways. The hypothesis inaugurated an empirical search to determine those linguistic universals.

The gap between evidence and theory need not be closed in such a way, however. The anti-realist closes it by denying that the theory does outpace the data in this manner. Acquisition is essentially tied to manifestation. There can be no more to meaning—there can be no more to acquire—than speakers of the language can manifest in their use. Two things are being denied here: first, that there can be a private element to meaning, an introspectible quality which cannot be made public. The phenomenology of meaning is often thought to belie this claim; we experience the phenomenon of knowing what we mean despite being frustrated in our attempts to express our ideas and achieve communication. But the logic of the situation tells otherwise. Wittgenstein's private language argument is the most famous attempt to establish this point. A private language would require private incommunicable rules; private attempts to accord with those rules would not distinguish between correct observance and breach of the rules; whatever seemed to the private linguist to be right would be right. But the notion of rule requires just this distinction, between correct and incorrect use, between what merely seems right and what really is right. As a corollary, there can be no aspect of meaning that is not publicly manifestable.

The second denial is that truth, understood as an evidence-transcendent notion, could be the central notion in the theory of meaning. The realist notion of truth is one, as I have repeatedly emphasized, that entails that a proposition could be true yet remain forever unknown by us. Truth consists in the properties of a structure conceived of as obtaining independently of our ability to know about it. The present claim is that such a notion of truth could play no part in the concept of meaning. We must be capable of manifesting our understanding of a proposition in the use we make of it. That manifestation consists in asserting or denying the proposition in the light of evidence for or against it. Hence, it is claimed, its meaning must consist in a grasp of what would count as a verification or refutation of it. That is, its meaning cannot consist in the obtaining of a situation regardless of our ability to recognize it as obtaining; it must consist in a capacity to recognize that situation as obtaining, if it does.

The canvas has now been widened. The problem is no longer restricted to the narrow case of mathematics—it encompasses empirical propositions too. Propositions concerning the past, the future, open classes (e.g. 'All emeralds are green'), counterfactuals, attributions of mental states, all must be tied, says the constructivist, to an effective method of verification. To manifest understanding of such propositions, a link must be set up to what would count as conclusive proof or disproof. This does not mean that one is necessarily in a position to establish their truth one way or the other. Those of which one can are the effectively decidable propositions. But even for those not effectively decidable, their sense must consist in an account of what would establish them as true or false, were one to obtain that evidence.

The challenge to the classicist is this: his philosophy commits him to the existence of propositions whose truth might be incapable of demonstration by us. Take an example: 'Jones was brave'. Jones is now dead, and never in his life was he placed in a position to reveal whether he was brave or not. The proposition has sense, says the constructivist. Its sense is that, had he been so placed, he would have acted bravely. We can manifest the sense of such propositions, namely, that on observing someone to behave in a particular manner, we commend them as brave. That sense extends to the undecidable proposition, 'Jones was brave'. Had he been tested, his reaction would have shown whether he was brave or not. But the constructivist refrains from asserting that either Jones was brave or he was not. Until there is some method of deciding which disjunct is the right one, there is, he claims, no fact of the matter. Its truth attaches to how he reacts, not to some hidden property, lying dormant and unrevealed. Yet such must be the classicist's assumption.

The classicist will answer that either Jones was brave or not—he is committed universally to Excluded Middle. There must, therefore, be some fact of the matter that decides the truth one way or the other. Yet that truth could—the classicist cannot deny—remain forever hidden from us.

The linguistic argument claims that such a classical understanding of the proposition could not be communicated, that it could not be manifested, and consequently could not be acquired. The classical account attempts to ground meaning in possibly evidence-transcendent facts, semantic structures divorced from methods of verification. The challenge is that such an identification of meaning with conditions for truth separated from conditions for verification will leave such propositions void of meaning.

What is good about the linguistic argument is what it shares with the earlier puzzles, about infinity; what is bad about it, is what it shares with scepticism generally. The acquisition argument poses a rhetorical question: how could the language learner discover, from the linguistic behaviour exhibited by competent speakers, any element of meaning not displayed in those speakers' sensitivity, in their claims, to the evidence available? It is a rhetorical question, in that the constructivist does not expect an answer; it is taken for granted that no answer can be given. It is surely no answer, even if tempting, simply to reply with the observation that we do attach realist sense to such propositions, realist sense which is proven by our affirmation of Excluded Middle generally, and in particular, for the undecidable class. That's no answer, for the present issue is whether that affirmation is justified, and whether there is such a coherent realist sense. On the other hand, the very fact that there appears to be such a sense, that is, that we are given to act as if there were, makes the situation one of paradox, not of immediate victory to the constructivist. We appear to attach a sense to such propositions as 'Jones was brave' that commits us to asserting Excluded Middle for it; yet such a sense would appear to resist manifestation. Who is right, the sceptic about realist sense or the believer in evidence-transcendent facts?

The behaviourist reaction in the 1930s to over-reliance on

phenomenological and introspective reports was salutary. Such reports cannot always be taken at face-value, and an adequate methodology for sifting them is needed. What was wrong with it was its narrowing of what could be accounted evidence. One upshot, within philosophy, was the scepticism about meaning which we find in Quine and certain interpretations of Wittgenstein's remarks, and in the linguistic argument for constructivism. The sceptic rightly challenges us to say how such propositions could be shown to be true. He wrongly declines to wait for an answer. A canonical way to prove bravery is to observe bravery in action. What is not so obvious is whether we do not think there is other evidence one might address, failing the canonical observation. Bravery is a quality making up a human personality, which consists of an interlocking matrix of virtues and vices. These do not come as a free assembly kit, unconstrained in their mixtures. Jones's possession, or lack, of other qualities can also count as grounds for attribution of such character as bravery or cowardice.

Such brief remarks are not a rebuttal of the constructivistic sceptic about meaning. What they are meant to do is balance the debate so that we see that the question is the coherence of certain conceptions. I started the chapter by contrasting the realist, objectivist conception of truth with the constructivist, epistemically constrained conception. The issue we end on is the central one in that debate: is the realist conception coherent and in particular can it be intelligibly elucidated and explained?

Summary and Guide to Further Reading

The realist conception of truth is one of the possession by propositions of an objective property, a relational property which they acquire in vitue of the properties of the objects mentioned in them. A metaphysical realist will search, as we saw in Chapter 1, for a single correlate, a fact, not reducible to other objects, whose existence makes the proposition true; a minimal realist will deny that truth is such a substantive property, and will seek to reduce truth to the possession by the objects mentioned in the proposition of the properties assigned to them. In either case, however, truth is objective, in that there is no hint that whether a proposition is true is affected in any way by our ability or inability to discover it. Facts could exist, or objects could have their properties, without any need for this to be evident to us.

The anti-realist denies that this classical, realist picture is intelligible or coherent. Traditionally it was seen as a special problem about infinity; more recently it has been extended by analogy to other areas—but themselves ones with a history of dispute over scepticism and idealism—the past, the future, other minds, universal generalizations, and so on. It is discussed in Pascal Engel's *The Norm of Truth*, ch. 6; two classic sources are Michael Dummett's 'What Is a Theory of Meaning?' (II), and Crispin Wright's review article on Dummett's collected papers, 'Anti-Realism and Revisionism', reprinted in his *Realism, Meaning and Truth*. The focus of criticism is on so-called 'verification-' or 'evidence-transcendent truth', the realist idea that a proposition might be true whose truth we had no possibility of discovering or establishing. Suppose, for example, that Goldbach's Conjecture, that every even number greater than 2 is the sum of two primes, is true. On the realist conception, there might be no general proof, no proof which took an arbitrary even number and showed how it must decompose into two primes. Perhaps it's a unique and particular fact for each even number that it so decomposes. If so, we could not establish its truth, for we could not complete the task of examining each even number in turn and verifying its prime decomposition. Its truth could be evidence- or proof-transcendent.

On the anti-realist conception, this is unintelligible. There is no reality to the collection of even numbers, beyond our ability to generate larger and larger numbers each divisible by 2. In the case of a finite collection—whether of numbers, or of sheep, or electrons, or daffodil species—it is in principle possible to check through them one by one and examine them. So each may be unique, each may be a particular with its own properties to be discovered. With an infinite collection—from the anti-realist viewpoint—the case is different. The realist is mistaken to extrapolate from the one to the other. The conception of a structure, of an infinite collection of numbers, say, is derivative from that of a construction, in the case of the numbers, the construction or operation whereby the successor of a number is generated. Hence anything true of such numbers must reside in the construction. Anything true of them must be verifiable by a general proof, checking of a particular number that its construction results in the supposed feature.

Why is the constructivist so fearful of a structure underpinning the operation, some totality on which realist truth can be based? His anxiety has good cause, namely, an array of paradoxes, both old and new. The paradoxes of the line go back to Zeno of Elea in the fifth century BC—see e.g. Aristotle, *Physics*, bk. 3 chs. 4–8, or A. Grünbaum, *Modern Science and Zeno's Paradoxes*. The philosophical problem with the notion of infinity—of the incompletable—is well described in Mary Tiles's *The Philosophy of Set Theory*. But mathematics seemed to need more than the Greeks, with their constructions and theory of ratios, could provide. The move to arithmetization, to treating the line as an actual infinity of points, gave rise to the calculus and the successes of its application in mathematical physics from the seventeenth century onwards. It reached its zenith in the nineteenth century, in the work of Cauchy, Bolzano, Weierstrass, and others. This work is carefully surveyed by Morris Kline in chapters 40–1, 43, 51 of his magisterial study, *Mathematical Thought from Ancient to Modern Times*.

The underlying philosophical motivation is that every potential infinity presupposes an actual infinity—e.g. generating successors suggests they are really all there already; cutting the line suggests that the point where the cut is made is already in place. It was particularly the latter, the line as a continuous linear ordering of points, which drove forward Cantor's work, as described so well in M. Hallett, *Cantorian Set Theory and Limitation of Size*. Infinite collections—sets—seemed to yield to straightforward extensional treatment just like finite ones. The realist approach, the concentration on the structure as revealed by our probing, seemed perfectly vindicated. But this was to reckon without the logical paradoxes, Cantor's, Burali-Forti's, and Russell's antinomies. These and others are described in a veritable gold-mine of information, *Foundations of Set Theory* by Abraham Fraenkel and Yehoshua Bar-Hillel, and with further contributions from A. Levy and D. van Dalen.

The realist reaction was conservative, to preserve as much as possible of the development of mathematical analysis, the classical work of Weierstrass and others. The constructivist reaction was radical; their scepticism was vindicated, they believed, and what was needed was completely to rework the mathematics of the infinite from a constructivist perspective. The details are set out in A. Troelstra and D. van Dalen's *Constructivism in Mathematics: An Introduction*, developing intuitionist and other constructions in parallel. The particular elaboration given by the intuitionists, led by L. E. J. Brouwer from 1907 onwards, is surveyed in M. Dummett, *Elements of Intuitionism*, which also contains extended philosophical discussion. A useful collection of articles is *Readings in the Philosophy of Mathematics*, edited by P. Benacerraf and H. Putnam, in which intuitionism is shown side by side with other philosophical analyses and accounts of the nature of mathematics.

Much of this chapter was spent developing the mathematics of the infinite, both realist and anti-realist, for it is not only the hardest to get to grips with philosophically, it is also where I think the essential philosophical debate lies. Either constructivism is justified by the fact that Cantor's attempt to treat the infinite by the realist methods of set theory led to paradox; or realism is a viable project, and mathematics can proceed as the study of structures whose properties may outstrip our investigative procedures.

None the less, more recent advocates of anti-realism have tried to show the incoherence of realism by other means. The main authors of these arguments have been Dag Prawitz, in a number of papers, including 'Meaning and Proofs: On the Conflict between Classical and Intuitionistic Logic'; and Michael Dummett, again in many papers, but most notably in his early paper, 'Truth' (to which almost all his subsequent work is an extended footnote) and in 'The Philosophical Basis of Intuitionistic Logic', both reprinted in his *Truth and Other Enigmas*; and in his recent book (based on lectures given in 1976), *The Logical*

Basis of Metaphysics. Their ideas are usefully summarized in G. Sundholm, 'Proof Theory and Meaning', in D. Gabbay and F. Guenthner (eds.), *Handbook of Philosophical Logic*, iii. There are really two arguments which they add to the above considerations. Dummett criticizes classical negation for non-conservatively extending the theory of implication; both Prawitz and Dummett more cautiously criticize classical logic for failing to keep a proper ('harmonious') connection between its negation rules. The argument traces back to a very short but provocative paper by Arthur Prior, 'The Runabout Inference Ticket'. He claimed that the attempt (started by passing remarks of G. Gentzen's in 'Investigations Concerning Logical Deduction', translated in *Collected Papers of Gerhard Gentzen* by M. Szabo) to give the meaning of logical connectives by reference to the inference patterns in which they appear, was absurd, since such an approach would permit the introduction of such a connective as '*tonk*' and the consequent ruination of logic. Nuel Belnap's reply, in 'Tonk, Plonk and Plink', was to propose a constraint on the definition of new logical constants by reference to rules of inference, namely, that their introduction be conservative, that is, that no new consequences in the old vocabulary should be occasioned by it. It is clearly a strong and effective constraint; what is not so clear is what justifies it. But if it is accepted, it is tempting to use it as a stick to beat classical logic, for in its natural deduction form tracing back to Gentzen, classical logic is not a conservative extension of its negation-free fragment; that is, the classical rules for negation, in particular, classical *reductio* and double negation elimination, permit the validation of inferences in the negation-free vocabulary not permitted by the natural deduction rules for that vocabulary alone.

Of course, this argument will not impress a hard-line realist, who would not concede that connectives should be defined by rules of inference—that already smacks of anti-realism, and the idea that the operations (here, the inferential operations) are paramount. Let us first define the connectives by reference to the structures on which they operate, it will be said (echoing Prior); only then can we determine whether the inferences are truth-preserving. But even if one is attracted by the smoothness and elegance of the proof-conditional manner of defining the connectives (in contrast, say, with the complexity and roughness of possible worlds semantics), one can still feel that Dummett's objection depends too heavily on a particular style of presentation of the relevant inference-patterns. Indeed, the point then is not that the classical negation rules are too powerful, but that the other rules, in particular, the rules for implication, are too weak. Those disputed, so-called 'classical' negation-free inferences should already have been included in the negation-free fragment, and it is the fault of the negation-free rules that they are not, not that of the negation rules that they add them. To effect this, we need to adopt a different style of proof. As D. Shoesmith and T. Smiley remark in their brilliant but difficult book, *Multiple-Conclusion Logic*: '[Material implication] causes difficulty ... It turns out that the obvious introduction rules ... characterise intuitionist, not classical implication; and to introduce the latter it is necessary to have multiple conclusions. Indeed, one would have to conclude that classical logicians, like so many Monsieur Jourdains, have been speaking multiple conclusions all their lives without knowing it' (p. 4).

The other argument for the incoherence of realism has been pressed repeatedly by Dummett, in, for example, the papers already mentioned, and in chapter 13 of his *Frege: Philosophy of Language*. The anti-realist's complaint about realism is its commitment to verification-transcendence, to the idea that a proposition might be true but whose truth we had no means of recognizing. That idea, it is said, is incompatible with a natural constraint on meaning, that one's understanding of the meaning of a proposition is capable of being manifested, and that manifestation can act as the only input to language acquisition. Realism entails a divorce between what propositions can mean and what makes them true. It is a gap which was bridged by Chomsky, in his postulation of innate species-specific knowledge, in his *Cartesian Linguistics*; and was eroded by Quine in his attack on the idea of determinacy of meaning, in chapter 2 of his *Word and Object*. Dummett practises a similar move in restricting and limiting meaning, so that it require by the speaker a capacity to recognize when the proposition is true.

Understanding a proposition must consist in a manifestable ability to recognize a verification or demonstration of the truth of the proposition when presented with one. There is no requirement that its truth be effectively decidable. There are many propositions whose truth we have no effective means of deciding. But we manifest our understanding, says Dummett, by exhibiting our recognition of the truth of propositions to which it is related by some appropriate compositional mechanism. Understanding is a recognitional ability.

Dummett's claim has been resisted by several authors; chapter 2 of Simon Blackburn's *Spreading the Word* puts out its own defence, and has references to others. The connection with Quine's scepticism about meaning should remind us of Saul Kripke's Wittgenstein (see his *Wittgenstein on Rules and Private Language*) and his sceptical paradox. So too should the reference to Chomsky, the instigator of a programme in linguistics taken up and extended by Jerry Fodor in, for example, *The Language of Thought* to argue for an innate linguistic ability— where he claims that no one could learn a language who did not already possess one, innately. It was this Augustinian picture which Wittgenstein argued against in his *Philosophical Investigations*. But Wittgenstein there gives an answer to the sceptic— an answer that has been variously interpreted, in interpretations which can be as paradoxical as the original puzzle. I think he is telling us that it is our future practice which decides what our earlier utterances meant. The rule-following puzzle is that many interpretations (rules) are compatible with any finite manifestation of meaning; what makes it determinate? Fodor thinks it is our inner thoughts, our private language; Kripke's sceptic thinks nothing is meant. Wittgenstein's solution is that we decide by our future practice what we meant, so that the order of explanation (puzzlingly) runs from future to past, not vice versa.

There lies a clue to the realist for an answer to Dummett, one which can now make sense of the idea, dismissed earlier, that our practice as realists in using classical *reductio* and so on is in fact coherent after all. That practice is not justified by our negation-free usage, but serves to reinterpret it.

Select Bibliography

ACKERMANN, W., 'Begründung einer strengen Implikation', *Journal of Symbolic Logic*, 21 (1956), 113–28.

ADAMS, E., *The Logic of Conditionals* (Dordrecht: Reidel, 1975).

ALBERT OF SAXONY, *Perutilis Logica*, tr. in N. Kretzmann *et al.* (eds.), *The Cambridge Translations of Medieval Philosophical Texts*, i (Cambridge: Cambridge University Press, 1988).

ANDERSON, A., and BELNAP, N., *Entailment: The Logic of Relevance and Necessity*, 2 vols. (Princeton, NJ: Princeton University Press, 1975, 1992).

ARISTOTLE, *Physics*, ed. and tr. E. Hussey (Oxford: Clarendon Press, 1983).

ARMSTRONG, D. M., *A Combinatorial Theory of Possibility* (Cambridge: Cambridge University Press, 1989).

ASIMOV, I., *The Gods Themselves* (London: Panther Books, 1973).

AUSTIN, J. L., 'How to Talk', reprinted in his *Philosophical Papers* (Oxford: Oxford University Press, 1970).

BARNES, J., 'Medicine, Experience and Logic', in J. Barnes *et al.* (eds.), *Science and Speculation* (Cambridge: Cambridge University Press, 1982).

BARWISE, J., *The Situation in Logic* (Stanford, Calif.: Center for the Study of Language and Information, 1989).

—— and ETCHEMENDY, J., *The Liar* (Oxford: Oxford University Press, 1987).

—— and PERRY, J., *Situations and Attitudes* (Cambridge, Mass.: MIT Bradford, 1983).

BELNAP, N., 'Tonk, Plonk and Plink', *Analysis*, 22 (1961–2), 30–4.

BENACERRAF, P., 'Skolem and the Skeptic', *Aristotelian Society*, supp. vol. 60 (1985), 85–115.

—— and PUTNAM, H. (eds.), *Readings in the Philosophy of Mathematics* (Oxford: Blackwell, 1985).

BENCIVENGA, E., 'Free Logics', in D. Gabbay and F. Guenthner (eds.), *Handbook of Philosophical Logic*, iii (Dordrecht: Reidel, 1986).

BLACK, M., 'Vagueness', *Philosophy of Science*, 4 (1937), 427–55.

BLACKBURN, S., *Spreading the Word* (Oxford: Oxford University Press, 1985).

BOH, I., 'Consequences', in N. Kretzmann *et al.*, *The Cambridge History of Later Medieval Philosophy* (Cambridge: Cambridge University Press, 1982), ch. 15.

BOLZANO, B., *Theory of Science*, tr. R. George (Los Angeles and Berkeley, Calif.: University of California Press, 1972).

CERVANTES, M. DE, *Don Quixote*, tr. T. Smollett (London: Deutsch, 1986).

CHOMSKY, N., *Cartesian Linguistics* (London: Harper & Row, 1966).

CICERO, *Academica*, tr. H. Rackham (London: Heinemann, 1972).

COOPER, W., 'The Propositional Logic of Ordinary Discourse', *Inquiry*, 11 (1968), 295–320.

CORCORAN, J., and SHAPIRO, H., review of J. Crossley *et al.*, *What is Mathematical Logic?*, in *Philosophia*, 8 (1978), 79–94.

CORNFORD, F. M., *Plato and Parmenides* (London: Routledge & Kegan Paul, 1939).

CROSSLEY, J., *et al.*, *What is Mathematical Logic?* (Oxford: Oxford University Press, 1972).

DAVIDSON, D., 'True to the Facts', reprinted in his *Inquiries into Truth and Interpretation* (Oxford: Oxford University Press, 1984).

DAWSON, J., 'The Compactness of First-Order Logic: From Gödel to Lindström', *History and Philosophy of Logic*, 14 (1993), 15–37.

DEVLIN, K., *Logic and Information* (Cambridge: Cambridge University Press, 1991).

DUDMAN, V., 'Interpretations of "If"-sentences', in F. Jackson (ed.), *Conditionals*.

DUMMETT, M., *Elements of Intuitionism* (Oxford: Oxford University Press, 1977).

—— *Frege: Philosophy of Language* (London: Duckworth, 1973).

—— *The Logical Basis of Metaphysics* (London: Duckworth, 1991).

—— 'The Philosophical Basis of Intuitionistic Logic', reprinted in his *Truth and Other Enigmas*.

—— 'Truth', reprinted in his *Truth and Other Enigmas*.

—— *Truth and Other Enigmas* (London: Duckworth, 1978).

—— 'Wang's Paradox', *Synthese*, 30 (1975), 301–24.

—— 'What Is a Theory of Meaning?' (II), in G. Evans and J. McDowell (eds.), *Truth and Meaning* (Oxford: Oxford University Press, 1976).

EDGINGTON, D., 'Do Conditionals have Truth-Conditions?', in F. Jackson (ed.), *Conditionals*.

ENGEL, P., *The Norm of Truth* (Brighton: Harvester, 1991).

ETCHEMENDY, J. *The Concept of Logical Consequence* (Cambridge, Mass.: Harvard University Press, 1990).

—— 'Tarski on Truth and Logical Consequence', *Journal of Symbolic Logic*, 53 (1988), 51–79.

FIELD, H., 'The Deflationary Conception of Truth', in G. Macdonald and C. Wright (eds.), *Fact, Science and Morality* (Oxford: Blackwell, 1986).

FINE, K., 'Vagueness, Truth and Logic', *Synthese*, 30 (1975), 265–300.

FODOR, J., *The Language of Thought* (Brighton: Harvester, 1976).

FRAASSEN, B. VAN, 'Singular Terms, Truthvalue Gaps and Free Logic', reprinted in K. Lambert (ed.), *Philosophical Applications of Free Logic*.

FRAENKEL, A., BAR-HILLEL, Y., LEVY, A., and VAN DALEN, D., *Foundations of Set Theory* (Amsterdam: North-Holland, 1973).

FREGE, G., 'On Sense and Reference', in *Translations from the Philosophical Writings of Gottlob Frege*, ed. and tr. P. Geach and M. Black (Oxford: Blackwell, 1966).

—— 'Further Remarks on Sense and Meaning', in his *Posthumous Writings*, ed. H. Hermes *et al.*, tr. P. Long and R. White (Oxford: Blackwell, 1979).

GÄRDENFORS, P., *Knowledge in Flux* (Cambridge, Mass.: MIT Bradford, 1988).

GEACH, P., 'Ascriptivism', reprinted in his *Logic Matters*.

—— 'Assertion', reprinted in his *Logic Matters*.

—— 'On *Insolubilia*', reprinted in his *Logic Matters*.

—— *Logic Matters* (Oxford: Blackwell, 1972).

GENTZEN, G., 'Investigations Concerning Logical Deduction', in M. Szabo (ed. and tr.), *Collected Papers of Gerhard Gentzen* (Amsterdam: North-Holland, 1969).

GOGUEN, J., 'The Logic of Inexact Concepts', *Synthese*, 19 (1968–9), 325–73.

GRICE, H. P., 'Logic and Conversation', in F. Jackson (ed.), *Conditionals*.

GROVER, D., *A Prosentential Theory of Truth* (Princeton, NJ: Princeton University Press, 1992).

—— CAMP, J., and BELNAP, N., 'A Prosentential Theory of Truth', *Philosophical Studies*, 27 (1975), reprinted in D. Grover, *A Prosentential Theory of Truth*.

GRÜNBAUM, A., *Modern Science and Zeno's Paradoxes* (London: George Allen & Unwin, 1968).

HAACK, S., *Philosophy of Logics* (Cambridge: Cambridge University Press, 1978).

HALLETT, M., *Cantorian Set Theory and Limitation of Size* (Oxford: Oxford University Press, 1984).

HARPER, W., *et al.* (eds.), *Ifs* (Dordrecht: Reidel, 1981).

HEIJENOORT, J. VAN, 'Frege and Vagueness', in his *Selected Essays* (Naples: Bibliopolis, 1985).

HOFSTADTER, D., *Gödel, Escher, Bach: An Eternal Golden Braid* (Harmondsworth: Penguin, 1980).

HUGHES, G., and CRESSWELL, M., *An Introduction to Modal Logic* (London: Methuen, 1968).

JACKSON, F., *Conditionals* (Oxford: Blackwell, 1987).

—— (ed.), *Conditionals* (Oxford: Oxford University Press, 1991).

—— 'On Assertion and Indicative Conditionals', in F. Jackson (ed.), *Conditionals*.

KEENE, G. B., *Foundations of Rational Argument* (Lewiston, NY: Edwin Mellen Press, 1992).

KLINE, M., *Mathematical Thought from Ancient to Modern Times* (Oxford: Oxford University Press, 1972).

KRIPKE, S., *Naming and Necessity* (Oxford: Blackwell, 1980).

—— 'Outline of a Theory of Truth', reprinted in R. L. Martin (ed.), *Recent Essays on Truth and the Liar Paradox*.

—— 'Semantical Considerations on Modal Logic I', reprinted in L. Linsky (ed.), *Reference and Modality*.

—— *Wittgenstein on Rules and Private Language* (Oxford: Blackwell, 1982).

LAMBERT, K., *Meinong and the Principle of Independence* (Cambridge: Cambridge University Press, 1983).

—— (ed.), *Philosophical Applications of Free Logic* (Oxford: Oxford University Press, 1991).

LEWIS, D., *Counterfactuals* (Oxford: Blackwell, 1973).

—— 'Counterfactuals and Comparative Possibility', reprinted in W. Harper *et al.* (eds.), *Ifs*.

—— 'Counterpart Theory and Quantified Modal Logic', reprinted in M. Loux (ed.), *The Possible and the Actual*.

—— *On the Plurality of Worlds* (Oxford: Blackwell, 1987).

—— 'Probabilities of Conditionals and Conditional Probabilities' I and II, reprinted in F. Jackson (ed.), *Conditionals*.

LINDSTRÖM, P., 'On Extensions of Elementary Logic', *Theoria*, 35 (1969), 1–11.

—— 'On Characterizing Elementary Logic', in S. Stenlund (ed.), *Logical Theory and Semantic Analysis* (Dordrecht: Reidel, 1974).

LINSKY, L. (ed.), *Reference and Modality* (Oxford: Oxford University Press, 1971).

LOUX, M. (ed.), *The Possible and the Actual* (Ithaca, NY: Cornell University Press, 1979).

MARCUS, R. B., 'A Backwards Look at Quine's Animadversions on

Modalities', in R. Gibson and R. Barrett (eds.), *Perspectives on Quine* (Oxford: Blackwell, 1989).

MARTIN, R. L. (ed.), *Recent Essays on Truth and the Liar Paradox* (Oxford: Clarendon Press, 1984).

MONTAGUE, R., and KAPLAN, D., 'A Paradox Regained', reprinted in R. Montague, *Formal Philosophy* (New Haven, Conn.: Yale University Press, 1974).

MOORE, G. E., *Some Main Problems of Philosophy*, ed. H. D. Lewis (London: George Allen & Unwin, 1953).

O'CONNOR, D. J., *The Correspondence Theory of Truth* (London: Hutchinson, 1975).

ORLOWSKA, E., 'Semantics of Vague Concepts', in G. Dorn and P. Weingartner (eds.), *Foundations of Logic and Linguistics* (New York: Plenum Press, 1984).

PARRY, W. T., 'Analytic Implication: Its History, Justification and Varieties', in J. Norman and R. Sylvan (eds.), *Directions in Relevant Logic* (Dordrecht: Kluwer, 1989).

PAWLAK, Z., *Rough Sets* (Dordrecht: Kluwer, 1991).

PEACOCKE, C., 'Are Vague Predicates Incoherent?', *Synthese*, 46 (1981), 121–41.

PLATTS, M., *Ways of Meaning: An Introduction to a Philosophy of Language* (London: Routledge & Kegan Paul, 1979).

PRAWITZ, D., 'Meaning and Proofs: On the Conflict between Classical and Intuitionistic Logic', *Theoria*, 43 (1977), 2–40.

PRIEST, G., *In Contradiction* (Dordrecht: Nijhoff, 1987).

—— 'Can Contradictions be True?', *Aristotelian Society*, supp. vol. 67 (1993).

PRIOR, A., 'The Runabout Inference Ticket', *Analysis*, 21 (1960–1), 8–39.

PUTNAM, H., 'A Comparison of Something with Something Else', *New Literary History*, 17 (1985–6), 61–79.

—— 'Models and Reality', *Journal of Symbolic Logic*, 45 (1980), 464–82, reprinted in his *Realism and Reason*, Philosophical Papers, 3 (Cambridge: Cambridge University Press, 1983), 1–25.

—— *Reason, Truth and History* (Cambridge: Cambridge University Press, 1981).

QUINE, W. VAN O., *Methods of Logic* (London: Routledge & Kegan Paul, 1962).

—— 'On What There Is', reprinted in his *From a Logical Point of View* (London: Harper & Row, 1953).

QUINE, W. VAN O., 'Three Grades of Modal Involvement', in his *Ways of Paradox and Other Essays* (New York: Random House, 1966).
—— *Word and Object* (Cambridge, Mass.: MIT Press, 1960).

RAMSEY, F. P., 'Facts and Propositions', in his *The Foundations of Mathematics and Other Essays*.
——*The Foundations of Mathematics and Other Essays*, ed. R. B. Braithwaite (London: Routledge & Kegan Paul, 1931).
——'General Proposisions and Causality', in his *Foundations of Mathematics and Other Essays*.

READ, S., *Relevant Logic* (Oxford: Blackwell, 1988).

RUSSELL, B., *Logic and Knowledge*, ed. R. C. Marsh (London: George Allen & Unwin, 1956).
—— 'On Denoting', reprinted in his *Logic and Knowledge*.
—— 'The Philosophy of Logical Atomism', reprinted in his *Logic and Knowledge*.

RYLE, G., 'Heterologicality', reprinted in his *Collected Papers*, ii (London: Hutchinson, 1971).
—— 'Discussion of Rudolf Carnap: "Meaning and Necessity"', reprinted in his *Collected Papers*, i (London: Hutchinson, 1971).

SAINSBURY, R. M., 'Concepts Without Boundaries', Lecture, King's College, London, 1990.
—— *Logical Forms* (Oxford: Blackwell, 1991).
—— *Paradoxes* (Cambridge: Cambridge University Press, 1988).

SHOESMITH, D. and SMILEY, T., *Multiple-Conclusion Logic* (Cambridge: Cambridge University Press, 1978).

SLOMAN, A., '"Necessary", "A Priori" and "Analytic"', *Analysis*, 26 (1965–6), 12–16.

SMILEY, T., 'Can Contradictions be True?', *Aristotelian Society*, supp. vol. 67 (1993).

SMULLYAN, A. F., 'Modality and Description', reprinted in L. Linsky (ed.), *Reference and Modality*.

STALNAKER, R., 'Probability and Conditionals', reprinted in W. Harper *et al.* (eds.), *Ifs*.
—— 'A Theory of Conditionals', reprinted both in F. Jackson (ed.), *Conditionals* and in W. Harper *et al.* (eds.), *Ifs*.

SUNDHOLM, G., 'Proof Theory and Meaning', in D. Gabbay and F. Guenthner (eds.), *Handbook of Philosophical Logic*, iii (Dordrecht: Reidel, 1986).

TARSKI, A., 'On the Concept of Logical Consequence', in *Logic, Semantics, Metamathematics*, tr. J. H. Woodger (Oxford: Clarendon Press, 1956).

—— 'The Semantic Conception of Truth', reprinted in H. Feigl and W. Sellars (eds.), *Readings in Philosophical Analysis* (New York: Appleton-Century-Crofts, 1949).

TENNANT, N., *Anti-Realism and Logic* (Oxford: Clarendon Press, 1987).

THARP, L., 'Which Logic is the Right Logic?', *Synthese*, 31 (1975), 1–21.

—— 'Three Theorems of Metaphysics', *Synthese*, 81 (1989), 207–14.

TILES, M., *The Philosophy of Set Theory* (Oxford: Blackwell, 1989).

TROELSTRA, A., and DALEN, D. VAN, *Constructivism in Mathematics: An Introduction* (Amsterdam: North-Holland, 1988).

URMSON, J., *Philosophical Analysis* (Oxford: Clarendon Press, 1956).

WALKER, R. C. S., 'Conversational Implicatures', in S. Blackburn (ed.), *Meaning, Reference and Necessity* (Cambridge: Cambridge University Press, 1975).

WILLIAMS, C. J. F., *What is Truth?* (Cambridge: Cambridge University Press, 1976).

WILLIAMSON, T., 'Vagueness and Ignorance', *Aristotelian Society*, supp. vol. 66 (1992), 145–62.

WITTGENSTEIN, L., *Philosophical Investigations* (London: Blackwell, 1953).

——*Tractatus Logico-Philosophicus*, tr. D. Pears and B. McGuinness (London: Routledge & Kegan Paul, 1961).

WRIGHT, C., 'Anti-realism and Revisionism', reprinted in his *Realism, Meaning and Truth* (Oxford: Blackwell, 1987).

—— 'Further Reflections on the Sorites Paradox', *Philosophical Topics*, 15 (1987), 227–90.

—— 'Language Mastery and the Sorites Paradox', in G. Evans and J. McDowell (eds.), *Truth and Meaning* (Oxford: Oxford University Press, 1976).

—— 'On the Coherence of Vague Predicates', *Synthese*, 30 (1975), 325–65.

—— 'Skolem and the Skeptic', *Aristotelian Society*, supp. vol. 60 (1985), 117–37.

—— *Truth and Objectivity* (Cambridge, Mass.: Harvard University Press, 1992).

ZADEH, L., 'Fuzzy Sets', *Information and Control*, 8 (1965), 338–53, reprinted in his *Fuzzy Sets and Applications*, ed. R. Yager (Chichester: Wiley, 1987).

—— 'Fuzzy Logic and Approximate Reasoning', *Synthese*, 30 (1975), 407–28.

—— *An Introduction to Fuzzy Logic* (Dordrecht: Kluwer, 1992).

Glossary

Addition traditional name for the inference of a disjunction from either of its disjuncts, that is, from A to 'A or B' and from B to 'A or B'.

a posteriori knowledge of the truth of propositions gained empirically, that is, from experience or observation.

a priori knowledge of the truth of propositions arrived at independently of experience.

atomic proposition a proposition which cannot be logically analysed in terms of simpler propositions; e.g. 'Socrates runs' or 'Snow is white.'

Bivalence (Law of) the claim that every proposition is either true or false.

conditional a proposition of the form 'if A then B', where A is the antecedent, B the consequent; e.g. 'If Ernest is a mountaineer (then) he is brave.'

Conditional Excluded Middle (Principle of) standard name for the claim that one or other of a pair of conditionals with the same antecedent and contradictory consequents must be true, that is, that all propositions of the form 'if A then B or if A then not-B' are logically true.

Conditionality name coined in this book for the relationship between conditionals and consequence, that a conditional follows from other propositions if and only if its consequent follows from those other propositions in conjunction with its antecedent. Sometimes known as the Deduction Equivalence or Deduction Theorem.

conditionalization standard name for the procedure of moving from one probability function to another by identifying the second with the conditional probability based on the first relative to some item of information. It measures the result of raising the prior probability of that information from a non-zero value to 1.

connexive logic any logic which incorporates what is commonly called Aristotle's Thesis, that no statement implies or is implied by its own negation. This thesis cannot be consistently added to classical logic, in which, for example, the Law of Non-Contradiction implies its own negation (and everything else). Connexive Logics usually lack Addition and Simplification.

consequentia mirabilis traditional name for the inference patterns 'if A then not-A, so not-A' and 'if not-A then A, so A'. When Bertrand Russell was criticized for basing his rejection of naïve realism about perception on physics, which in turn depends on naïve realism, he countered by using *consequentia mirabilis*: if naïve realism is true then (so is physics and so) naïve realism is false. So naïve realism is false.

constructivism an anti-realist position, primarily in the philosophy of mathematics, which requires each assertion to be backed by an explicit construction. The assertions mainly affected are existential claims, where exhibition or construction of an object witnessing to the truth of the claim is required; and disjunctions, where a proof of one or other disjunct is required, so the constructivist refuses to assert the universal validity of the Law of Excluded Middle.

Contraction, or Absorption standard name for the inferential principle which identifies many uses of an assumption as one. It is often used in the form of inferring 'if *A* then *B*' from 'if *A* then if *A* then *B*'.

Correspondence Theory of Truth the claim that truth consists in correspondence to the facts, that a proposition (belief, etc.) is true if and only if it corresponds to a fact.

Disjunctive Syllogism traditional name for the inference of one disjunct from a disjunction together with denial of the other disjunct, that is, from '*A* or *B*' and 'not-*A*' to *B*.

empiricism the claim that all real knowledge derives ultimately from empirical observation, that is, from the senses.

essentialism the claim (often attributed to Aristotle) that some attributes belong to their subjects of necessity, that is, that some singular statements are necessarily true, e.g. 'Socrates was a man.'

Excluded Middle (Law of) the claim that all propositions of the form '*A* or not-*A*' are logically true.

Ex Falso Quodlibet literally, 'from the false, anything (follows)'. Traditional name for the inference of an arbitrary proposition from an explicit contradiction, that is, from '*A* and not-*A*' to *B*.

Existential Generalization standard name for the inference of an existential proposition from one of its instances, that is, from '*a* is *F*' to 'something is *F*'.

'Fido'-Fido Principle name coined by Gilbert Ryle for the idea that the meaning of a word or expression is an object corresponding to it, as the dog Fido corresponds to the name 'Fido'.

Goldbach's Conjecture every even number greater than 2 is the sum of two primes. (No counterexample is known, yet neither is any general proof, as yet.)

haecceitism the belief that everything has an individual essence, a set of properties which are essential to it and distinguish it from everything else.

Indiscernibility of Identicals (Principle of the) standard name for the claim that whatever is true of something is true of it regardless of how it is referred to, that is, that if *a* is *F*, and *a* is *b*, then *b* is *F*.

König's Lemma theorem of non-constructive mathematics which says that any infinite finitely branching tree has an infinite branch.

meta-language the language which is used to talk about another (possibly the same) language.

minimalism name for recent deflationary and reductionist trends in art, music, philosophy, and other spheres. It rejects any attempt to invest linguistic and other elements with special expressive, representational or transcendent properties. Minimalism about truth is the claim that Tarski's T-scheme (see below) says all there is to know about truth.

modal Platonism the claim that how things are (this world) is only one of countless really existing concrete possible worlds.

modus (ponendo) ponens traditional name for the inference˙ of the consequent of a conditional from the conditional and its antecedent, that is, from 'if *A* then *B*' and *A* to *B*.

Non-Contradiction (Law of) the claim that no proposition and its contradictory can be true together, that is, no proposition of the form '*A* and not-*A*' is true.

Occam's Razor methodological principle: do not multiply entities beyond necessity, that is, do not postulate more things in an explanation than are strictly necessary.

paraconsistent logic any logic which allows the formulation of inconsistent but non-trivial theories. In classical logic, a contradiction entails an arbitrary proposition by *Ex Falso Quodlibet* (see above), and so it is not paraconsistent.

particular technical term for a particular object, something which cannot itself have instances, though it may be an instance of something else, namely, a universal, with which it is contrasted.

Plato's Beard the claim that everything, even what does not exist, must in some sense be, for how can empty names have meaning?

Principle of Independence the independence of so being from being: whether an object has certain properties is independent of whether it has being or exists.

prosentential neologism, by analogy with 'pronominal', to characterize expressions which have the force of a sentence, but are used deictically or anaphorically to refer to other sentences.

Ramsey's Test the proposal (by Frank Ramsey) that one should believe a conditional in those cases in which, on adding its antecedent hypothetically to one's other beliefs, one should come to believe its consequent.

realism general name for the belief that some class of entities exist independently of our knowledge of them, and are not merely apparent, nor simply the result of our way of thinking or investigating.

reductio, or *reductio ad absurdum* standard name for the inference to the falsity of a proposition from demonstration that its truth leads to contradiction, that is, for inferences of the form, 'if *A* then both *B* and not-*B*, so not-*A*' and, in classical but not intuitionistic logic, 'if not-*A* then both *B* and not-*B*, so *A*'.

reductionism a proposal to solve a philosophical problem by replacing problematic terms, possibly in context, by others that are less problematic, but arguably none the less equivalent to the first.

Simplification traditional name for the inference of one conjunct from a conjunction, that is, from '*A* and *B*' to *A*, and from '*A* and *B*' to *B*.

Strengthening the Antecedent standard name for the inferential move of adding extra assumptions to the antecedent of a conditional, that is, from 'if *A* then *B*' to 'if *A* and *C* then *B*'.

Transitivity as a rule of inference, it can take two forms: either that of a hypothetical syllogism, from 'if *A* then *B*' and 'if *B* then *C*' to 'if *A* then *C*'; or the principle of lemma, that if we have a proof that *B* follows from *A* and we have a proof of *A*, then we have a proof of *B*.

T-scheme, or T-sentence any instance of the T-scheme, '*S* is true if and only if *p*', where what replaces *p* is the sentence, or a translation of the sentence, whose name replaces *S*, is a T-sentence. Tarski's material adequacy condition on theories of truth was that they should entail all instances of the T-scheme.

universal what, if anything, is common to all the things we call by the same name. The belief that there really is something in all such cases is realism (about universals), that there is nothing real apart from our conception of it is conceptualism, and that there is nothing real apart from the name is nominalism.

Universal Specification, or Instantiation standard name for the inference of a singular proposition from a corresponding universal one, that is, from 'everything is *F*' to '*a* is *F*' for each term *a*.

Index

OXFORD

MORE OXFORD PAPERBACKS

This book is just one of nearly 1000 Oxford Paperbacks currently in print. If you would like details of other Oxford Paperbacks, including titles in the World's Classics, Oxford Reference, Oxford Books, OPUS, Past Masters, Oxford Authors, and Oxford Shakespeare series, please write to:

UK and Europe: Oxford Paperbacks Publicity Manager, Arts and Reference Publicity Department, Oxford University Press, Walton Street, Oxford OX2 6DP.

Customers in UK and Europe will find Oxford Paperbacks available in all good bookshops. But in case of difficulty please send orders to the Cash-with-Order Department, Oxford University Press Distribution Services, Saxon Way West, Corby, Northants NN18 9ES. Tel: 0536 741519; Fax: 0536 746337. Please send a cheque for the total cost of the books, plus £1.75 postage and packing for orders under £20; £2.75 for orders over £20. Customers outside the UK should add 10% of the cost of the books for postage and packing.

USA: Oxford Paperbacks Marketing Manager, Oxford University Press, Inc., 200 Madison Avenue, New York, N.Y. 10016.

Canada: Trade Department, Oxford University Press, 70 Wynford Drive, Don Mills, Ontario M3C 1J9.

Australia: Trade Marketing Manager, Oxford University Press, G.P.O. Box 2784Y, Melbourne 3001, Victoria.

South Africa: Oxford University Press, P.O. Box 1141, Cape Town 8000.

PHILOSOPHY IN OXFORD PAPERBACKS
THE GREAT PHILOSOPHERS
Bryan Magee

Beginning with the death of Socrates in 399, and following the story through the centuries to recent figures such as Bertrand Russell and Wittgenstein, Bryan Magee and fifteen contemporary writers and philosophers provide an accessible and exciting introduction to Western philosophy and its greatest thinkers.

Bryan Magee in conversation with:

A. J. Ayer	John Passmore
Michael Ayers	Anthony Quinton
Miles Burnyeat	John Searle
Frederick Copleston	Peter Singer
Hubert Dreyfus	J. P. Stern
Anthony Kenny	Geoffrey Warnock
Sidney Morgenbesser	Bernard Williams
Martha Nussbaum	

'Magee is to be congratulated . . . anyone who sees the programmes or reads the book will be left in no danger of believing philosophical thinking is unpractical and uninteresting.' Ronald Hayman, *Times Educational Supplement*

'one of the liveliest, fast-paced introductions to philosophy, ancient and modern that one could wish for' *Universe*